7/6/09.

Best wishes.
to Dear Patricia
Whitely

Thou Shalt Not Forget

Thou Shalt Not Forget

by

Israel Lapciuc

KTAV Publishing House, Inc.
Jersey City, NJ

The Sue and Leonard Miller Center
for Contemporary Judaic Studies
University of Miami
Coral Gables, FL

Library of Congress Cataloging-in-Publication Data

Lapciuc, Israel, 1934-
  Thou shalt not forget / by Israel Lapciuc.
     p. cm.
  ISBN 0-88125-822-9 (hc)
  1. Lapciuc, Israel, 1934- 2. Jews--Ukraine--Belz--Biography.
Jewish children in the Holocaust--Ukraine--Belz--Biography. 4
Holocaust, Jewish (1939-1945)--Ukraine--Belz--Personal narra
Belz (Ukraine)--Biography. I. Title.
DS135.U43L37513 2003
940.53'18'092--dc22

                                        2003022326

Published by
KTAV Publishing House, Inc.
930 Newark Avenue
Jersey City, NJ 07306
Email: info@ktav.com
www.ktav.com
(201) 963-9524
Fax (201) 963-0102

Contents

Acknowledgments   vii

Foreword   ix

The Wait   1

The Ghetto   27

The Train   75

When the World Turned Dark   96

The Devil's Whip   128

A Desperate Leap   181

The Tunnel of Misery   219

Good-bye to a Friend   257

Getting Out of the Sewer   294

On the Path of the Dead   329

Fall Back, Comrade   358

The Exit   386

Epilogue   398

Index of Names and Places   400

Acknowledgments

Special thanks to Betty Heisler for translating this book from its original Spanish version into English.

To Maxine Schwartz, all my gratitude for being so instrumental in editing and arranging for the publication of the English version of this book through the Sue and Leonard Miller Center for Contemporary Judaic Studies at the University of Miami. Without her help and motivation, this book, which chronicles the darkest moments in my life and in the history of the Jewish people, would not have been available to the English-speaking world—so that future generations will never forget.

Special gratitude to Dr. Haim Shaked, Director of the Sue and Leonard Miller Center for Contemporary Judaic Studies, for his advice and guidance in bringing this book to fruition.

With all my love to my wife, Tania; my children, Marcos, Isaac, and Yair, and their wives, Tiffany, Sandy, and Bassy; and all my grandchildren. They have given me the strength to live a normal existence and not to superimpose in my mind the images of horror that still linger. They turn my nightmares into the fresh, sweet air that I breathe every day and allow me to believe in the goodness of life, especially as I contemplate the innocent faces of my grandchildren

To the six million Jews who perished, and to God, who inspired me to tell this story, so that these memories will not be forgotten.

⚜

Foreword

I srael Lapciuc's memoir *Thou Shalt Not Forget* is an ode
to a certain type of memory. Lapciuc was only seven
when the Germans invaded his hometown in 1941, in
territory that was under Soviet rule but culturally
Romanian. One hesitates as to how to describe its terri-
toriality: "part of Ukraine," "part of the Soviet Union,"
"part of Romania," each of these descriptions has politi-
cal overtones. They presume that the history of a place is
settled, its national identity secure. This is easy for
Americans to suppose, for in the United States the
demarcations of states do not signify a change in language or culture. But there are certain parts of Europe
where people have lived in several different countries
without ever leaving home. So in which country Israel
Lapciuc lived is but one part of the mystery.

Israel was only seven when it all began. Though he
was merely a child, he was soon forced to become a man.
But however brave his actions, he had but a child's grasp
of history, a child's grasp of time. Israel Lapciuc, the
man, remains faithful to his experience and deliberately
refuses to impose an adult's way of ordering time and
space by imposing chronology, politics, and history on
the events he experienced so very personally. Such is the
charm of the work, but also a potential cause for some
confusion, because adults tend to see events in a
space/time configuration and write of dates and places,

times and locations. Israel writes from experience, and his chapters have headings relating to his experience. They are called: "The Wait," "The Ghetto," "The Train," "When the World Turned Dark," "The Devil's Whip," A Desperate Leap," "The Tunnel of Misery," "Goodbye to a Friend," "Getting Out of the Sewer," and so on. Only the epilogue (written recently at the request of the publisher) is an adult's way of organizing reality. Ironically, it is in the epilogue that Israel is most restrained, suggesting in a bare outline form the world after the Shoah: emigration, survival, struggle, and achievement. The journey from childhood "to the years of one's strength," to use the psalmist's phrase, and the transformation from being a descendant to an ancestor are passed over in one page as if they were someone else's story, seemingly unrelated to the twelve chapters that preceded it.

Whether their authors were children or adults at the time of their survival, the memoirs of Holocaust survivors order time as *before*, *during*, and *after*. Israel is no exception, though in his case the *before* and *after* take just a few sentences. His focus is unerringly on *during*.

"The first of the victims were the children, for from them a new generation would be born," said the famous poet of the Shoah, Yitzhak Katznelson. Yet the last of the witnesses will be the children, for they will indeed be our final direct link between the world of the Shoah and our world. And child survivors have had to wrestle with how to bear witness as adults to what they experienced when they were children. Child survivors often report that they have to fight for the integrity of their memories, because those who were older when they went through the Shoah frequently challenge them, asking: "What can you remember? After all, you were only a child." And child survivors have to distinguish between what they know of

❖

their past through their own memories and what they have learned of their past through the stories that have been told to them by others. It is never an easy task to recover the past, as psychologists, artists, rabbis, and writers know so well. Child survivors would be wise to learn from Israel's example—that is, to tell what they remember and not to embellish on their memories by giving a history told by others.

So let me, in this foreword, describe a bit of the history that Israel rightfully omitted, so that adult readers—and this book will be read mainly by adults—will be able to understand what Israel could not understand then: his personal history within the context of the time and place.

In the 1930 census, the last before the war, the Jewish population of Romania consisted of 759,000 souls and constituted the third-largest Jewish community in Europe. Only Poland and the Soviet Union had more Jews. Romania historically was a traditional ally of France and therefore lost territory after the fall of France in 1940. Thus, in the regions of northern Transylvania, Romanian Jews from towns such as Elie Wiesel's Sighet and Satu Mare (Saint Mary's), the ancestral home of the Satmar Hasidim, came under Hungarian control, which, until March 1944, kept them outside the orbit of the German policy of the Final Solution to the Jewish Problem. In March 1944, Germany invaded its former ally, Hungary, and imposed its rule and the Final Solution. Confiscation of Jewish assets began immediately. Ghettoization followed swiftly in April, and in the less than two months from May 15 to July 8, 437,402 Jews were deported on 147 trains, mostly to Auschwitz. Of the 150,000 former Romanian Jews under Hungarian control who resided in these territories 135,000 perished.

In June 1940 the Soviet Union occupied some of Romania, taking control of that part of Bessarabia which is located between the Prut and Dniester rivers and of northern Bukovina, along the Carpathian Mountains. This area, which was the locale of the author's hometown of Beltsy (Balti), was ceded to the Soviet Union, while southern Dobruja was ceded to Bulgaria in the Vienna Arbitration Awards of 1940. Believing in the inevitability of a German victory, Romania became a partner of Germany in November 1940 and adopted a policy resembling the Nazi policy of Aryanization, called Romanization. Jews were identified, their assets were confiscated, and they were excluded from commercial life. Soon, 40,000 Jewish homes were seized and handed over to Romanian non-Jews.

The Romanian army was at the side of the Wehrmacht when Germany invaded the Soviet Union in June 1941. As a result, Romania recaptured Bessarabia and northern Bukovina, which had cities with large Jewish populations, such as Chernovtsy (Czernowitz), Kishinev, Tulchin, and Mogilev-Podolski. Then the slaughter began. *Einsatzgruppen* (mobile killing units) went from town to town, to cities, hamlets, and villages, and rounded up Jews, Soviet commissars, and Gypsies, killing them one by one, bullet by bullet. In Romania and in the areas adjacent to Romania, the Romanians cooperated fully with the *Einsatzgruppen* and also engaged in their own slaughters.

Within three days of the invasion of the Soviet Union, a massive pogrom took place in the northern Romanian town of Iasi (Jassy). Four thousand Jews were killed, and thousands more were deported in sealed trains. On June 30, two trains were loaded with 4,332 survivors of the pogrom. One train was scheduled for the town of Calarasi, some 300 miles away. The cattle cars simply shuttled back and forth until their human cargo perished from hunger and dehydration in the heat of the Romanian summer. Before the journey was over, 2,594 people had died. Somewhere on Romanian soil, the mass graves of these Jewish dead are yet to be found.

Those of us who have read many memoirs of the Holocaust have become accustomed to a certain sequence of events. In Poland, invasion was followed by ghettoization, which then led to the struggle to survive, followed by the German decision to murder, and finally by deportation to the death camps. Even narratives dealing only with the deportation to the death camps have a familiar sequence of events. Arrival, *selektion,* tattooing and cutting the hair (or, to use the parlance of America's West, branding and shearing) was followed by slave labor for the few who were not murdered upon arrival. This sequence was identical with regard to Hungarian Jews, though in their case the process of ghettoization took days, not months, and the period during which they remained in the ghetto lasted weeks, not years. Western European memoirs tend to be different, but in Israel's memoir the German determination to kill the Jews of Eastern Europe is clear even before the deportations. He had to adjust to Soviet rule and later to German rule. Israel's recounting of the train sequence in Chapter 3 seems to be a journey to nowhere—as it was—because in trying to mirror Nazi policies, the Romanians didn't get it quite right. They did not establish death camps, but used the train to starve and freeze Jews and even to kill them *before* they arrived at their destination. Hence what may seem a child's confusion to some is, in reality, a correct

❖

narration of sequence and of the seeming absence of destination.

Israel is compellingly clear on the violation of the victim's privacy, the absence of even elementary sanitation and food and the nature of the odors. Children are more vivid in their descriptions of what the late literary scholar of the Holocaust Terrence Des Pres, in the final chapter of his masterful work *The Survivor: An Anatomy of Life in the Death Camps*, called "excremental assault." Israel's description is as riveting as it is painful to read. Dehumanization preceded the killing because it made the killing easier for the killers, who could pretend that they did not share a common humanity with the stinking folk who stood in front of them. The latter were seen as denizens of a different universe.

The Romanian army, acting on its own, murdered Jews. For example, in Odessa, the Soviet port on the Black Sea, the Romanian army murdered Jews by burning, as part of a reprisal against Jews and Communists. This attack was ordered by Marshal Antonescu in response to an attack on Romanian headquarters. On October 23, 1941, four months after the beginning of the German-Romanian invasion, 19,000 Jews were taken to the square at the harbor. Gasoline was poured on them and then set aflame. That afternoon, another 20,000 Jews were taken to the village of Dalnik. Some were shot. Others were locked in a warehouse, which was then set afire.

Romanian army teams joined *Einsatzgruppen* in the slaughter of more than 100,000 Jews in the territories of Bukovina and Bessarabia, which had been occupied by Soviet troops in 1940. In many instances, the local Romanian and Ukrainian populations were willing par-

⚜

ticipants in the killing. Israel clearly differentiates between the Germans and the Romanians. He calls the former beasts and the latter slaves, He also makes a distinction between Romanians and Ukrainians, although both were dangerous in their own ways. Germans were clearly the leaders. He also clearly delineates the mood of the Germans and the dangers of being in contact with them as the wartime fortunes of Nazi Germany deteriorated and the Germans themselves felt imperiled.

The 120,000 Jews who remained in Bessarabia and Bukovina were expelled and forced to go on foot to Transnistria, an area between the Dniester and Bug rivers 60 miles away. During these death marches, tens of thousands of Jews died. Many were shot, but hunger, thirst, and exhaustion claimed the lives of many more. During the next three years, 90,000 Jews—three out of four— perished in Transnistria, victims of famine, disease, cold-blooded murder by the Nazis, and of mayhem.

As Germany's military situation deteriorated in 1942 and 1943, policy toward the Jews shifted. German defeat was a matter of time, and European rulers, who in 1940 and '41 and well into 1942 had adjusted their *Realpolitik* to the idea of Germany dominating Europe, had to readjust their thinking and hedge their bets. A German victory was no longer assured after Stalingrad, and by 1944 Germany's eventual defeat, though not its timing, was presumed. Suddenly sensitive to the prospect of an Allied victory, Marshal Antonescu, the ruler of Romania, was hesitant about deporting the Jews of "old Romania," including the regions of Walachia, Romanian Moldavia, and the city of Bucharest. He did agree, however, that Romanian Jews living in the Reich could be sent to concentration camps. Antonescu also approved plans for the

❧

deportation of Romanian Jews to the death camp at Belzec, although the plans were never carried out. He decided to use Romania's surviving Jews as hostages, valuable commodities to be traded to the Allies for cash. For the moment, Jews were worth more alive than dead. In December 1942, the asking price for a Jew was $1,336. At that price per head, Antonescu was willing to send 75,000 Jews to Palestine. He even repatriated Jewish orphans from Transnistria to increase the number of Jews he could use as bargaining chips.

By war's end, more than 400,000 Romanian Jews— 135,000 Jews under Hungarian control, 20,000 Jews from old Romania in the pre–World War I boundaries, and 250,000 Romanian and Ukrainian Jews—were dead. Romanians and Hungarians, not Germans, had killed two-thirds of them. More than 300,000 more remained alive, waiting to be ransomed, which is one way to read the history of the "secret" migration of Romanian Jewry to Israel during the Communist era. The idea of ransoming Jews for money had a long life in Romania.

Israel Lapciuc had no idea of this historical context while he lived it. For him the story was far more elemental. It consisted of parents, grandparents, family, and later friends, beasts and slaves, suffering and starvation, fear and revenge. We should read Israel's story as he wrote it—as one child's experience in a complex and brutal world during the darkest moment of Jewish history, when humanity revealed the worst of its capacities and occasionally, and all too infrequently, the best.

Michael Berenbaum

Los Angeles
October, 2003

⚜

1

The Wait

Czernovitz, 1941. That afternoon a whole battalion of German troops went by. The faces of the soldiers did not look all that serious for having been the victors. They had destroyed our army. The Red Army troops were retreating, and no one in the city knew what to do or which way to go. Everyone was simply dumbfounded. The atmosphere was heavy as the Germans paraded past with their characteristic goose-step, holding the swastika banner in the arrogant posture of occupying troops.

I saw them go by from the window of my house. At the age of seven, everything was new to me. Those square-faced soldiers had something strange in their look. They walked very straight in their brown uniforms. For a boy like me, who did not know any soldiers other than the Romanians with their horses, the troops going by were a real spectacle. I could finally see what the old people talked so much about, particularly the shoemaker. He used to say that horses were no longer good for battle, and that in Germany he had seen soldiers riding motorcycles and cars. At the beginning they had laughed at him, but now everyone could see the motorcycles and cars roaring through the street.

At home nobody said anything. My mother tried not to seem nervous but she kept moving about, always looking for something to do. She was worried about my father, a soldier in a defeated army.

Many stories would be circulated, all of them about dead and mutilated men. All night I would hear my mother crying, but I never asked why. Even at my age I could sense her feelings.

The afternoon that the soldiers paraded past our window, I trembled as I nestled in her bosom. It seemed as if all her hopes had dissipated and now she was trying to infuse me with her life, to get me inside of her so as not to lose me. Outside, some curious people looked with misgivings at the parade of the occupying army, and some even hailed them as victors.

Life in our city remained mostly the same over the next few days, but with some changes, of course. At a certain time a siren would go off and I knew it was time to go home. All of a sudden everything changed. The women talked about arrests and executions outside the city. Nobody trusted anyone, and the slightest movement seemed suspicious, even a shadow appearing in a corner. We kids were hardly allowed to go out, and food was rationed. Sometimes we would eat some bread with cabbage soup. Other times our only sustenance would be a bunch of dried vegetables and then we would go to sleep. My mother kept crying, her eyes swollen and a strange tremor in her hands.

She probably had given up on my father. She never said anything when I asked about him. "He will come," she would tell me, "Everyone who goes to war comes back." Those were sweet words, but with a tinge of sadness. When the subject of the war was broached among

❧

the women, they would look at each other knowingly and tried to give their words a meaning they really did not have. They tried to revive their dead. They would make us children study a bit, and later they would make us do some work around the house.

It started to rain. Autumn had come, and a great many dead leaves began to fall on the ground. The streets were wet, and every once in a while we would hear the roar of a motorcycle or the hollow sound of the steps of a German patrol making its rounds. One rainy afternoon I had to go get bread and I saw the arrest of a thin man with an enormous beard. The soldiers were having fun insulting him and hitting him with their rifle butts. They were screaming the word "Jew" at him together with a stream of profanities I had never heard before. I was shocked by his swollen eyes and the blood spurting from his mouth.

He writhed on the ground as if he were scratching the dirt, but he did not speak, nor did he emit a single sound. We children watched in horror. No one knew why the man was being beaten so savagely. I was afraid and almost ran to hide behind my mother's skirts. Without understanding why, I seemed to see the image of my father. I came home afraid, with the loaf of bread clenched so tightly under my arm that it was about to break in two. The image of the blood spilling from the man's mouth was fresh in my mind and haunted me. I told my mother what I had seen, and she said nothing, sensing perhaps that my father would never come back. She now seemed sadder than usual, going about her tasks without paying too much attention to the daily conversations of the neighbors about the developments of the war. I began to feel afraid and I made myself comfortable at home, knowing that the streets were now a dangerous place.

I hardly looked out the window. I would spend long hours stuck in a corner, thinking about my grandparents' farm. How I enjoyed the time I spent with them! Going on sleigh rides in the winter, listening to the sound of the snow under our boots, looking at the white shroud of snow in the distance that would cover the roofs, the trees, the mountains and the valleys. Covered by a warm leather coat, I would breathe the humid air and touch my face to see if my cheeks were as red as my grandfather's. I would hear his laugh and the whip on the backs of the horses. We would go fast, swallowing up the road, thinking about the beauty of the coming spring.

And now I was hiding in a corner, waiting for something to happen, with the image of the beaten man still fresh on my mind. I waited for my father, looking for him in the walls, trying to see his figure through the windowpanes that looked out at the street. But to no avail. The days went by. Slow, rainy days, with my mother looking more haggard with every passing minute. Young as I was, I began to feel the solitude that is a product of waiting, that continuous ambulating in a vacuum that hardly gives the heart a break. I was cold and would put my hands inside my pockets searching for some warmth. To keep track of the days, I started breaking away pieces of cork that I would insert into a rope, creating a makeshift calendar of my wait. The faces of the women seemed to get grayer and more mysterious, as if they were hiding something from me. They would come in from the street with their big scarves wet from the rain and eyes swollen by tears. They talked in whispers, stopping after every phrase, trying to steal a little time from the wooden clock we had in the house.

⚜

Suddenly I began having nightmares, dreams charged with distorted images that haunted me and made fun of me, images of the corks, of the rope, and of the window-panes. Shadows that would lift me by the throat so that I could see how those square-faced soldiers beat up the thin men with long beards. I would wake up sweating and would cuddle up to my mother, who seemingly was never asleep. Every time I opened my eyes I would see her awake, looking always at the door. And that is where I directed my eyes. Something directed me to look at the wood. I was sure that any minute it would open up to give way to my father's figure. They were cold, heavy nights that threatened to crush us all. The wait continued slowly, and outside the rain poured down ceaselessly. For the first time I was conscious of the slow death of autumn that starts to strip the trees of its leaves and deliver them naked into the hands of winter.

The square faces of the Nazi soldiers went by without looking at anyone. Their bodies were wrapped in big coats and their feet were encased in black leather boots. They were watched by people frightened and anxious for news from the front.

One morning, the neighbor's wife came crying to my house and began to pull her hair right in front of my mother. The poor woman, eyes wide open, dragged my mother by her apron and forced her to accompany her home. In my childish curiosity, I dared to follow my mother, since her presence felt reassuring. So I went to the neighbor's house to find out what was the source of her anguish.

When I came in I saw a man with a deformed face and a missing leg sitting in a chair. He was staring without blinking, his eyes dull. It was the neighbor's husband. Between sobbing and hugging her two children, she was

⚜

saying: "They brought him in last night. But look at him. He's barely a shadow of himself. I swear I almost didn't recognize him." The children were staring, frightened, at their father. "He doesn't say anything, he doesn't even move from where he is. He's a living corpse, a rag. This is the war, that's how the Germans brought him back to me," and she stomped at whatever was nearby, striking the walls with her fists and her head. The children huddled close to each other, with their frightened little faces, not understanding what their mother was doing.

I too was frightened by that man who did not move from where he was. I felt a shudder that came up to the base of my brain and a terrible upset stomach. I couldn't believe it was our neighbor, the same man who used to spend hours at a time talking and playing chess with my father. It couldn't possibly be him. The man I had known was polite, always smiling and joking, with pockets full of candy and a whole list of stories about the butcher and the baker. But now this figure was a stranger, something far removed from the image I remembered of our neighbor. I couldn't help but run and hide in my mother's apron. She put her hands on my head and I felt her trembling, for she too was affected by the image of the man with his face destroyed and eyes that looked without seeing. Suddenly my mother lifted me against her chest and we left the room. Inside we left two children who did not move and a woman who, in her despair, was knocking herself against the wall and wailing that she was going to kill herself.

I didn't eat a thing at lunch. The cabbage soup remained in the plate untouched. And, even though my mother did everything she could to make me eat, she didn't touch a thing either. She was upset, nervous, looking

❧

out in desperation toward the door, awaiting a husband who had unconsciously taken on the image of the neighbor. But she didn't say anything to me.

I went to my corner, and she took up some old rags and started to fashion a coverlet for the winter. The street noises came in ominously, heralding tragedy. The wooden clock moved slowly, marking hours that now mattered to no one. It was a time without shape, cloaked in shadows, auguring strange things and harrowing noises like that of the bombings. I looked at the ceiling and could see the damage done by the bombs that had been falling for several days, almost always from five to six in the afternoon, when my mother would come running in, take me in her arms, and run out to the street to get inside the communal shelter for our block. There were many of us, and we looked like sardines cramped in that underground built of stones that were always wet and moldy. People prayed, screamed, or cried. Only a few remained quiet, unresponsive, as if what was happening had been preordained. There was an old man who caught my eye. Whenever the bombing started he was the last one to come in. There was no hurry in his steps. He would sit in the back, clean his mother-of-pearl-framed glasses, and light a short pipe that let out a very pleasant aroma. Whenever a bomb exploded nearby, he would bring his fingers to his earlobes and pull lightly at them. He didn't do anything else. He talked very little, and I never heard a word from him. Only once did I see him smile. And his smile was directed at a little green-eyed girl who shuddered every time there was an explosion. Other than this old man, everyone was trying not to let their thoughts be known, for fear they would turn into reality. Some talked about the front, and a few of the mothers spoke of the let-

⚜

ters and notes they had gotten from their sons. Of course not many notes actually reached their destinations, since most were lost on the way. It was a devil's post. Messages would come in at random.

After the bombing we would go outside to find our way through the hot, smoking rubble. The roofs of many houses had disappeared completely, and some of the walls, cracked by the impact, threatened to fall down at any moment, trapping and burying passersby. Suddenly the bombings stopped. Three days later we found out that the Red Army was retreating before the advancing Germans, who were displaying a new military strategy— attacking in masses, tearing away whole sections of an army, and trapping the bulk of the troops. It was a lightning war. We children did not understand the situation very well, but the grownups spent hours at a time discussing these things.

At this time there weren't many men around, since most of them had been drafted and were now on the run. Women and old men carried out the daily chores. We were hardly good as messengers and water carriers. Our youth did not compensate in any way for the work of those who were gone, but we did the chores for the women.

Altogether we felt the drama of the war and its weight on our shoulders. At first we took the whole thing as a game in which we could play the role of fathers. A freckled redheaded kid used to boast that in his house his mother and sister would do anything he said. When he told them it was time to sleep, they would simply go to bed. We admired and even respected him. At only ten years old, he was a real man, an example we all wanted to follow. We never saw him again. After a while we found

⚜

out that a patrol had shot him while he was crossing a roof that led to the bell tower of the monastery. The Germans shot the boy, and those who saw him fall swore that his stomach was completely perforated and his guts were falling out.

This impressed me as much as seeing the man with the beard being beaten. I didn't see the redheaded kid die, but I had seen the man beaten, dragged, and cursed.

This first image of degradation became rooted in my subconscious and I couldn't let go of it. It got into me with more force than the noise of the bombings, drilling into my brain like an alarm ready to warn of ever-present danger. This was my first vision of what the occupying forces did. And the worst was the relationship between this incident and the image of my father. Without realizing it, I fell asleep in the corner. I wasn't hungry and my memories stopped suddenly. I dreamed a pleasant dream devoid of images that represented anything. I simply wandered in space in search of a bit of warmth, of more light for the gray days of fall. After a while I felt someone playing with my hair. It was my mother. She was squatting, watching me with eyes sad from waiting for the door to open. She smiled when I opened my eyes. "You must be cold, my son. Come and put on a sweater so you won't catch a cold." I rubbed my eyes, yawned, and let her lift me up from my place in the corner. I went with her to the room and let her put a sweater on me that was getting raggedy at the elbows. She smiled, happy to see me covered with something warm that would protect me from the cold that already started to dampen the walls and the windowpanes. I wanted to ask her about my father, but I couldn't pronounce the word. I seemed to see him sitting in a chair, like the neighbor, with a spacey look in his

⚜

eyes, oozing blood from his mouth, not uttering a word and being hit with rifle butts by the square-faced soldiers with tall, shiny leather boots.

I started to cry and my mother seemed to understand my feelings. "Don't cry. Remember, you are now the man of the house, and for nothing in the world—" She was unable to go on. She too began to cry, and her tears rolled down to my mouth. Their strange salty taste infused me with renewed strength and confidence. My mother's silent crying reaffirmed my desire to be, as she said, the man of the house. I smiled, thinking that with this she would stop crying, and presently, making a supreme effort, she smiled back.

Somewhat relieved, I ate my soup and looked for something to pass the time, to avoid the images constantly passing through my mind. I went to my room and took out some wooden toys my maternal grandfather had bought for me from neighboring farmers. The day I got them had been a happy one. With them in my hands, I dreamt of being a great lord, like that giant who sat at the eastern wall of the synagogue. I was always impressed by his size, bigger than anyone else around him and so full of life. But he did not come close to my father who, even though he was smaller and poorer, always had a piece of candy in his pocket for me. The tall man I could only look at, but my father I had always by my side, filling me up with warmth, explaining every detail of the ritual. And now, with my wooden toys, I was dreaming once again of the green pastures that extended in the summer around my grandparents' farm.

I would run after the ducks, and my grandmother would clap when I corralled one and brought it back unharmed, holding it under its wings, to the pen from

⚜

which it had escaped. My wooden toys helped me forget, up to a point, the situation we were going through. They were pulling me toward the past, looking to get me out of the gray present, out of an autumn with our country in the hands of the occupying troops of Nazi Germany.

I don't know how long I was half-dreaming with my toys. I only know that I woke up from my imaginary world when I heard some soft, quick knocks on the door. The first one to get to it was my mother. She opened up and found herself facing the neighbor's son, who was shaking all over, his face white as chalk. The boy, without asking to be invited in, came through the door and went to hide behind a leather chair close to a bookshelf. I stayed in my place, waiting to see what would happen. My mother, on the other hand, closed the door and walked slowly to the place where the boy remained, rolled up in a ball. Upon seeing my mother, he tried to hide his pale little face between his small dirty, yellow hands. At first I thought my mother lacked the words to ask the reason for his sudden visit.

For a few minutes there was nothing but silence. The walls were wet and we all felt the cold that had come in when we opened the door. I put my hands inside the sleeves of my sweater and waited. My mother finally began to question the neighbor's son. "Moshe, what happened? Why have you come in like this, like something bad has happened? Tell me." The boy looked up and, with terror in his eyes, muttered a few words: "My father shot himself in the head!" I noticed the shudder that went through my mother's body. It was as if an electric charge had risen from the floor to make her take a step back, petrified. In order not to scream, she took her apron to her mouth and bit it. The man she had just seen

⚜

sitting in his chair with a deformed face and a missing leg now had a bullet between his eyes and was probably oozing blood from his mouth like the man the Germans had beaten up in the street. Once again my father's image came to my mind. I saw him lying in an open field, with his face destroyed and a huge hole in the side of his head. I couldn't control myself. I ran to my room, where I lay on my bed, crying. I was desperate, feeling that the front door would never open to let my father in. It was terrible. My mind did not put ideas together very well, and only reacted in response to the stimuli it received from the outside. I cried until my throat started to hurt and I felt a void in my mind. My eyes stung. The figures that adorned my headboard became distorted, swaying in a slow movement that did not incline them in any direction but moved them nonetheless. They were gesturing to me, calling to tell me that my father wouldn't come back and that the front door couldn't be crossed by a man with a bullet in his head.

When I came down my mother had gone out. I was afraid to face alone the street that had been witness to the "treatment" given the thin man with the beard. I counted to three before running out in the street, and a few seconds later I was crossing the threshold of the neighbor's house. Everything was in motion. The wife of the neighbor had fainted and was prostrate on a small table. Her two children were crying, and a few women, my mother among them, were trying to revive her by rubbing her temples and her cheeks. Others were covering the corpse with a blanket and discussing the reasons that could have brought the man to take his own life. One of the orphans was saying, as if talking to himself, "I saw him take the pistol, cover the barrel with a rag, and shoot. He didn't utter a sound, he only turned his eyes and his head fell to one side. When my mother saw him, she either fainted or died. What's the difference?" The boy talked hoarsely, and had difficulty pronouncing the words. I watched him as if in a trance, seeing him grow older by the minute. His eyes shined and were getting smaller and smaller. A story I had heard in school came to mind. It said that dwarfs had small eyes that gleamed with a strange light.

My mother told me to leave and wait for her at home, since what I was seeing was not for a child's eyes. Afraid as I was to go out in the street, I was getting ready to leave when the widow let out a deep scream that rolled through the windows of the room. We all turned to her. Her two children were the only ones who did not stir. They didn't seem to understand the scope of their tragedy, the terrible burden they were going to have to carry from now on. Moshe, the one who had come to our house to tell my mother what had happened, took his father's hands in his. He seemed to be saying good-bye or maybe trying to leave with him. I felt my stomach turn into knots, and my fear of going out into the street intensified. I was trembling, my hands were sweating, and I did not dare to take another step. The images in my head were scrambled, and I couldn't put my thoughts together. It was all like the nightmares that frequently came to me at night. I put my hands in my pockets, seeking some warmth and comfort. The women passed by my side, going from one place to another. Their voices rebounded like an echo, tearing at my ears, penetrating with force and bringing to light the sense, until then unknown to me, of the war. An old woman, with her hair pulled back in a bun, was whispering some prayers. I hadn't seen her

❖

come in. I didn't trust her, she was a stranger. Perhaps she had been walking down the street and came in when she heard the commotion.

The mother of the orphans got up and bit her lips until they almost bled. Her eyes opened slowly, as if she had just woken up from a long sleep. She moved her head and started to cry, ignoring the women who surrounded her. She called her two children and hugged them as she sobbed, crying:

"They killed him. He was already a corpse when he came back. The war killed him like they are going to kill all of us. To live! I don't know what it means! We believe we are alive because we feel cold and hunger: they are lies. In this God-forsaken time we are all corpses, people who smell bad as they walk. My husband was alive before this damn war started. He moved without leaving a bad odor behind him. But he was drafted and I saw him pale, completely decomposed. He had already begun to smell when he said goodbye to the family and swore he would come back. No, the dead have no reason to return. They go slowly to their graves, led by others, without allowing the cold to fill their chests and the raindrops to flood their caskets. No, I shouldn't have harbored any hopes! I was a fool to think there could be a life for us after he returned!"

She kept talking for a long time, holding her two children very tightly. I watched the scene and looked at the old lady from the side. To see her so old, with her lips moving, scared me. My grandmother did not look like that in spite of her years. She was always smiling and kept a good supply of sweets in her pantry. On the other hand the woman at my side did not even try to smile, to give a little warmth with her gaze. For all I could see, it

❖

wouldn't surprise me if she was death itself. This thought made me close my fists inside my pants pockets. If my father did not return it was because the old woman had taken him away. She would be responsible if I did not see him again.

I ran to my mother. Realizing that I had ignored her command to go home, she began to reprimand me, but held back when she saw me signaling at the old woman who was constantly moving her lips. It was true that the woman had a funereal look about her that bothered everybody. Another pair of women, who had also noticed the stranger, looked at her in fear. Finally, smirking in an attempt to smile, the old woman nodded her head in greeting and left. Her back was so bent that she looked like a hook. She stopped at the door and, taking out a big talisman hanging from a copper chain, she turned to us and said: "God help you, you Jews!" and she was lost in the rain that had started to fall again, covering the street with mud and making puddles in the holes in the sidewalk. Everyone looked around, asking one another who was the old lady who had just left.

I did not want to leave by myself. I went home with my mother. She understood my fear. Sitting on my bed, with my hands under my chin, I asked her: "Mom, what did that lady mean? What does God have to help us with?" She ran her hand through her hair and looked at me for a while before answering. She was looking for clear words to give me an answer that would satisfy my curiosity. Finally she said: "Look, Israel, the old lady probably didn't know what she was saying. That happens to some people when they are old and alone. The say the first thing that occurs to them, they say things that no one understands." She did not say anything else. It was diffi-

❖

cult for her to talk. And I was not satisfied with her answer. What was going on with the Jews?

It seemed strange to me that the non-Jewish men in town were always addressing each other by their given names, Stephen, Julian, Andrew, while when they addressed us they simply used the word "Jew," as if we all had the same name. That's why I was impressed by the old woman's words and gestures, and the way she twirled that talisman in front of us. I saw no reason not to believe that the woman was death itself. I did not say anything to my mother, not wanting to frighten her. I realized that things were getting worse and worse, and I did not want to aggravate the situation. I had to be careful about what I said. I realized that the time would come when we wouldn't be allowed to talk.

That night I had a hard time falling asleep. I closed my eyes to make believe I was sleeping, but I kept hearing the raindrops hitting against the window. My mother prayed and sighed. She was praying to God that my father would come back safe. The figure of the dead man kept creeping into my mind. He was sitting in his chair, showing me that he was missing a leg, pointing with his long fingers to the cuts in his face and the hole through which the bullet had entered his head. His two children were playing by his side, as if nothing had happened and their dad was the same man as always. Moshe even sat on the leg stump and, narrowing his eyes, put his little finger through the hole the bullet had made, which kept getting bigger and bigger until his whole hand fit through it. Thus, between nightmares and associations with my father's image, dawn finally came.

Some flashes of steely light hit my face and I woke up. My body hurt and my right hand was totally numb. I

⚜

pulled back a lock of hair that was falling in my eyes and I jumped up from bed. My mother had awakened much earlier. Her side of the bed was already cold. Just like every morning, I went to the window and looked out. I was convinced that my father would return with the morning light. There was hardly anybody outside, only a couple of guards and Moshe, who was in front of his house letting a stray dog lick his feet. The dog had become attached to us children because we used to feed him. I used to sometimes bring him a piece of bread. Others would bring vegetables and even marmalade for him to eat. He was our dog, since nobody had claimed him.

When I came down I found my mother reading a letter in the kitchen. I didn't tell her that this morning I had not seen my father come in either. When I got closer I saw two big teardrops rolling down her cheeks, which were reddened from the heat of the fireplace. She was crying after reading once again the only letter my father had sent from the front, long before the Germans had marched into our city. She held on to the hope of his return in those lines written down in small characters:

"Dear Perla, I haven't stopped thinking about you for one minute since I left. Don't worry. I promise I will come back home in one piece and we will resume our lives. None of us is despondent. On the contrary, we are hopeful that the Germans will not cross the border. The Red Army is big and strong. Maybe this war will end soon and the countries involved will reach an agreement. We live in civilized times and military men know that the last big war was not a good experience. Don't think that this will be like 1914. Men don't have that savage urge to kill each other. How is Israel? Have you heard from your parents?

❧

Hugs and kisses for them and Israel. I'll be back soon. See you soon, dear Perla. Until then, I send my thoughts that always cling to you."

Just a few words sent from the front at a time when hope still reigned.

When she saw me she hid the piece of paper in her apron and dried her tears. "Did you sleep well? You are not as afraid as yesterday, are you, dear? You know what? We should be calm, happy, sure that dad will come back to us in a few days. Many have returned—" Then she stopped. Our neighbor was one of those who had come back. She got up and signaled for me to sit down and have my breakfast. Later, sitting in front of me, she changed the subject: "Israel, how would you like to go spend some time with your grandparents this winter? You will have a good time sleigh riding and helping grandfather light up the fireplace. I will start knitting a wool coat and some mittens. Would you like them yellow?" She spoke slowly, believing that her words would have an effect on my child's mind. But they didn't help. Meanwhile I was thinking of Moshe standing in front of his house, no longer able to wait for his father. If mine suddenly showed up, how could I tell him? It would be like calling him an orphan, which would be the same as calling him a thief, for I had heard the butcher saying that the orphans were cleaning him out with their constant robberies. "They are like birds of prey, ruffians who steal the first thing they see, even if it is to throw it out someplace else. You have to mind your things!" said the man, and his big mustache would move, affirming his words. And orphans happened when children like Moshe lost their father. I couldn't go on eating. My stomach ached thinking about yesterday: the old woman and her

⚜

talisman; Moshe's mother screaming that everyone who had gone to the war was already dead from the moment they left; Moshe hiding behind the leather chair.

Everything had changed, even my mother's face. Now I saw bags under her eyes, a strange light in her pupils, more wrinkles on her forehead. Her hair was falling out of place from behind her ears and she did not mind. The sense of autumn was getting into me along with the cold and rain seeping in from the street.

When I got up from my chair, my mother took me by the arm and said: "Israel, promise me you won't go next door. Something happened there that small children like you should not witness. They are things meant for grownups." I nodded, but something impelled me to go to Moshe's house. Curiosity was getting the best of me. I looked at my mother to tell her that I wanted to go there anyway. I couldn't very well stay home and play with my toys. It was impossible, especially considering that I still hoped that Moshe's father, even though dead, would be able to tell me things about my father. If he had come back sooner, then he could tell me when my father would be back. I went out of the kitchen and sat down on the leather chair. There I thought about how to get out of the house without my mother noticing it. It would be for only a few minutes. I was sure to find the rabbi and the cantor there. I would watch them talk, quote the Talmud, and console the widow. It was not the first dead person I had seen, and I already knew the ritual.

But my mother, perhaps anticipating my thoughts, locked the door. This new development threw me, and I sat there, lost in my thoughts, for close to five hours. I was infuriated by my helplessness, separated from the neighbor's house by a door I couldn't go through. In the

❖

middle of the silence I started weaving strange situations
that took the shape of stories in which I was wounded
and put in prison. All those stories about pogroms and
massacres came to me, and I saw myself arrested and
chained to the wall, my body covered by wounds. There
in my chair, memories came back to me. My subconscious rebelled and I reacted to the tensions suffered
during the last few days. At the end of my seizure, I
began to turn into somebody else—the man of the house,
as my mother had said. I felt sorry for Moshe and
promised myself to share my father with him. I wanted to
tell him that we could have the same father between us
and that he would take us to the synagogue on the holidays, and after services we could go out and enjoy ourselves, eating sweets. Unconsciously something bound
me to Moshe. He with his dead father and mine far away,
still alive in a letter that had come many days ago. How
silly I had been, back when I hadn't known who the
Germans were. Now I could identify them from 300 feet
away. During these five hours I didn't dare look at my
mother for fear of turning red. I loved her and was afraid
I would weaken if I let my feelings take over. This was
something not fit for the man of the house, the one who
would have to protect her if my father turned into one of
the dead of whom Moshe's mother had spoken.

With my hands in my pockets I went to the table to
eat my soup. When I lifted the spoon, my mother's eyes
became fixed on the plate. Against my will I had to get up
and wash my hands. I ate slowly, thanking God in a way
for the nourishment. It was almost certain that most people, due to the circumstances, would not have had even
half of what was on my plate. When I finished my mother looked happy. For the first time in several days I had
almost cleaned my plate. "You were hungry, weren't you,

✤

Israel?" I couldn't answer. Yes, it was hunger and love, fear and hope of seeing my father come through the door. I felt all that, and I also felt the cold that came through the windowsills. I went up to my room to go back to my toys. I did not even try to open the box they were kept in. The window called to me. I wanted to know what was going on in the street. I wanted to know if Moshe's father had been taken to the cemetery. I looked out and did not see anything. Only some passersby walking fast, their hands in their coat pockets. Aside from the Germans, everything was the same as any autumn afternoon in Czernowitz.

I saw rain, mud, and hazy figures through the glass, wet flashes of dull light and a long street. I couldn't distinguish very well the figures walking through the street, but I kept inside myself, very vividly, the desire to see my father again. My mother did not say anything, but she would let her feelings out at night, when she had conversations with herself thinking that I was asleep. I heard her perfectly and felt her labored breathing under her repressed sobs.

I looked toward the neighbor's house and it was closed. Surely they were now at the cemetery, opening up a hole in the ground, shoveling in the required soil and adding some soil brought from the Holy Land by one of those pilgrims who roamed the world. If I were Moshe, how would those shovels full of earth falling on the casket sound to me? What's more, since his father had taken his own life he probably had been buried to one side, near the wall and had not been allowed to be washed beforehand.

Of course many laughed at these things. Elias, the tailor's son, did not believe there was anything after death. I heard him say that after dying you decayed like

❖

a toad. The old men in the community thought he was crazy, but some of the young girls were very taken with him and, because of my age, they didn't mind talking in front of me, thinking I did not understand. The truth is that I did not understand about these things and even less when the words come from women's gossip. The red-headed kid the Germans had killed was right to reprimand his sisters. I believed that women only changed after they were married, and then not much. Many women came to my house after my father left to tell stories about neighbors and friends. They only talked when the one they were talking about was not present. You would have to be a woman to understand these things.

It did not stop raining. I imagined Moshe's mother weeping in front of the covered grave. Everybody cries when the corpse is covered with dirt, especially if the burial takes place in the winter or, like now, in the fall.

The landscape itself, with its sadness, helps tears flow more freely. "Tomorrow morning around ten, I will go to Moshe's. He will tell me in detail how the burial was and how one feels when one's father comes back half-dead and then kills himself." I talk to myself in front of the window, intent on hearing my own words like my mother does at night. It wouldn't be strange if my father heard them and then came to us to tell us about his battles. But the image of the thin man with the beard whom the Nazi soldiers beat up so brutally came back to haunt me. A shudder ran down my spine and I felt suddenly faint.

My mother let me sleep, not waking me even for dinner. I slept until 5:00 a.m. and then woke up to see the gray dawn that barely gave signs of life amidst the cloud-covered sky. I went back to bed to find some warmth in between the covers. It would be another rainy, cold day.

⚜

Not thinking about anything I fixed my eyes on the ceiling and started to draw imaginary scenes: men on horses crossing the fields and brandishing sabers, like the hussars in the books in our town library. Small funny figures that laughed while turning, playing drums and trumpets . . .

My mother moved to one side and later opened her eyes, a bit startled to see me awake so early. She stroked my forehead with her hand, testing for fever and she let out a sigh of relief at finding me healthy, or at least appearing to be. I was proud to have a mother who worried so much about me. I would tell my friends, once I was allowed to go out again. We got up and I went to the washbasin to wash my hands and my face. Wow! How cold that water was! All traces of sleep disappeared once I touched the icy liquid.

I noticed that my mother was moving faster than usual. She was coming and going without accomplishing anything. She opened drawers only to close them again. She cleaned the table more than once and then stirred the water that was boiling on the stove. Her gaze examined every bit of space, smiling when it stopped at me and then turning serious again. I could tell she was worried, as if she was foreseeing something. She did not say a word during breakfast. Finally I decided to ask her: "Mom, could I go to Moshe's today?" She nodded.

I went out around nine, without feeling my usual fear. That day I had woken up feeling sure of myself, without the cruel uneasiness that often filled me after my usual nightmares. I took the first few steps walking very close to the wall. It was a habit everybody had adopted ever since the Germans invaded Czernowitz. The wall gave us a kind of protection against those square faces that

❖

looked at us without seeing us. They would patrol the streets and every once in a while would detain a passer-by, asking for identification.

When I got to Moshe's house I stopped to decide whether I should knock on the door. I was a bit scared. I felt that seeing my friend would be terrible. What could I say to someone who would never again be able to see his father? I stood still against the door until I saw some vehicles coming around the corner. They were somewhat different from those of the soldiers in brown uniforms. The passersby looked at them with apprehension. We felt there was a heaviness in the air. Two old men pointed to the letters on the front of every truck: "It's the SS," said one, who was holding an unlit pipe in his mouth. "They're here. God help the Communists and the Jews!" I felt a knot at the pit of my stomach when I heard those last words. Once again I was feeling the words lashed at me less than two days before: "God help the Jews!" What did we have to do with anything? Wars were always waged between great lords, those with a coat of arms emblazoned with an animal of some kind. Yes, I had seen pictures of such men in books we kept in our house. They had everything. I was annoyed for a while and did-n't pay much attention to the rest of the old men's con-versation. The trucks went by slowly, leaving behind a trail of black smoke that dirtied the paving stones, still wet from the evening rain. When the last truck turned the corner the street came back to life. Something told me that the so-called SS were not good people because of those black uniforms with the skulls on the collar and because of the way they looked at us.. I did not dare to knock on Moshe's door and came back home.

My mother, seeing me come in with my head down asked why I had come back so soon. She had expected

⚜

me back around noon. I stood before her and asked: "Mom, what do you know about the SS?" I could see her face change and her eyes open in terror. She raised her hand to her mouth to muffle a cry. After a while she calmed herself and asked: "Israel, what did you hear, who told you about them? I don't know anything. I don't even believe they exist!" There was something hidden that she did not want me to know. "Mom, I just saw them parading down our own street. They wear black uniforms with a skull on the collar. They stare at us coldly and I heard an old man say: 'God help the Jews'."

My mother let her arms fall in a gesture of surrender and said in a hoarse voice: "Israel, for God's sake, don't go out in the street again. I have arranged with a woman to bring us the food we need. Oh my God, it was true what Pessia and the others were saying and we didn't believe them!"

I didn't understand anything. As my mother kept talking, everything was getting more and more confusing. What had Pessia, the druggist's wife told her? Why was my mother adopting this attitude? Why couldn't I go out in the street? What was the reason for a woman having to bring us the food? Several minutes went by without us saying anything. The house seemed dark, shrouded in black like the uniform of the SS men. The silence became overwhelming, and more than once my mother took me close to her bosom to try to protect me whenever she heard a vehicle approaching. I became more and more bewildered.

The noise was turning into something strange that was making my mother react, staying close to me to give me some warmth. I felt sick and went upstairs to lie on my bed. It was a rather strange day, and I felt sorry for poor Moshe, who would never see his father again.

❧

Uniforms paraded along the ceiling. They were black, and time had given them dried-out faces that were almost skeletal. They looked at us and exclaimed: "God help the Jews!" Fast, strong knocks resounded on the door. My mother did not move. Her face turned white and a strange tremor shook her hands. I came down running. The knocks became stronger. "Open up, Perla!" It was a familiar voice, somewhat resembling my father's. My mother hesitated, but I decided to open.

Two men came in quickly, as if they were being followed. They looked like old men, with their faces and feet covered with rags. One of them took the rag off his face and hugged me, covering me with kisses. Then, holding me by the hand, he went over to my mother and kissed her on the cheek. My father had returned and was in one piece, with none of his body parts missing, but filthy with mud up to his forehead and wearing a beard. His teeth were yellow, either from not cleaning them or from chewing tobacco, but he was smiling and his eyes were not fixed on the wall like Moshe's father. My father had come back safe from the front. "What happened, Perla, that you didn't want to open? We went through a lot to get here. But we're together now and nothing will separate us again." And he was kissing us and touching us, surely to make sure we were also alive.

The man who came in with him fell asleep against the wall, without even sitting down.

✤

2

The Ghetto

With the arrival of my father, the situation in our house suddenly changed, but not for long. He told us about all his adventures when his battalion had to scramble. The Germans had destroyed most of the army and killed half of the men. My father, together with some comrades, was able to run away from the siege and wandered in the forest for several weeks, eating nothing but herbs and roots.

I would fall asleep listening to his stories. I can't recall everything. All I know is that my father came back to us after crossing the German lines. He took a big risk, since he would have been shot on the spot if found, as he told us. Very few came back. Some died in the attempt, either from cold or hunger or from their wounds. One of the men who had run away with him had half his body rot away from gangrene. He cried out to be shot in the head and finally did it himself. There was no time to bury him, he was simply covered with leaves and someone put a rose on top to mark his grave. My father's eyes would turn red when he talked about this.

The man who came with him hardly stayed a day in our house. When he had recuperated a bit from his ordeal he made his farewell, saying: "Comrade, take care of yourself. You know what we went through." He wished us good luck and went out in the street, walking slowly, with his head covered and the same old look with which he had come. My father and he exchanged meaningful looks, sharing some private knowledge that my mother and myself were not privy to. Days went by and my father sold everything we owned, barely leaving what we needed.

I looked around without understanding anything. My mother, though more at ease, still showed a growing anxiety. Sometimes we could not talk to her too much, because she would only get flustered.

Something similar was happening with my father. It was evident that he was nervous and eager to dispose of everything we owned. At first I thought we were going to live with my grandparents. That's when I began to dream. I was hoping to be able to go on a sleigh ride with my grandfather through the fields of his farm. It would be wonderful, and, if my parents allowed it, I could invite Moshe so that I could share my father with him and have some fun for a while.

I built many imaginary castles in the sand that first week. But Shabbat came and we could not go to the synagogue. The men in the black uniforms did not allow Jews out in the streets and every gathering was terminated as a violation of the occupation rules. The streets were being patrolled by the so-called SS, and one rarely saw the brown-uniformed soldiers who had come in at the beginning. My mother started to gather things in a corner of the house. Obviously the SS could come into any house and take whatever they wished. Those who resisted would get a bullet in the head. I knew about this because our friends would come to the house with new

⚜

stories every day. We spent Shabbat at home, trying to make the best of it. When the meal was over I went to the window and looked outside. The street was emptier than usual. There were no people walking by. I did not wish to ask any questions, but I knew that something was wrong. Very wrong!

On Sunday, after the church bells announced that it was eight o'clock in the morning, a truck equipped with a loudspeaker announced that all the Jews were to present themselves at the commissariat in order to register for work. My father turned white. My mother went up to embrace him and looked at me in despair. They knew what was happening but did not want to tell me. Uncertainty filled my heart and the men in the black uniforms seemed more suspicious than ever. In their proclamations they referred to "Jews" with a certain irony. My father put on a white shirt and went to the door, gesturing that we should follow him. "Come on, we need to go to the commissariat to register. It will be worse for us if we don't." He shut up and looked at the floor for a few minutes. It seemed that he was seeing something in the stone surface, but he kept quiet, wordlessly suppressing his misery.

My mother took me by the hand and I went out with her, next to my father. With every step we took our feet were covered with snow and mud. The street was not the same one I used to know. Now it seemed full of shadows, with weeping walls and closed windows. Some of our Gentile neighbors turned away when we tried to say hello. I had no idea why they were avoiding our greetings. Before the war they always would say good morning to us, but now it was as if we did not exist. They did not want to see us. I was hurt and so were my parents. We felt alone, as if we were walking though a dark tunnel, closer to the walls than before. We walked with sad and silent steps. The soles of our shoes emitted strange sounds when pressed against the pavement, like those of old mice. We walked that way until we got to the commissary. A very long line of people was standing at the door, guarded by a pair of SS men with their dogs. On the wall, above our heads, we could see the Nazi swastika flag flapping in the wind.

While we waited I had a chance to look around. There were people of all kinds. Men and women, old and young, all looking at their neighbors with indifference, wrapped up in themselves and perhaps wondering what was coming. However, there was still a ray of hope. We all were certain that things would come out all right. The guards in the black uniforms were yet to manifest themselves. They simply stared ahead, as if the line of people did not exist. Their dogs moved around uneasily but were held on a tight leash that did not allow them to lunge at anyone. Several women were trying to warm up the children they held in their arms, some of who were turning blue from the cold. Some cried, some slept and shuddered every once in a while. A little boy was coughing. He would open his little mouth and let out a low sound that resonated in his chest. His face was red from the effort. His mother was quiet, unable to help her baby. Some children my own age clutched their parents' coats, looking for a bit of warmth in the heavy material.

We looked at each other without understanding what was going on. One of the boys, with a head full of curls, was squeezing his brother's hand. I noticed he was limping, and his foot probably hurt. He would grit his teeth and bring his foot up for a few moments, surely to escape

⚜

the cold that was tormenting him. He had no socks, just shoes. His foot was covered with a brown scab that came up to his ankle. I turned away, feeling that my foot hurt too. Suddenly a snowball hit the man in front of us in the face. Before he could do anything, a burst of machine-gun fire kept him in his place. The SS man with the smoking gun looked serious, as if nothing had happened. On the other side of the street a group of anti-Semitic boys were readying a bunch of snowballs to throw at us. They knew we wouldn't be able to do anything. They laughed and cried out: "Hey Jews, it's about time, it's about time!" My father shook as a snowball hit him right on the nose. He managed to control himself while my mother held him so that he wouldn't try anything foolish and end up gunned down by the guard.

The snowballs kept hitting the people on line, and the laughter increased as more and more struck their targets. But one boy could not control himself and left the line to face his aggressors. We stood quietly, waiting for the shots, but they did not come. Instead the SS man let the dog loose after giving him a command in German. The animal lunged at the boy, biting his neck until it broke. The women brought their hands to their mouths to contain their cries, and I hid in my mother's skirt. It was a terrible spectacle. The boy's neck was broken and the dog kept biting his face. We were immediately surrounded by men in black uniforms. An officer with a white skull on his cap stood in front of us, shouting: "Any of you who makes trouble will end up like that one. We have brought you here following orders, and we will not tolerate any misconduct. You have to stay in line. Period. Whoever disobeys will pay. And don't forget, from now on you must do as we say." His eyes were red with anger as

❖

he finished this statement. The line continued its slow progress toward the door. We kept quiet, barely breathing and with fear showing in our faces. The body of the boy was picked up by two men who threw him in a cart like a sack of potatoes.

Even though I had my parents next to me, I was afraid. I think I finally began to understand some things that up to then had not been clear to me. The war was not over. It was barely starting, and we Jews were going to be its worst victims. But the situation was still not clear. Whey did we have to stand in line in front of the commissariat, and why were we the butt of everyone's jokes? And what had we done to those SS men that they looked at us with such contempt? I started to cry silently, trying not to make too much noise. The image of the boy with the broken neck was going around in my mind. When I opened my eyes the red stain was still fresh on the snow and the men with the black uniforms had not shifted one millimeter from their places. I lowered my head and thought about Moshe's father, with his mutilated leg and his eyes wide open, staring into space.

After two hours of waiting in the cold we found ourselves in front of a little man with a round face and small glasses that covered a pair of gray eyes. He sighed when he saw us, drank from a cup of tea that he kept in front of him, and picked up a piece of paper. My father was firm, but his voice quivered when he answered the German's questions. "Jew, what do you do? Where do you live? How did you escape the siege?" My father answered with short sentences, not volunteering too much information, because he knew the possible misunderstandings his poor command of German might cause. He answered the questions in German, which seemed to

❖

please the man. He identified my mother and me as his family. The Nazi made a note and gave him a ticket. He then said a few more words and told us to get out. My father walked slowly toward the back door of the building. He was white, rereading the ticket he had in his hands. He later told us that we had to leave our home and go north to an old, poor neighborhood. All Jews had to move there by order of the occupying authority. We came back tired, our legs and arms numb from the cold, and tried to think about something other than the need to leave our home. Moshe was standing in front of his house. We exchanged brief greetings. They too were going to the north of Czernowitz.

Around six o'clock a neighbor came in to tell us about the latest developments. All the businesses owned by Jews were being plundered by crowds acting under the protection of the SS. An old man had been dragged by his beard until it tore away and then was shot in the back. The synagogue was being guarded and there were rumors that it would be burned. The latest Nazi edicts forbade Jewish children to attend school. We were also prohibiting from going out at night, and anyone who did business with us would be punished. It was the first time in my life that I felt the true impact of anti-Semitism. I knew that some Romanians did not like Jews, but I had never imagined that they harbored such hatred for us. We were considered guilty simply because of our religion. Now we were being driven away like mice, forced to abandon our homes and live on the outskirts of the city. It was as if we had all contracted the plague.

That afternoon I couldn't touch a thing. Nobody did. An opportunist who was risking his life, so he told us, bought the house from my father for a third of its real

❖

value. His condolences looked to me like smiles of triumph at winning twice. He shed crocodile tears for the fate we were facing but did not give in one inch on the purchase price. He said he was doing it to help us out. The truth is that he was getting our house at a bargain price and had been lusting for it even before the war. I went up to my room. Downstairs my parents were talking with some people who wanted to buy our things for next to nothing, taking advantage of our situation. I heard my father trying to bargain with the buyers.

Suddenly there was a loud noise from the street. Some SS men jumped out of a truck and went into the house opposite ours. Some Jews lived there who had not reported to the commissariat. The SS men did not knock at the door—they kicked it in after forcing the lock with a crowbar. They went in swiftly, not saying a word. I watched from the window with my eyes wide open. People disappeared from the street, which remained silent and covered by snow. Every once in a while we heard some hollow sounds from inside the house. The guards did not move, as if afraid of the closed doors and windows. Suddenly the owner of the house came out. His head was bloody, and a yellowish-red liquid was oozing from one of his ears. Two men followed him, hitting him with the butts of their rifles. The man turned in the snow, raising his hands and pleading for mercy. Later his wife and two daughters were brought out.

They didn't look any better than the father. They had been beaten up, and their clothes were tattered. In the middle of the street the SS men gave them all another terrible beating. The man's eye came out of its socket. The woman was crying, trying to protect her face with her hands. A square-jawed blond officer told the SS men to stop the punishment. Staying in the doorway with his

⚜

hands on his hips he shouted: "We gave an order, right? And all the Jews have to obey it! What right did you have not to go to the commissariat? How are you different from the rest of your race? What we are about to do will teach others that our orders have to be respected!" He brought up his arm and six huge dogs lunged at the four people, who still laying in the snow, very close to each other and with their faces gripped by terror.

The first target of the jaws of the animals was the old man. He died almost immediately. He may even have been dead already, because I didn't see any sign that he reacted to the dogs. His wife and daughters, however, began screaming and tried to fight back, much to the amusement of the SS men, who laughed at the spectacle.

My mother pulled me away from the window, giving me a strong reprimand. "Israel, how can you look at the street without your parents' permission. Don't you know that everything you do has to be checked first with us?" And she began crying. I did not understand. Why would they forbid me to look out the window when I had always done it before without asking for permission? The situation was getting worse and worse. I lowered my head but did not become angry. If my mother said so, there had to be a reason. After what I had seen and felt that morning, nothing seemed strange anymore. From now on, I would have to live a different life. I would live differently. I knew instinctively that the blood of that family would still be on the snow like that of the boy the SS dog had torn apart in front of the commissariat. Some gunshots made us shudder. My mother hid my face in her bosom and held me tightly against her.

"Tomorrow we leave for the place they indicated on the card," said my father. And while he talked he rubbed his chin distractedly, not explaining what awaited us there. I

⚜

understood that this was the last night we would spend in our home, which I knew inch by inch. I even knew the holes though which the mice came into the pantry. I went through the house mentally; there was not a corner I did not know. I used to draw lines on the walls, and later erased them to avoid a beating. With my toys I paraded through the tiles up to the headquarters, an empty wooden box. How my grandfather would rejoice when I told him that I used to have a small city in my house where the toys he had given me used to live. And this was to be the last night I would sleep here. It seemed like the dogs of the men in black uniform were biting me as well. I looked at my father and was unable to say anything when I saw that his eyes were filling with tears just like mine. My mother's sobs could be heard from the kitchen.

That night my father's two brothers came to visit. They shut themselves in a room and talked for a long time. My mother prepared some suitcases and pointed to some clothing for me to put in a canvas bag. I sneaked my toys inside a wool coat, together with some socks and my father's underwear. We were leaving, and my toys and my memories were leaving with me.

My father and his brothers opened the door and called out to my mother. The following day at eight we would move to our new home. We would have to be careful, since the Germans had picked out a group of Jews as a "government" to run things in the neighborhood we had been assigned to. My uncles said goodbye and were supposed to come for us the next day. I couldn't sleep that night. The cold, wet night slid through the walls, crying. The fireplace remained unlit, the pots and pans were in a linen bag, and my mother was coughing with the beginning of a cold.

✤

A long, cold night. The worst night of my life. I tried to sleep, but my head would fill up with images and I mentally toured the house. I remembered every detail; the repairs my father would do in the summer so that in autumn water would not come in through the cracks. I could almost see the spider in the kitchen weaving its unending web waiting for a fly, walking proudly with its long legs over a thread so thin that I always thought spiders walked on air. As the time passed, my mind evoked more and more forms: the loose brick under the cistern, the back door that led to the apple tree from where you could go to Moshe's house. The windowpanes always clean, transparent by starlight, letting in whatever happened in the street. At this point my body began to shake from the cold. The bloody forms of the day's dead came up to me like stones, hitting each other. Blood, the red liquid filling the streets up to the end of the city, mixing with water from the wells, staining the white uniforms of the schoolchildren.

I bit my lips so as not to cry out in fear. I could see the dogs in front of me. I clearly heard the orders of the man in the black uniform. I was finally able to get some rest when I saw the first light of dawn and, even though my eyes were burning, I was filled with tranquility when the light came in. At least with the light the specters that had surrounded me during the night disappeared.

I was completely free of these nightmares when I heard the steps of my father coming in to wake me. I pretended to be asleep, for I did not want to worry him. When he gave me a soft tap on the shoulder I made believe I was waking up. "You'd better get ready, for they'll be coming for us soon," he said. I nodded and got up. Everything was spinning around me. I looked at him

❖

sideways. He had big circles under his eyes. I was sure he had not slept either.

When we came out of the house, my mother began to weep on my father's shoulder. My uncles and their children were waiting for us in the street. They all had the somber face of a night without sleep. They carried their belongings in leather suitcases and canvas bags. They had some mattresses in a wooden cart. We began walking toward the northern end of the city, the area where the Germans had decreed we Jews could live for the moment. We walked slowly, covering the tracks of others before us, of people who had woken up a little earlier, so as to arrive at their destination a little sooner. In the main street we saw a caravan of people walking in the same direction we were. They were all carrying things on their heads, backs, and shoulders. They were bent over, in a slow procession that became a show for the few passersby on the sidewalks. Some looked at us with compassion, feeling like accomplices to the fact. Others took the opportunity to hurl insults and swear at us. Many pointed at us as if we were animals. The procession grew bigger toward the horizon, and also a bit darker due to the worn-out clothes and the mud that stuck to our boots as we walked northward.

Strangely, no one said anything. We took for granted what was going to happen. What could we expect, since we had already seen the SS in action? They solved everything with violence, with their dogs, rifle butts, and machine guns. It was clear that our fate was sealed. The grownups knew it but said nothing, waiting for a possible change or perhaps a miracle.

Still, we had not yet given up all hope on this freezing march. We dreamed about the long-shot possibility that

⚜

things would not be as dark as we expected. After what seemed like a very long time, we reached the zone indicated by the authorities. It encompassed several square blocks, and that is where the Jews of Czernowitz had to assemble, together with those coming in from neighboring towns. It was clear that we were too many for such a small place. Hundreds of faces looked at one another fearfully, not understanding what was happening. It seemed to me that even the houses were sad. My father looked at his card, talked to his brothers, and they pointed to a street that got narrower the closer we got to it. Many of the people around us seemed dumbfounded, uncertain which way to go. The children shivered in the cold, and some had already began to wander aimlessly with no one to claim them. It wouldn't surprise me if they had come by themselves, following this human tide that had finally reached the beginning of the end.

The SS were watching and their hands pressed against their rifles in preparation for any possible disturbance. We all understood that any *faux pas* would be madness. A woman with a baby in her arms, barely covered by a blanket, was laughing without any apparent reason. Her dull, wide-open eyes denoted that madness was clouding her mind. The baby, in the meantime, looked around without understanding what was happening. A group of old men were chanting the morning prayers. Their voices hit against the wall and came back to us as we walked to the place designated on the card.

Our backs ached, and we were looking for a reprieve in order to began putting away our belongings. Twelve people were supposed to share a room. We had expected to be crowded, but not this crowded. We were like sardines in a can. The room was small, with a small window

✣

that barely admitted a ray of light. The wet floor seemed to give in under the weight of our bodies.

It was clear that the men in the black uniforms had chosen this place beforehand in order to start killing us slowly. A rat scurried in between my legs, letting out a squeak that made my aunt Sarah scream. Simon, my father's oldest brother, said, "If things go on as I see it, pretty soon we'll have to eat these animals," and remained silent, ruminating on the thought of being locked in and isolated from the rest of the world simply for having been born a Jew.

We put away our things as well as we could. When we finished we sat down on the floor, looking at one other and asking the silent question that had been on our minds all along: "Why?" The answer did not come, and we only felt the cold that increased as the day went on. Staring at the floor we searched for a reason that would explain this sudden change in our fortunes. Barely two days before we still had a house and had never imagined that we would soon find ourselves sharing a space of five by six meters with nine other people. My father cracked his knuckles and looked at us without saying a word. He had nothing to say to us. We had almost nothing, and there was no need for explanations.

The women put together a sort of kitchen in a corner of the room. From the other rooms we heard the desperate cries of an old couple who seemed to have lost their minds. Some children walked aimlessly in the hallway with wet clothes and pale faces. They went in and out of every room, not saying a word, as if looking over the neighbors.

A red-haired boy who had lost his front teeth came in. He was the leader of a group that followed him every-

⚜

where. Although he didn't say anything, he would nod and pat his lambskin jacket whenever he saw something in order. I stood in the doorway with my four cousins. We too wanted to go out, walk around the house, find out what was going on in the other rooms—things like how many people were living with us, and where the bathroom was. Without my mother noticing I went out with two of my cousins, Elias and Reuben. We went in formation, led by the redhead. We walked fast, without stopping anywhere and much less when our other cousins called us. In the room next-door there were at least fifteen people, mostly girls. One of them lifted up a hand when she saw us, shouting at us to go to hell. Some friends tried to calm her down. We heard them saying that this would soon end, that the SS were not as bad as they appeared to be, that the pogroms were nothing but old wives' tales. However, a woman of about thirty-six or thirty-seven stood up on a wooden box on which she had been sitting and said: "Don't you know about Warsaw? My brother, who is now a fugitive, said that Jews there are starving to death in the ghetto. Why harbor any illusions? The Germans, like the Russians and the Polacks, are thoroughly anti-Semitic. Who's going to rescue us? Romania is defeated, Germany rules, and the rest of the world couldn't care less about us. In many countries they don't even know we exist. We don't have a country that will raise its arm in our favor." And then, suddenly, she shut up.

She looked at us and said nothing. She only bit her lip and ran her fingers through the brown hair that fell to her shoulders. The old man with her was either asleep or perhaps already dead. Reuben pulled at our shirts and our hearts stopped when we looked in the direction he

❖

was signaling. Walking toward us down the hallway toward us was a man with no ears, nose, or hair. His eyes were half-shut and bloodshot. The pink hole he had once breathed through made him look like a skull. It was horrible to see him without ears and hair, and that tragic way of dragging himself, the hissing sound of his breathing and the saliva running from his mouth.

He tried to smile when he saw us, but only succeeded in spooking us even more, grimacing with those black holes where his teeth were missing. He walked past us, leaving behind the smell of putrefaction. Some doors closed on him to spare other children the spectacle. Only one woman approached him to offer a drink of water. He refused it and kept walking toward the floor above. We went to the door, led by Elias. On our way we saw long, pale faces with red eyes from sleepless nights. Our neighborhood was nothing if not heterogeneous.

Some people had no shoes. Instead, their feet were wrapped in rags, with a piece of wood by way of a sole. They were Jews who had come in from other parts, forced out of their homes and now in the same desperate situation as we were. You could see everything in their faces. They were maps of humiliation, open books where a whole life could be read.

In the room next to the door, a man was sitting on a bench against the wall. His clothes indicated that he was a man of means, a learned man, like the doctor who once had come to see me. But he was now staring into space while he smoked one cigarette after another, thinking who knows what. He surely had attended a university, befriended talented people, and he was probably married. I walked over and asked where he was from. He looked at me, his face half-hidden by the smoke from his cigarette.

⚜

"Where I come from doesn't matter. I am now in the ghetto, like you and your friends." "They're my cousins," I said. "Well, your cousins, what's the difference? I do like the rest of us. I wait. That's a characteristic of our people. We Jews spend our lives waiting and never get tired of doing it. Look at me. I'm waiting for my wife and daughter. A month ago they weren't there when I came home. I looked for them, asked about them, and no one could give me an answer. After fifteen days I went back to my office and the Germans had ordered it closed. You see. I had already been excluded from my home and my work. Yesterday I went to the commissariat, and they told me that I had to come here, and here I am. Waiting. Believing with blind faith that this has to end somehow, even if it is with us. You know, at the university—" He closed his eyes and began to whistle a long, sad melody. He threw away the cigarette butt that was beginning to burn his fingers and dropped his hands in a sign of impotence.

He wasn't interested in talking to me or to anybody. Reuben and Elias looked at each other and then at me with inquisitive eyes. I was unable to give them an answer, trying myself to understand the meaning of the words of the man on the bench. We left slowly, trying not to "wake him up."

The street was in an uproar. Men and women went around swearing. A cold air froze the beards of the old men and covered the faces of everyone with frost. Hundreds of bags and suitcases were at the entrances of the houses. There were still many people who had not settled in. Some dogs walked around sniffing and trying to open the bags. They were thin animals, with watery eyes and visible rib cages. Elias put his hands in his pockets and exhaled, trying to get some warmth.

⚜

Yes, it was cold, and the dampness came in through the soles of our shoes. We were reprimanded when we got back. Our mothers had become almost hysterical when they realized we were gone. In the situation we were in, you thought of nothing but the worst. We had to listen to the reprimand with our heads down. We had done wrong in going away from our room without letting others know. After a while everything went back to normal.

Some smoke in the improvised kitchen indicated that food was cooking, but even though we were hungry, we tried not to show it. Elias, Reuben, and I had made a pact that we were not going to complain or ask for. We had made it in the street, when we saw all those miserable people looking for a hole in which to crawl in order to get a bit of warmth.

There was an outcry from the hall. The women went around crying and bringing in the little ones. Something strange was happening upstairs. Everyone cautiously went up to the next floor; the man on the bench opened his eyes and stood up. My father and my uncles grabbed some knives, thinking that the SS was on the way.

My mother picked me up and held me to her face, clinging desperately to my body. My other cousins were in the same situation. Our eyes widened, and fear crept up our throats, making our stomachs ache.

But it wasn't the men in the black uniforms. The man without the nose and ears had gone into the upstairs bathroom and hung himself with his belt. His mutilated body was dangling from the showerhead and his tongue was hanging from the left side of his mouth. His eyes were bulging out. Everyone commented on the terrible death, but at the same time people were relieved that the noise was not due to an incursion by the SS. You could

⚜

tell the grownups suffered more as we waited to know our fate. The children were more at ease, perhaps because we did not truly understand the situation. Grownups knew many things that they did not want to tell us, or else they kept quiet in the hope that whatever they feared would not come true.

I was beginning to get used to the new life, to the daily appearance of fifty people living in a house with two bathrooms and three water faucets. We had a salty hot broth for lunch. Nobody complained. At four o'clock, a siren went off and the street filled up with SS men, machine guns ready to fire at the least provocation. The grownups paled. "It's the end," muttered a fat little man with a big double chin.

We stood still in our places. The presence of the men in the black uniforms did not lead to good thoughts. Using loudspeakers they laid down the law that from that moment on would rule the life of the Jews. "From now on, it is strictly forbidden to leave the neighborhood we have assigned you. Those who do will be shot on sight. The public administration is in the hands of the Jewish Council, a group duly elected to take care of any problems that arise." The SS spokesman paused for a moment. He felt like a king, the messenger of the gods. People looked at him in terror, listening to every sound that came from his thin lips. The guards watched everyone. They did not feel secure in the ghetto. The official took up the microphone again. "You will have to register every three days, and if anyone dies of a chronic illness or of old age "—he said these last words in a clearly ironic tone—" the members of the council will have to be informed. Anyone who disobeys these regulations will be severely punished. Anyone who does business with peo-

❧

ple in the city will be sentenced to death. No transactions are allowed outside this zone. You are required to denounce anyone who does not obey the law, otherwise measures will be taken." Having said this, he came down from his platform and motioned the troops to leave.

Night fell and we tried to accommodate ourselves as best as we could, almost on top of one other. The space seemed even smaller when we lay down on some newspapers obtained from a nearby building. The walls were damp, and even though we huddled very close to give each other warmth, the cold made us shiver. I tried to sleep, but felt my extremities go numb, especially my feet, despite my boots and socks. It was a long night, too long. Every once in a while you could hear a child crying, the shouts of a woman, or the snores of an old man. Thousands of strange sounds filled the atmosphere, and the air we breathed became heavy with odors from the nearby rooms. My father and his brothers kept talking and gesticulating in a corner of the room. Elias and Reuben had covered themselves with the same blanket in order to give each other some warmth. My mother kept rubbing my chest. Some soft lights illuminated the downstairs hallway. Upstairs everyone was in motion. I could hear the noises.

Toward midnight I felt something biting me. It was fleas. The house was full of insects, especially cockroaches that ran on top of our blankets and sometimes even on our faces. It was a freezing sensation to feel the bugs crawling on our skin. But the fleas were the worst. Theirs was a strong bite that made us feel prisoners in a world so far away from the one we knew.

Our enemies had set us apart because we believed in one God who could not possibly be depicted and who

❖

spoke to us from the scrolls of the Torah. We were considered delinquents simply because we were practicing Jews.

I couldn't understand any of this. What evil were we perpetrating by attending the synagogue? All we did there was pray, asking God's grace for all men, thanking Him for the full crops that belonged to everyone and not only to one group. We even prayed for the laws and the government of the country in which we lived. What was wrong with that? But now they had us trapped, away from the city, like you do with crazy people and those who had the plague. The more I thought about all this, the more I felt the weight of the night. The cold intensified, and you could hear the howling of the hungry dogs that ambulated in the snow that did not stop falling, covering the street and the half-torn roofs of the houses they had designated for us. Dawn came slowly, with an opaque light that tried to come in through the small window of our room. We got up. No one had been able to sleep. We all had pale faces with half-closed eyes and skin covered by red bites, the mark of the bugs we had to share the house with whether we liked it or not.

Many chose to relieve themselves outside rather than wait for the bathroom to become available. The water faucets were not enough. The women, pots in their hands, waited patiently for the trickle of water to fill their receptacles. My mother, among them, tried to control her growing nervousness. Standing by her side, I tried to figure out the reason for her fidgeting, which everyone had noticed. She didn't say anything, but she sighed when she saw two old men and began to cry. When our turn at the faucet came, it was I who filled up the pot. My aunts tried to console her but to no avail. Finally, after listen-

⚜

ing to them I realized what was bothering my mother. She
had not heard from my grandparents. From one moment
to the next all communication with her parents had
stopped. She had not heard from the old people and suspected the worst. The only Jews in their town, they had
probably had been killed. Who would have protected
them? Remembering my toys, I relived the time spent
with my grandfather. He and my grandmother loved me
like no one else. I was the only son of their only daughter, a kind of promise into the future. It hurt not to know
about them. What if they had been thrown to the dogs?
The men in the black uniforms were capable of anything,
and for them the age of a Jew apparently didn't matter.
They were against men and women, children and old
people alike. From then on I began calling them beasts.
Yes, they were uniformed beasts who instead of growling
talked in German.

The beasts were waiting for us all in the ghetto. You
could see them around the clock at the end of the street.
The beasts patrolled and smoked.

One of our neighbors went crazy and ran into the
street crying that her belly was full of mice. She was an
eighteen-year-old girl, not very attractive but with fine
features. Her roommates later said that Ruth—that was
her name—had not been well for a whole month, ever
since her brothers and her father had been killed in the
invasion. Later her boyfriend was captured by the
Gestapo and after a couple of days was found in a trench
with his head and arms broken. He survived for just a
few hours. Ruth's mother had died of tuberculosis three
days before we were summoned to the commissariat.
Everything came together and she went crazy, running
over to the beasts.

⚜

We all watched the scene. An old man with a fur hat said Kaddish for the girl. When she got to the beasts they took her by the waist and went inside. They came out an hour later. She came out afterwards, with her dress in her hand, completely nude and with her skin touching the snow. One of the men threw a snowball at her and she cried. At that moment the other one pressed the trigger of his machine gun and the body of the girl filled up with holes that gushed out blood. She fell without letting go of the dress she was holding. The beasts later kicked the body outside of the ghetto.

The murder had been justified. Anyone who tried to leave the zone would be shot on the spot. I was beginning to understand many things. Elias told me that some boys knew of a place from where you could leave the ghetto without the guards finding out. He said it in a serious tone, like someone who knows that life depends on a certain degree of risk. He looked at me in a way that let me understand I was not to say a word. I nodded. Reuben, who also knew about it, pretended he didn't know anything and whistled a tune. In less than two days the people of the ghetto were finding ways to survive. Many were ready to risk their lives to defy the laws of the beasts.

That afternoon, after telling my mother that I was going to stretch my legs with Elias and Reuben, we went to a three-story house. There we found some boys our age who were eating dried vegetables. I was surprised, for it was not mealtime and we did not have food to spare. Elias smiled and introduced me to the group. They all raised their hands.

The oldest was about sixteen. He gave me a strong handshake. "Elias told me about you, and it looks like you will be able to help us in important ways. How old are you?

⚜

"Eight."

"Well, whether you are or not, your height will do."

I looked and listened in amazement, without understanding what it was all about. The boy, who identified himself as Red, perhaps because of a red mark he had on his chin, took me by my waist and lifting me up threw me about five feet away. The others looked satisfied. "You're all right, you know how to fall and you're very light." I felt offended when I realized they were calling me thin.

Red was explicit. "Israel, do you see what's happening in the street? People are dying slowly, they're cold and at home there is not much to eat, is there? Well, we have opened up a tunnel that leads to a street that ends up in the city in a place where there are never any German patrols. There are people there who are willing to trade food and medicine for the things we give them. Those who don't want to have anything to do with us, we steal from. Yes, I know that stealing is ugly, but what are you going to say when your mother is sick or your cousins are hungry? " He talked without hesitation, sure of himself. You could tell that even before coming here Red knew his work.

He was a kind of teacher, Elias told me. His father had no legs and he supported him. He even hid him from the beasts when they came to take him to the "hospital." His mother had died when he was still an infant. In some parts of town he was known as "the serpent" because he was able to slide down a roof without anybody seeing him or hearing him. When something was needed at home he would go get it.

And here in the ghetto he was the first to look for a way out, something that would keep him from aimlessly walking around and suffering from the cold.

⚜

I trusted Red, but I didn't say anything to my parents, just as my cousins had told me. If they knew, they would have locked me in to avoid a situation as dangerous as the one I was about to face. Life in the ghetto was becoming unbearable. Every day more Jews would join us from different parts, which resulted in real chaos. To the lack of housing was added scarcity of food and medicine. In our room we began to feel the effects of hunger. There was little to eat. Sometimes potato soup, other times some half-baked chestnuts. One of my father's sisters-in-law was beginning to show signs of malnutrition. She was very quiet, her eyes were sunken, and her skin was beginning to have a yellow tinge. Elias would sometimes bring her some vegetables, but it was not enough, she needed a tonic and no one could give it to her. She was dying in front of our eyes.

One night in early spring I was initiated in one of Red's jobs. Because of my height and my weight I could go to the city with three other boys. One part of the mission consisted in stealing the medicine my aunt needed.

We were to meet Red at eight in the morning. The night before he gave us precise instructions as to how to walk unnoticed in the streets of the city. He told me to keep my shirt open in order to show a medal with the face of a saint on it. That would keep me from looking suspicious. We were ready at eight. Red took us to the back of the ghetto and there he gave us last-minute instructions. We climbed a wall and had to slide down the roof of an old house that served as the boundary between the city and us. The building was half-destroyed and in serious danger of coming down on us. The beasts had a well-armed patrol in the surroundings, since this was one of the logical points to leave the area. When I saw the guards my stomach almost came out of my mouth. My other three companions motioned for me to keep calm. One of them slid down a pipe to the ground. He came down very slowly, keeping his body close to the wall. The place was dark and was only suitable for somebody small and slim. Somebody bigger than us would have been discovered. Red obviously planned things very well, but how were we going to avoid being seen once we were on the ground?

I came down swiftly, and very scared. So as not to make any noise, the boys who were already there caught me in their arms when I fell. No one made a sound. We waited for the last boy to descend. He came down as light as a feather. He was one of the more experienced ones, having come out of the ghetto at least fifty times. Moritz, the oldest, who was no more than nine, moved along close to the wall for a while until he reached a specific point. From there he motioned for us to follow. We crouched so as not to be seen by the beasts. Morris plucked out some grass and smiled. Underneath there was a tile that could be lifted. He put his hands on the sides, and after a bit of a strain we found a hole that led to a kind of gallery. We went in and Moritz placed the tile over us again and covered it with grass. Moving ahead of us and lowering his voice, he told us to hold hands and walk slowly. At first I was afraid that I might fall in a hole, but we kept very close to the grainy wet wall, putting our feet softly on the slippery floor.

The air was heavy and difficult to breathe. We walked this way for about a half an hour, unable to see anything even after our eyes had adjusted to the darkness. As we walked the tunnel kept getting narrower. I began to regret having gotten into this. I did not see much possibility to

❖

get out and started to lose confidence in Red. Suddenly we saw a faint light up ahead and I was happy not to be trapped. The floor there was firmer and made of a mixture of sand and stone.

When we got to the mouth of the tunnel Moritz made us stop. We were standing in front of the patio of the public school, which was right above us. Moritz told us that Red and another friend had discovered the route, but they had to enlarge the opening because it was barely a small window that served as a sewer. To get out we would wait until recess and leave one by one, mingling with the schoolchildren.

Moritz made us feel at ease: "I've done it many times, it's very easy."

We had to wait almost an hour. Finally the kids came out and I found myself thrust into the patio. At the beginning I did not know what to do. I was completely disoriented. The second boy out took me by the arm and I ran with him to a gate. We stopped there to wait for the others. They came almost immediately. Obviously Red knew all the details. The hole through which we had come was barely visible. It was covered and there was a statue in front of it. But the best part was that the spot was off limits to the schoolchildren because it was a storage area for some stones that the principal considered valuable. That's why at recess any of us could run to the patio and then go to this spot, which in fact was quite ugly, full of thorny bushes and wet, but hardly visited by the rest of the children.

Moritz crouched and lifted some bricks. There was an opening under the gate through which we slipped. People in the street took us for schoolchildren trying to cut class. An old lady confronted us: "What are you doing, kids?"

❖

Moritz, who had faced similar situations before, answered:

"Don't say anything, ma'am, we're trying to escape because the math teacher wouldn't let us go see a friend who's dying. TB, you know."

The woman put her hand to her throat and said, "Poor boy, is he very poor?"

Moritz, a bit more sure of himself, answered: "Too poor, as poor as the Jews they've locked up in the north."

The woman raised her hand to bless us. "God should punish that principal. Here's some money so that you can buy something for that poor boy. Charity is an obligation. The priest said in his last sermon that whoever allows a child to die in misery will not enter the kingdom of heaven."

Moritz gave her such an innocent look that the woman gave him a second blessing. "Go, my children, to your little friend. Oh, my God, how can you allow a child to die?" and she pressed her rosary as she walked off.

Moritz took the money and motioned us to follow him to a nearby house. There, inside a hole that led to the basement, he told us what we must do in the city. "Walk in twos, without looking at anybody, as if you were taking a stroll. If someone stops you, tell them you're hungry, that you don't know anything about your parents and you're waiting for Simon's mother to come back. Do you understand, Israel?"

"And that woman?"

"Don't worry, she's the wife of one of the town officials. She's always giving away a few bills to anyone who tells her about sick children. She's mad, poor woman. Red told us the Germans killed one of her sons in the war. But enough talking, let's go, we have barely enough time to get back. Simon and Israel, to the market.".

❖

Simon put his hands inside the sleeves of his coat and started to whistle as he walked. I followed him, a bit scared. I was afraid of the streets. I could still see the people in the windows, talking in whispers, not daring to say hello to us. Some ignored us as they walked past. Others saw us go by, but their thoughts were far away, perhaps waiting to hear from a loved one. We saw many women, always commenting about how hard life was getting to be. Some, knowing that the Jews had been deported to the north, blamed everything on them. It was the result of the Nazi propaganda.

Simon looked seriously at them, but he did not stop. We walked toward the market, for our mission was to bring something from there. We would steal fruits and vegetables and, if possible, a piece of meat. I was trembling just thinking that the beasts might get hold of us. I had already found out about some boy who had fallen in the attempt to escape. They were shot against a wall of the ghetto. The SS followed orders to a T, as if they were trained animals. That's why Red liked it when I referred to them as beasts.

We got to the market. There were many stores with goods for sale. A man with a black mustache shouted: "Here, people, here it's cheaper. Tomorrow I may not be able to give you the same price."

Simon stopped and told me: "Israel, go to the corner and wait for me. I'll give you something as I run past. We'll meet a block away. Understood?"

I did as Simon said. Waiting there, with my legs shaking slightly, I looked around. It was my first time, and I did not want the plan to fail because of me. I took out a linen bag that I had brought with me and applied my five senses to the task. I was trying to remember, step by step, the training Red had given us in the ghetto. I had to

⚜

wait for Simon. He would give me his booty on the run and I would start shouting that he had stolen the vegetables I had bought for my family. It was very simple in theory but dangerous nonetheless. I began to bite my nails. I imagined that I would fall into the hands of the beasts and would never see my parents again, who probably thought I was somewhere in the ghetto. How could they even imagine that their son was in the middle of the city, risking his skin for a pack of vegetables? Some of the passersby gave me a pitying look, thinking perhaps that I was an orphan.

Suddenly I heard a commotion from one of the stores. I saw Simon heading toward me fast as an arrow and some men coming after him with sticks and knives. When he got to the corner he took my bag and left his with me. Some policemen who collaborated with the Nazis took out their whistles. I pissed in my pants and was unable to speak. Frozen by fear, I began to run in the same direction as Simon. I couldn't see him, but I felt the people shouting at my back.

As we crossed a street the door of a house opened and I ran in, not realizing what was happening until they closed the door.

My muscles paralyzed by fear, I saw a shadow approaching me. It was the woman who had seen us leaving the school. She looked at me for a long time before she asked, "Why were you running? What were people shouting after you?"

I swallowed and hid the bag behind my back. "I don't know, ma'am. People are always running for something, you know, they keep running."

The woman rubbed her hands. "It's true, child, people run for fear of the war. This damn war is going to end

❖

with all of us. Every once in a while I see them running. All of them, men in the street as well as soldiers. Some because they are afraid, others looking for people to shoot or take into their prisons. Don't you have a relative in prison?"

A bit more confident, I answered: "Yes ma'am, my brother." I was trying to go slow, in order to put my ideas together. "They took him out of the house one night because, according to the soldiers, he was doing business with the Jews in the north. We don't know what happened to him. My mother has not been allowed to visit him."

The woman looked at me without blinking. I thought I had been caught in a lie when she asked "What is your brother's name? I could find out about him."

With my mouth dry and a terrible pain in my stomach I dared to say "Isaac, yes, that's his name," and I started to cry. I was crying from fear, but the woman thought it was for my brother. She stroked my face, "Don't cry, little boy. He'll get out, many have. Of course your brother's crime is a serious one. Don't you know that it is forbidden to trade, even to talk with the Jews?"

Drying my tears I asked the woman to do what she could to find out about my "brother." She smiled and before I left asked me to wait for her. She went to the back of the house. I wanted to leave, but a huge dog sitting by the chair made me change my mind. I began to get impatient. Surely Simon was waiting for me. Finally the woman came back. She was carrying a piece of bread with butter. "For you to eat," she said and added, "Tell me something, haven't I seen you before? In school, wasn't it?"

I shook my head no while I ate. The hunger pangs had been bothering since early morning and it wasn't the

✦

right time to start giving explanations. I realized that I had to save a piece for Simon, since he had not eaten yet either. I said goodbye to the woman promising to come back to find out about my "brother."

She gave me a blessing and followed me with her eyes until I turned the corner. From there I had to get my bearings. While running I had passed the meeting point and now I had to go back to find Simon. I went around the block a few times and finally started to go back. My whole body tensed with each step. I was terrified every time I encountered someone along the way. I saw all the people in the street as enemies. I kept close to the wall to find some measure of protection. At an intersection I felt someone tap me on the shoulder. I felt lost. One of the beasts might be behind me waiting to put a bullet in my head. I didn't move and barely breathed.

The hand made me turn on my heels and I found myself facing Simon. "Where did you go?"

In my relief, I gave Simon a hug. Alarmed by my behavior, he turned away and asked once again, "Israel, where did you go?"

I couldn't say anything. Instead I handed him the bag he had given me and also gave him the piece of bread with butter I had saved for him. He bit into it heartily while checking the contents of the bag. "Tell me later. The others are waiting for us down there," he said with his mouth full of bread, and taking me by the hand he started to walk fast, avoiding the crowds and the guards.

In about ten minutes the group had reunited. Moritz looked at our work and let out a whistle when he found a whole salami inside the bag. Simon shrugged while he smiled. "I found it in the hands of the wife of a German official," he said. "What an ugly woman!" Moritz let out a big laugh and asked, "How did Israel do?"

⚜

Simon put his hand on his chin: "Not bad for the first time." He was covering up for me. He did not want to make me look bad in front of the others. There were still some breadcrumbs on the side of his mouth. When he realized this he wiped his mouth with his sleeve, feigning a cough. The church bells chimed one o'clock. Moritz told us it was time to go back.

The morning had gone by very fast, full of thrills. We walked separately, leaving between thirty and forty meters between us on different sidewalks so as not to arouse suspicion. Red had been very clear about this. And if any of us was arrested we would have to say that we did not know anything.

Forget about parents. In the city we had to be orphans, whether we liked it or not. They had taken the orphans to the ghetto and it was not unusual to see them wandering around there. After all, what could a child know about his identity? This was at least what we had planned. We did not know the plan of the beasts or their intentions.

When we got to the gate, Moritz put the bricks together again and indicated for us to run to the statue. One every three minutes. At that time there was no one in the school, so going back was more difficult. We had to be careful not to be seen by the watchman, who was a sleepy old man, or some teacher who was going out to lunch later than usual. We managed without any problems, waiting in the hole until everyone was there.

Our return through the tunnel was very slow, just the way we had come. We had to be very careful not to slip or cry out. The beasts might hear us, and then we would never get out alive. They would not bother to ask who was there. They would simply shoot to kill.

⚜

When we got to the tile, Moritz stuck his head out. "We still have to wait a while. When they change the guard we'll go out and climb up the pipe. Be careful not to leave anything behind. Red won't like it if we only come back with part of our booty. That would give us away, and they would intensify the surveillance. No one throws away food or medicine these days." Moritz spoke slowly, enunciating very carefully so that what he said would stay in our minds forever. No one asked any questions. Our boss stuck his head out once again.

He slipped out first, pushing the tile to one side so that we could all get out without any difficulty. He covered it again with straw and took the three bags, tying them around his waist, then started up the pipe we had slid down before. When he got to the top he took a rope he had hidden under a few tiles and tied it to a wall. That way it was easier for us to climb up, especially for me, since I was a beginner. Once we were all out, we crawled on the roof again until we got to the place where the ghetto met the city. Moritz was about to jump down when he stopped and motioned for us to keep quiet.

Right where we were supposed to jump down, the beasts were making a reconnaissance and were forcing some old people to get out. They boarded them on trucks and burned their prayer books. One of the beasts, with a hat too big for his shaved head, switched on a loudspeaker and announced: "Every book where your religion is manifested will be considered subversive. God knows what plans you have written in that strange language! Anyone found reading such a book or anything similar will be shot on the spot. And now go to sleep, you pack of dogs."

Moritz tightened his fists and tensed his body. The other four of us were livid and broke out in a cold sweat.

⚜

We breathed a little easier when we saw the trucks leave. Simon pointed out that the trucks did not let out smoke like the others, but we were too nervous to speculate about that.

When Moritz was sure that the beasts were gone, we jumped down. Red whistled from a hiding place near where we had landed, and we showed him our booty.

"Boys," said Red seriously, "I congratulate you for your work, but I don't think we should take any more risks for now. The T group fell into the hands of the Gestapo. It's best that we all go home and not see each other until next week. At that time I will show you how to again go about our business. And you," he said to me, "how was it? Thank Moritz that you came back alive. I know everything." That was Red, always full of surprises. Before leaving I was given a bag of flour, two bottles of medicine, and a good piece of sausage besides a pack of cigarettes. We went our separate ways.

On the way back to the room Simon said to me: "You know who was in the T group? They were older boys. Their mission was similar to ours, but included bringing weapons. I doubt they will come out alive. And you should be more careful. You don't know what I went through when you didn't come back," and he left without saying goodbye. Without realizing it, I was growing up. Age did not count in the ghetto. Only the capacity to survive. We were men like any other, only without beards.

Before going into the house I ran into Reuben and Elias. When they saw me, they came over and touched my face and body. "Israel, alive," said Elias, "alive like us, Israel, you're alive!" I didn't understand what this was all about. Elias told me later that a rumor had gone around the ghetto that one of the groups that had gone outside was in the hands of the Gestapo. The children had been

❖

mentioned, and Elias thought I was one of them. Very proudly I showed them my bag. It was my first trophy, my certificate of membership in one of the groups that went into the city, defying the beasts' orders, to obtain food, and making it possible for many in the ghetto not to die of hunger. We were not about to let them to exterminate us like mice.

I came into the room. My father wanted to know why I was late. I did not answer. My soup was on top of a wooden box, covered by a small dish. I was sorry not to have a piece of bread and butter, like the one I had shared with Simon, to offer them. I sat down to eat, but my bag did not go unnoticed.

My mother was the first to ask what was inside it. "A few things I found," I said.

"Where did you get this from?" asked my mother when she opened the bag. "What's in these bottles?" I wiped my mouth and told her that it was the drug my aunt needed. They looked at me astonished, uncertain what to say. Elias and Reuben kept quiet, even though they knew everything. They did not want to compromise anybody.

Elias knew about every decree signed by the Jewish Council of the ghetto, which had been established by the occupation authorities and was continuously supervised by the beasts. He and Red kept in close contact in order to exchange information and pass on the most important intelligence to the Aleph group, which had been formed by youths and mature men who went from one ghetto to the other in order to keep abreast of everything that happened. I did not know much about this, due to my age. But Elias was my first survival teacher. I felt very old, capable of undertaking complex operations that needed daring people.

❧

My father and my uncle asked me many questions from different angles to see if they could catch me in a lie. But I always said exactly what Red and my cousins had told me. Deep inside I was sorry to have to lie, but what else could I do?

We needed to survive and in the ghetto we learned that we could not sit quietly and watch small children die, as well as women and old people, not to mention the sick. Those of us who were still strong and capable had to form groups and go out and barter for what we needed, or steal it. What was the difference! The beasts were tightening the knot, waiting for us to hang ourselves like the man on the second floor. But I, and many others, already knew that we could get into the city without encountering the guards. And in the city was the key to our survival: food and drugs!

I think my father knew everything from the beginning, but he did not say anything in order not to make things worse. He probably thought that I acted as a lookout inside the ghetto and received a few things in exchange.

Three days went by and none of the boys from the group showed up. We were dispersed and very careful, always trying not to be caught. The danger increased when I found out that there were spies in the zone.

Reuben told me that some of the boys were in the hands of the Gestapo, but we did not know how they had been caught. The operation was very simple. There were some people who watched for anything usual and then ran to inform the beasts. Later the Gestapo would come in, kill the old people, and take the accused with them.

Reuben told us that one of the boys had jumped from the truck where they had put him and tried to run away. The driver had followed him. The boy put out his hands up looking for protection, for an open window to crawl

❖

into, but before he could do anything the truck ran him over, crushing him against a wall. His brains spilled out on the stone. Not content with this, the beasts ran over him several more times until their tire tracks were imprinted in his smashed body. Several meters away from there the truck had stopped and the guards had made the terror-stricken occupants get out. The officer had pointed a few out, and they were immediately taken to a wall where they were shot. Among the dead were a woman and a boy our age.

Life was becoming more complicated. The system imposed by the Nazis was beginning to bear fruit. It was psychological. We were all careful not to talk in front of anyone, for there might be an informer among us. No one spoke about the daily events of the ghetto in our room.

Everyone knew about certain things, but we did not talk. We all knew about the deportations to the labor camps in the east. They could come for us any morning, seize our belongings, and take us to the main city square from where they would transport us to a nearby camp. From there, we would be sent by train to our destination, and rumors abounded about that. Nobody knew for sure about factories in the east. Those who came from Poland talked about death camps where people were put into strange chambers and then into common graves. Others talked about large numbers of people being shot in the back of the head only to fall directly into their graves. But it seemed too fantastic, and most of us did not believe them. It was impossible that the Germans would go to such extremes of cruelty. That was what we believed in the ghetto before our turn came for deportation.

People kept disappearing. They left in the dark, without being able to say good-bye to anybody, for the beasts

❖

would not permit such things. Women crying, trying to take along a piece of bread, an empty bottle, and the baby that kept crying from hunger. Men with their heads bowed, carrying half-empty bags and dragging their feet to leave their marks on the floor, knowing perhaps that they would not return.

One afternoon I was at the door of the house where we lived, talking to the man who sat on the wooden bench, when I saw Moshe. I called him three times, but he did not answer. When I got a close look at him I felt dizzy. His face was dirty and a green crust covered part of his neck. The eczema had spread to his hands, and he was limping. He looked at me without recognizing me. His mind was gone. It made no difference whether I talked to him or not, whether I yelled or talked softly. He was in a world of his own. His eyes were bleary and wide open. Somebody said behind me: "Watch out, boy, don't get too close to him or you'll catch the plague and give it to everyone else!" Moshe had the plague everyone was talking about. I stopped myself from running away. I don't know how I was able to smile at Moshe while watching him go past, limping as if he were going to fall by the wayside. I cried; besides being sick, Moshe's pants and shoes were falling apart. I came back with my mind blank.

The man on the wooden bench tried to console me. "There are many children in that condition. Be thankful to God that you've been spared. He will die soon. Those who contract that illness don't last long. And he has even less a chance, being the son of the madwoman!"

He saw the expression of terror in my face. I asked what he meant by "son of the madwoman." "I don't know the story very well," he said, "but I've heard that the poor

❖

boy lost his mother. She went crazy and started hitting people in the street. She began throwing stones at a guard in front of the Jewish Council. The last I know is that the SS took her to the hospital. You know more about those things than I do, isn't that so?"

I did not say a word, and without saying good-bye I left the man. I spent the rest of the day thinking about Moshe and his body full of sores. So much had happened in such a short time!

My aunt got better with the medicine I brought her. She recovered some of her color, but continued to lie on her straw bed. My father leaned over to me and said, "Israel, don't trust the man at the door." I looked at him, waiting for an explanation, but he only stroked my head and winked for an answer. Apparently he too knew many things and probably belonged to his own organization, which he kept quiet from children like me.

I promised myself I would ask Red about it first chance I got. The ghetto organization was functioning. Half of us worked without the other half knowing it. Without realizing it, we learned how to live in silence, to look ahead and risk our lives around the clock. Very few people could say that they were not involved. That's why so many people were worried when news of the informers leaked out.

Elias scratched his head constantly, swearing at the bugs that were tormenting him, and he couldn't stop blinking. It was a nervous tic he had picked up when he joined our group. When he stopped for a minute I approached him. "What do you know about the man by the door?" He shrugged, squeezing a flea between his fingers and said: "Why are you interested in him? Those who know already have him on their list. I've told you too much already, damn it!"

⚜

I began to suspect that he couldn't be trusted. He was probably an informer. It was strange. We were short of everything, but he seemed to always have whatever he needed. Always sitting on his box, lighting one cigarette after another. Too comfortable a life for a man in the ghetto. Of course, he might also be a counterfeiter. It was puzzling, but after all, I was still playing with a double-edged sword.

Spring had come, but in the ghetto we had no flowers and no fresh air. We didn't give a damn about spring. It wasn't a time for us who only cared about surviving. The deportations went on almost daily. There were no longer any new Jews arriving in the ghetto nor any more beasts at the entrance. Someone said that the zone was going to be demolished at any moment and us with it. The news hit us like a cold shower.

The man at the door disappeared suddenly without a trace. Obviously he had gotten tired of waiting for a wife and a daughter who never showed up. As spring went on things became sadder.

Red disappeared also, and the boss was now a girl with very black hair. Over time she had learned about a dozen escape routes to the city and went out every other day.

Once she held up a food truck. Samuel and I had to jump into a ditch that led to the city dump. The attackers passed us. One of them was the man from the door. He was covering the retreat with a machine gun he had taken from the guards. He was wearing a brown uniform with a red band on his arm. Samuel explained that he was one of the partisans who had taken up arms against the Germans. Samuel, who used to get excited when he talked about this group, was deported one night together with his family. He waved his arm in farewell and dis-

✤

appeared into the shadows. His father had fallen into the hands of the Gestapo and was shot after being tortured. One by one, my friends were being taken to the work camps in the east. Every day I could see a house being abandoned. I could see the bent heads of the occupants, and sometimes I would hear the sobs.

They took the sickest old people in the car that did not let out smoke. Summer came and the heat became unbearable, bringing out the stench that made the women run out into the barbed wired fences the beasts had put up as barriers between us and the rest of the world.

Our escapades became more difficult because, with so many fewer people still in the ghetto, it was easier to find out who was missing. We were the informers favorite bit of news. And we knew who they were, or at least we suspected it. The Jewish Council was a big problem Some of the members, in order to curry favor with the beasts, had set up a complex system of information that reported all of our actions to the Gestapo. We were almost lost. Only the counterfeiters managed to accomplish their objectives. They must have been paying people outside. I don't know how this worked, but it did, and sometimes we would pay a fortune for half a dozen half-rotten potatoes.

The girl who had replaced Red as commander of our group killed herself by jumping from a third floor in order not to reveal the names of her comrades. That night the Gestapo came into the ghetto and arrested more than a hundred people. They were shot the next morning for being partisans. Among the group was Simon, my first comrade in our incursions into the city.

One of our neighbors kept a diary in which she wrote down the names of everyone who disappeared. She was

⚜

an ugly woman, but very intelligent, and through her hands ran the threads of the most important organization in the north. It suddenly became clear why sometimes I would find a piece of fresh baked bread with onions on top of our table. My mother would sometimes take care of Nora's father while she was away. Nobody knew her real name, and she made us call her Nora. What difference does a name make? Life is made up of forms, not names, as my uncle Aaron used to say. By the end of summer, when the first autumn breezes came, we no longer saw Nora again, or her father. No one knew where they were. The house we lived in was beginning to crumble and empty out. The back wall fell down, exposing two rooms to the elements and putting the rest of the structure in danger of collapsing. Water became scarce and the dampness seeped in through the cracks. The bugs increased and it was almost impossible to sleep at night because of the bites, the worries, and the constant state of alert in which the men in the black uniforms kept us.

There was not a night without the sound of sirens announcing that a good number of us would be taken away to another place. In every face you could see the ever-present question: "Who will be next?" In our room we were in a state of panic. The nervousness was taking a toll on my father and his brothers. They would jump up at anything. Sometimes they would confess that they wished everything would end once and for all. The uncertainty, the continuous wait, the silence that pervaded the streets, and the nightly siren were taking their toll. Those of us who remained in the ghetto were losing control of ourselves. I did not go out again when I found out that Moritz had been arrested in the patio of the school just as he came out of the tunnel. They gassed him together

❖

with three of his friends and later exhibited their bodies
at the gate of our zone. That afternoon the Jewish
Council gave the Gestapo a list of people suspected of
"sabotage." Three entire families were taken in the
strange trucks to the outskirts of Czernowitz. This time
we were even more confused because twenty-five minutes later the trucks were again driving through the
streets near the ghetto.

The men no longer concealed the nature of our fate.
In our room we began to talk about death as if it were a
new neighbor. Elias couldn't sit still. With his hands
behind his back he kept pacing around. "What then,
should we let them kill us? Can't we act like the partisans?" His questions remained in the air, hitting the
grownups with full force.

Yes, I too was thinking, why not do something? We
already knew that the intentions of the beasts were not
good, that all their malice was directed against us. Our
only hope for survival was to be taken to an unknown
place. Maybe we were still waiting for this. It was a faraway light that we could barely see, but in the end it was
our last hope and nobody was ready to play the last card.
In that move there could be life.

Autumn came with a constant cold rain. The women
put their pots out to catch the water that fell from the
sky, for the Germans had cut out our water supply two
weeks before. When we walked out of our rooms what we
saw was heartbreaking: old people dying in the streets,
letting themselves go without a whimper in order to save
their rations for the young children.

We seemed to be playing at being alive. Numbers of
children, most of them orphans, walked aimlessly. They
walked on the sidewalks, looking among the papers for

something they could use. It was not unusual to find, underneath some cartons, the body of a five-year-old dead from hunger and cold.

The smaller ones were being eaten by rats. A woman went out looking for something to eat and when she came back found out that rats had eaten her one-year-old. Yes, those who still remained in the ghetto had to fight for survival with insects, rats, and dogs. The different species fought for their right to survive. Surely this too had been planned by the beasts.

The sirens went off once again. This time the trucks stopped just beyond our house. The door was broken with rifle butts and the occupants were taken out by force. As usual, the old people had to go inside the strange trucks.

The rest were taken outside the ghetto on foot. From there they would go to the square and would then be taken to the east. I had already checked out the itinerary.

But this time something unusual happened. One of the trucks in which the old people were taken skidded on the wet pavement and overturned. To our surprise we saw black smoke coming from inside it. The few survivors came out coughing and with their eyes bulging from asphyxiation, but they were immediately finished off by machine-gun fire.

The discovery clarified one of our most serious doubts about the strange trucks. It was a cruel system. The exhaust system was directed inward, that's why we never saw any smoke going out. The carbon monoxide killed the passengers. It was a form of murder without anybody noticing what was going on. We had finally found out why the beasts preferred the old people and the sick for this treatment. And God help those who resisted. They were taken in by force, kicking and hitting them with rifle butts.

That night we hid in a basement dugout prepared by some of the men. The beasts, after what had happened, intensified their raids. They blew up houses, killed people in the middle of the street, and massacred most of the street children. The final extermination of the north zone was under way.

Even under the ground we felt the floor tremble and the noise of the flames that ate up the wood buildings blown up with grenades. My mother had a terrible nervous crisis. My two aunts cried without stopping, holding their two younger children. Reuben, Elias, and I sat in a corner of the basement, waiting for the end. Every once in a while we would glance sideways at each other to check out our state of impotence. After thirteen hours we were able to leave the dugout. We didn't see any beasts anywhere. We kept believing, even in the midst of the destruction. For the next three days there was a strange, total calm. My father, together with his brothers, was getting things ready. They had come to the conclusion that we would be the next to go to the work camps in the east.

The beasts knocked on our door. Two guards with machine guns stood against the wall. Three of them and an officer came in. "With your hands on your head, up against the wall!" he shouted.

We did as he told us. My knees were trembling. The man shouted once again with his guttural voice: "Pick up what you have and let's go!" We picked up the bags we already had prepared and went out. The beasts followed with their machine guns ready as if we were dangerous criminals.

Once in the street we found other people in the same circumstances. We looked at each other blankly.

⚜

Although we had seen so many other deportations, we still could not accept ours. Uncertainty was reflected in every face, in the dull looks we exchanged, looking for an answer, for a bit of solace and strength.

We walked toward the city square. It began to rain. When we crossed the boundary between the ghetto and the city we felt like we were leaving a secure place, a piece of our lives, behind us. A piece of something that did not offer a future. We walked in a long line. The passersby, accustomed to such processions, did not pay much attention. We turned up our faces to look at the leaden sky and the rain that manifested our hopelessness.

We were completely soaked when we reached the square, our feet covered with mud and our backs aching from the weight we were carrying. The square was surrounded by a great many soldiers. My mother rested her head on my father's shoulder and held me against her bosom. She was crying, feeling perhaps that this was the end. A woman fainted, and when the person standing next to her tried to help her, we heard machine gun fire going over our heads. The man had to stay quiet at his assigned spot, looking sideways at the pale face of the woman. A group of beasts got to her and put her on a cart. "She's dead and we're going to bury her so she won't spread the plague," they said. We kept waiting.

At the end, toward the place where they had taken the woman, we heard gunshots. We understood. "They had to kill the dead woman," a man said, and he put his hands in the tattered pockets of his jacket. The door in front of us opened. A tall man with square shoulders stood in front of us. He rubbed his hands and put them behind him. "From now on you will be workers of the German Reich. You will be taken to the camps." I fell asleep. The hunger, the cold, the constant nervous tension had taken

⚜

their toll on me. My mother slapped me lightly on the face to wake me, and I realized that we had to start walking again.

It had stopped raining but the sky was still gray. I did not want to ask where we were going...

We left the city behind, our boots muddier than before.

❖

3

The Train

The walk was painful. Our boots were heavy with mud and our toes felt numb. It rained without letup, and the road was a sea of mud. After a while they made us stop. The beasts scattered around us and menacingly took up their machine guns, all the while shouting orders. The sound of motors broke the monotony of the falling rain. We looked up. Perhaps we already knew what was going to happen, but we harbored a strange hope, the force that had kept us from giving in once and for all.

Amidst the fog and the rain we saw some lights. It was the trucks. I froze. I didn't want to get into one of those death vehicles. But what to do? Any attempt to escape would mean death. I closed my eyes, trying to escape the cold and the fear. The noise got stronger and suddenly stopped. The trucks were here!

I opened my eyes unwillingly. My thoughts were a riot ready to explode. But the end had not yet arrived. I relaxed when I saw that the vehicles they were forcing us to climb into, using their rifle butts, were open trucks. The beasts were in a hurry. Once in I was unable to sit down. We had to stand up, leaning against each other and holding onto whatever we could so as not to fall. I believe about fifty people were forced into that truck. We could hardly breathe. Once we were all on board, an officer gave the order to start. As soon as the trucks started to move, we fell on top of each other. As far as the driver was concerned, we were as good as animals. He drove without paying attention to the potholes or the curves in the road. He would go anywhere and stop at the last minute, probably to frighten us, which he succeeded in doing. We held on fast for we were sure we would end up hitting our heads against the rocks. We took the road that led out of Czernowitz. The trees along the way had lost their leaves. Every once in a while we passed peasants, none of whom dared to raise their heads, perhaps for fear of the Germans. Terror reigned in the countryside as well as in the city.

The only ones who dared look at us, but without understanding what was happening, were the animals: cows, sheep, and dogs. Next to me, leaning against my father's back, an old man was coughing. You could hear his muscles contracting, but he did not complain. He simply coughed and chewed on a small piece of wood. I looked at him, trying to place him, but he was a stranger to me. Something attracted me to him. His white hair, covered by a tattered felt hat and a pair of broken glasses, made him look like quite a figure. Could the old man be a great rabbi? Or one of those righteous men my grandfather talked about when he told me stories about the Jewish people? I looked at him, and he coughed again. It was a dry cough that made him shudder. My father didn't say anything and let the old man lean against his back. He coughed again and had to put his hand to his mouth. I could see that it was covered with blood. The old man coughed and blood came out of his

❖

mouth. I swallowed and said nothing. If word got out, the old man would probably be shot in the middle of the road. I kept quiet.

The first thing I had learned in the ghetto was how to keep quiet. In our situation words were ammunition that could get back at us at any time. Red used to explain this very well: "Boys, everything will come out all right as long as we keep our mouths shut. Any word is a clue, and if we're alive, it's because we know how to keep quiet. We only think, and once this is over, whoever can, should write about it. The fish dies by the mouth."

Looking at the old man I thought about Red. How much he had helped me. Because of him I had been able to bring a few things home to eat. He had trained me, and his training had spread through every corner of the ghetto. Anyone who wanted to survive had to go to Red.

Another cough and the old man doubled up, grasping his chest. His breathing was a kind of wheezing that would stop suddenly and give way to a long hoarse sound. Through his glasses, I saw a pair of dull eyes, full of wrinkles. His nose was covered with red spots. There were a few red spots in his beard as well. When he breathed he blew the air out with full force, as if he had a pair of bellows instead of lungs. The old man did not look at me. All his concentration seemed to be focused on leaning against my father's back. I turned my head. I was ashamed not to be able to help the old man, covered with rags and bleeding with every cough.

My eyes surveyed the mountains. I saw the wet paths that led to the woods. Somebody stepped on me. I looked up and saw a young girl. She did not excuse herself; her light eyes looked out into space, perhaps dreaming. All of us in the truck were trying to do something that would

❧

take us away, even if only in our thoughts, from that miserable truck in which we were packed like sardines. If somebody had died on that journey, it would have been standing up.

The rain kept on. It got into our hair and slid down our skin. Some children were shivering from the cold, others slept or died. A woman had a baby in her arms with a huge head and a face completely blue. His eyes, deeply set in two holes, were covered by a kind of thin gray veil. From his expression I was sure that he could not see. I was shocked to see a blind baby, in the dark, with his eyes open to an abyss without light. I touched my mother's hands and she answered by pressing mine. She was cold, but alive!

I consoled myself, realizing that at least I was not like that boy about my same age who kept looking at a wrinkled photograph he kept inside his jacket. I was too shy to talk to him, but his tears made me understand that the people in the photo were of great value. I had seen him alone on the line, and he had not joined anyone when he got on the truck. I looked and found his eyes looking at me. I smiled, but he remained serious, barely lowering his eyes. I must have turned red, for I felt heat rise up to my head. I opened up my mouth to the rain.

By our side the beasts rode on their motorcycles. They carried machine guns and were wearing raincoats.

Suddenly the caravan stopped. Four men were running toward the fields. They had jumped from one of the trucks and were trying an escape, which they had probably planned beforehand. We all watched. I prayed for their escape, but the beasts and their dogs soon caught up to them. They were brought back by kicks. When they got to us they forced them to kneel. Then, under the

⚜

threat of the dogs, they were forced to make their way forward on their knees over the rocks. The men in the black uniforms laughed as the poor men did what they were told to do. After half an hour of this, one of the men was told to get up and was taken in front of the ranking officer, who criss-crossed his face with a whip he held in his gloved hand. Then he dug the handle into the man's stomach. The man doubled up in pain. They made him get up, hitting him in the ribs with their rifle butts. After that the officer gouged out the man's eye. The man held back a scream while the eye jumped up from the socket, a red blotch gushing blood.

The officer rubbed his hands and cleaned the bloody handle on his pants. He ordered the three others to be brought up to him. After what they had seen, the three men tried to hold on to the slippery ground. One of the beasts let out a burst of machine-gun fire at the legs of the three men. They doubled up like puppets. The old man who was leaning on my father's back coughed, but this time he did not clean the corners of his mouth. The girl who had stepped on me was trembling and made a fist in a vain effort to do something. The baby with the blue face closed his eyes and leaned his head to one side, probably dead. The boy with the pictures in his jacket looked over the shoulder of a man who was watching the scene without blinking,

Down on the muddy road the officer yawned and, with his right boot, kicked the chin of the man whose eye he had taken out. He raised his arm, and his comrades understood. They started kicking the four fugitives and hitting them with their rifles. The poor men squirmed on the ground, trying to protect themselves from the blows, while their bodies kept getting covered with mud. They

❖

bit their lips to hold the pain until they tore them with their teeth. Their mouths were bleeding and several teeth jumped out into the muddy road. When they stood them up again, they looked like sacks of decaying meat. The only glimmer of life was in their frightened eyes. The beasts tore their clothes off and, in sight of everyone, proceeded to break their ribs and arms by kicking them.

The men no longer screamed. They were half dead and totally disfigured. The officer, having made sure that they were brutally punished, now ordered the coup de grace. One of the beasts rolled up his sleeves and took a pistol in his left hand. The other SS men smiled.

Four shots went off and we could see the broken necks of the men who had jumped out hoping for a freedom that they now only found in death.

Those of us in the truck tried not to scream. Some women fainted and some boys threw up. The four bodies lay naked in the open, which made their deaths even more humiliating. The dogs of the beasts licked the blood off the bodies. On command the animals returned to their masters, and I heard one of the beasts telling his dog: "Did you want to poison yourself with that, Darling, I must tell you who the Jews are so you won't take any more chances." He said these words aloud, so that all of us would understand what kind of protection we could expect from them during the journey.

The trucks started up again, this time slower so as not to crash into each other. The beasts were worried about their own welfare. Ours, after all, was already sealed.

My mother stroked my hair and, unable to help herself, began to cry. The girl who had stepped on me was also crying. I was already suffering the consequences of

❖

what I had seen. My childhood was being taken away from me, my imagination tainted with bitter reality. I touched my wooden toys and felt like I was touching the bodies of the fugitives. I couldn't play any more. What could I use to build a dream? Hunger, the massacre, and the cruel despotism of some assassins? I was a child who was beginning to feel old. Maybe that's why I took an interest in the old man who was coughing up blood and leaning against my father's back.

We finally got to our destination, an open field on the outskirts of Czernowitz. We were totally numb. The long walk, the constant rain, and the unending hunger and thirst had taken their toll on us.

The beasts indicated a spot and left us standing there while they decided where to put us. The old man with the cough was shaking, about to collapse at any moment. My father and another man held him up by his armpits. They knew that once he fell the beasts would rush up to give him the final treatment reserved for the sick: a bullet in the back of the head or a quick bite in the neck from one of the dogs. Sometimes it surprised me that I would think in these terms, like a grown man. But what the eyes see the mind reasons, and I had seen too much not to reason. I had to analyze each scene to give it a place in my mind. I had to be an eyewitness so that afterwards I could tell the rest of the world, like Red had said we should.

While the rain soaked our bodies I thought: "They've been moving us for a long time. First they mobilized my father. Then they took us to the ghetto, and now we are being drenched in this camp. Is all this part of a man's life? Are hunger, cold, and moral and physical destruction what they teach in the schools? Does one have to die like Red? What have the Jews done to be treated like this?"

"Is it worth that much to be Jewish?" I wanted to ask this last question, but when I saw the shaking, wet bodies of those around me, I kept quiet, feeling a terrible burden. What was happening? No, life the way my grandfather used to tell me when I visited his farm was not like this. He used to talk about flowers, of summers when the sun ripens the fruit, and of an autumn when you planted seeds. But this last spring I had seen no flowers, and in the summer I had to steal dried-up potatoes, and this fall I had seen holes, not waiting to be filled with seeds, but with the bodies of people who had done nothing worse than try to live.

I swallowed and my stomach hurt. But in the ghetto I had learned with Simon not to say I was hungry, even if I was consumed by hunger pangs. I had taken my first lessons in the school of life in the streets of the ghetto, inside the tunnels that led to the city. And now, getting wet in this camp, I was not ready to die. I would talk to Elias and Reuben to plan something. But before I had a chance to look for them, since they had been in a different truck, the beasts began to separate us into groups,

Each group of thirty-five was assigned a piece of wet land. A lieutenant with a skull on his cap said in a sarcastic tone: "Gentlemen, I hope you enjoyed your trip. Now, make yourselves comfortable here while waiting for the train that will take you to the east. Any inconveniences that may arise should be endured with patience. We couldn't find a better place, as we wanted to do, so please make yourselves as comfortable as possible until the train arrives." He saluted, clicking his heels, and my father and the other man were finally able to let go of the old man and lower him to the ground so he could rest a

⚜

bit. The old man sat down and put his head between his knees after coughing once again. My mother also sat down and put her head on a woolen bag she was carrying. My father and I were at her side. The rain had begun to abate, but the cold was worse every moment. It was five in the afternoon and the horizon had begun to turn dark blue. I looked at my mother and saw that she was asleep, her hair parted in strands on her forehead. The poor woman was exhausted. I went over and put my head on her lap. My father caressed my wet hair and smiled to inspire some confidence. I closed my eyes and started to dream about my grandfather's farm.

For a few moments I went back to being a child of seven again. I had a right to dream, to get away from reality. I could see my grandmother calling the ducks to feed them. My grandfather would tie together some logs and twirl his golden mustache. I would ride the horses and run through the summer fields. Like images, the memories would appear. I would smile seeing everything so near, and then it would evaporate. Finally, without realizing it I fell asleep.

They made us get up very early. My body was numb and my mother had to massage my legs, which felt like cement. When I finally opened my eyes completely, I looked around. People were waiting without knowing what for, but waiting nonetheless. The men were talking about the situation and the women were trying to light a fire to warm us up and give us a cup of salty water. The beasts were allowing us to do so. It was their technique, a false calm that would encourage us to dream about the "work" camps of the east.

The psychological game confused us, and sometimes we did not know for sure what they were going to do with us. It did not rain that morning, so we were able to

⚜

walk through the field where they had taken us. People were putting their clothes out to dry. I found Elias. He was going to come with Reuben to implement a plan he had.

I've been looking at the boy with the picture. He's still alone, not talking to anyone. I'm going to see if I can talk to him. He may be useful to our cause. Like Red says, in this war, even the stones are useful. The old man with the cough is still coughing, but there is no longer any blood coming out of his mouth. My mother offered him a lump of sugar, but he refused it and asked only for some water to wash his hands. He must be a Hasid. Of course he can't expect anything kosher. That would be too much. The girl who stepped on me hasn't been seen again. God knows what happened to her. I haven't seen her since yesterday, and it's strange, I think I dreamed about her. Perhaps I associated her with our neighbor who went mad. I'm obsessed with insanity. We live in a time of crazy people. Just looking at the beasts, it's enough to go mad. We all know they're a bunch of murderers, but what is more disconcerting is not knowing who will be their next victim.

They could point to me at any moment and that would be the end. The boy with the picture hasn't raised his head. He seems pensive. I'm going to get closer to him. What can I lose? A yes or a no is the same. I'm getting used to the insanity. I walk slowly, looking at the boots that have begun to crack because of the rain and the mud, and I wonder about Moshe and his sores. Some people look at me, thinking that I'm just another orphan. I'm next to the boy and notice that he has red hair and his nose is bent, as if he has received a big blow. I touch him on the shoulder and his small eyes look me up and down. He sighs and asks: "Do I also have to tell you that

❖

I've walked all the way from another town to get into the ghetto? They all ask and the answer is the same."

His high-pitched voice bothers me. I move my left foot and say to him without hesitation: "How about a piece of bread? We have some today, but what about tomorrow?"

He lifts the hood of his jacket and looks me straight in the eye. "What? Do you bake bread?"

I smile at him the way Elias taught me. "No, I don't bake it, but it can be had, if you're interested." I can't understand how that came out. Who am I to talk with such confidence? Me, younger than him and talking like an old man. He licks his dry lips with his tongue. "Aren't you interested in my story? They all want to know, and then they send me away when they realize they can't do anything about it."

I shake my head no. "I want you to meet some boys. Don't ask for explanations."

He looks around, rubs his eyes, and smoothes his hair to one side. "How about the bread?"

That takes me by surprise. Where am I going to get bread? The ideas turn in my mind. "If you're hungry enough you'll know where to find it, or where to find me," he says. Obviously he too has learned a few things in the ghetto. You have to be careful. Reuben told me that we still haven't gotten rid of the informers, so it wouldn't be odd for them to be among us. "My name is Isaac," he says, standing up and extending a dirty hand. I take it. "I'm Israel." We start to walk in the field. Although she doesn't know what is happening, my mother keeps track of me. I can see her observing each of my movements. How long are mothers attached to their children? As far as I'm concerned, up to their death. Isaac follows me, his dirty hands in his pockets. His fingers are sticking out of the tattered fabric of his jacket.

A woman's sobs bring me out of my reverie. Her sobs are broken. It's the mother of the child with the blue face. He's dead. The woman tries to revive him by putting her nipple in his closed mouth. Isaac shrugs. "She'll go crazy in a few minutes. I've seen it happen many times. In the ghetto I lived inside a chimney. It sounds crazy, doesn't it? But it's true. I made my home there and I lived as best I could. I used to go out to Czernowitz every couple of days. Enough to get me a bottle of beer, half a loaf, and a chunk of cheese. A Jew who escaped from the Germans gave them to me. The fact that he lived alone saved him. But the Germans smell us, they know who we are. Last time I looked for him he wasn't there. Later I found out that they broke his head. They wanted him to confess I don't know what. He died during the interrogation, and that's how I found out about life in the ghetto.

"I saw a widow go crazy. One of her sons died when he ate something foul. He died without a word. The other one caught the plague and started to decay. His name was Moshe, and his mother was killed by the SS. Well, they took her to the,' which is the same thing."

When I heard Moshe's name my stomach turned. "Did you know Moshe—wasn't he—?" I couldn't finish because Isaac interrupted me: "Yes, that one. He pointed you out to me once, but he didn't want to get near you. He was ashamed to show you that he was rotting away. I already knew who you were. We all know each other, even if we don't realize it. Nobody is a stranger here. Only we keep quiet because we're afraid of saying the same things. Yes, I know you want to ask me about Moshe. He rotted away and they put him in a common grave. They threw him in like garbage. He must have still been alive, but he didn't say a word." I feel like throwing up.

❖

Isaac talks without showing any emotion; his narrative is very cruel. While he talks his fingers move inside the holes in his jacket. "I told you I saw many crazy people in the ghetto, and it's true. My mother, may she rest in peace, went crazy and started hitting herself in the head with a frying pan. One day she aimed right and died. She never got to know the ghetto. She went crazy after the war began. She couldn't get any news about my father and she never slept again. Later she started to talk to herself, to see things, and finally she killed herself with the frying pan. I was used to crazy people even before they brought us to the north. And you know, to be honest with you, craziness has become a part of my life." He seems almost to be talking to himself.

I didn't want to ask about the picture he had inside his cap. That was up to him. Isaac stopped in front of an old lady. His hands went out to her. The woman smiled unwillingly and allowed him to take her yellowed, wrinkled fingers into his hands. Afterwards, Isaac nodded for me to join him for a walk. "You know?" he said, "I don't know how that woman hasn't died yet. I lived with her in the ghetto, and more than once I saw her take a piece of bread out of her mouth to feed one of the children. I think she came alone and is going to die alone. Well, we can't all live the same way, I guess."

Elias looked at Isaac for a long time. "Wasn't it you who used to jump across the roofs without asking anyone for help? Elias knew a great deal about what went on in the ghetto, and Isaac had not escaped his attention. Isaac said nothing. He let Elias talk and every once in a while answered with a soft yes.

Some of us in the camp would wander about looking for something to eat. People would negotiate with the

❖

farmers for a piece of bread or a plate of soup. I saw a woman take out her wedding ring and exchange it for two loaves of bread and half a bottle of milk. The child she had in her arms ate with such relish that my own stomach seemed full at the time. The fact is that I was not hungry that afternoon. Three old men bargained with a mountaineer for a plate of soup.

It was dangerous to do business with us, but people in the neighboring towns took the risk because the prices they got from us exceeded their wildest expectations. A man exchanged a pair of winter boots for two loaves of bread. He was left in a pair of slippers, and winter was around the corner. I knew this because the birds were flying south. My grandfather had taught me that.

Isaac went for a walk. Elias, Reuben, and I stayed behind, waiting for him and watching him disappear. Some people who were gathered around a fire told us: "You have to be careful with him. He's not an informer, but his fingers are too long. That's why he's able to live on his own. He could steal a machine gun from the SS. In the ghetto he didn't want to get involved with any group. He's a strange character."

We talked about him for a while, but no more than speculations. None of us could say anything concrete about him. The guy was a mystery, and that bothered us.

My parents had bartered a few of their belongings for a couple of loaves and some dried-out chestnuts. Everybody exchanged something for something else, especially for the old people and the children. I ate five chestnuts and did not want any more. I was thinking about Isaac and his jacket with the torn pockets. I thought Elias was thinking the same thing, for every once in a while we looked at each other without any par-

❖

ticular reason. Reuben went to sleep on the grass. A soft sunlight shone over our heads. It didn't rain, which was strange, for lately it had not stopped raining.

I was trying to remember. There was nothing else I could do for the moment. One of the beasts passed close to our group and stopped. He looked at each of the items we had around us and then went away whistling. Perhaps it was a scare tactic of some kind.

When the SS went to their guard post Isaac came back. He looked serious and was carrying a package under his jacket. He signaled for me to approach him. I was intrigued, but finally got up and went over. I waited for him to say something. He wiped his nose and let the package fall. It was a piece of dried meat, ready to eat. I opened my eyes wide—it had been some time since I had seen a piece of meat that big. He took a knife from one of his pockets and cut off a slice. I ate it fast and with relish. "It was good, wasn't it?" I nodded. When I finished swallowing I saw Isaac's face. He was looking at me, satisfied with his present.

I tried to think of something to say, but finally settled for a sincere "thank you." He understood and immediately went over to my parents. I followed him. They were surprised at the offering, which was about ten pounds of meat. "It's for you to eat now; it would be inconvenient for the owner to find out it's missing." A devilish smile spread over his face. I wanted to legitimize him by introducing him to the others. "His name is Isaac, and he came in the same truck we did," I said. But he, not much worried about anything, began: "Don't worry, the meat is good. Israel already had a piece." I turned red. "Yes, I know you're wondering where I found it. Well, if people don't take care of their things, they end up with those

❖

who need them most. Sir," he added, turning to my father, "weren't you in the brigade that looked for informers? Don't worry, I know you didn't turn them in, but I was very happy with the beating you gave them. Don't look at me that way, everything is known in the ghetto." My father swallowed hard.

Thank God, Isaac was talking to my father in a way my mother couldn't hear. I pulled at his coat to get him to shut up. He understood and asked for a piece of meat. He ate slowly without bothering too much about chewing properly. Elias drew near. My father did not take his eyes off Isaac. Reuben was waiting for him to speak.

Isaac burped and said: "I just heard that we're leaving soon. The SS are waiting for a train that will take us to the east. We're better off getting ready. Don't worry, in a while I'll bring some bread that I put away somewhere. Start storing some water. The trip is long and only God knows if they will let us off the train. I know a lot about those so-called trips." He got up and left without explaining this statement. We saw him jump a small fence and finally disappear. My father and his brothers called Elias, Reuben, and me. They were nervous. Elias's father said: "Who is he? He could be the end for all of us!" His voice broke, "This is not a fair where one can befriend the first person who approaches us. That boy is the devil himself, and if he falls in the hands of the SS we are lost."

Elias, looking angrily at his father, said: "I'm sorry, dad, but he isn't what you think. We saw him operate in the ghetto. He didn't bother anyone, but he never made— well, he never got anyone in trouble either." My aunt grunted back: "What do you know about people? You're just at the beginning of your life, and already you think you understand the world. I can't believe it!" These words made Elias lower his head.

❖

Reuben, however, took some bottles and went to fill them with water. My father and I did the same thing. It wouldn't be bad idea to do what Isaac told us. The boy was right, after all. My father broke a long silence. "I think we were wrong about the boy. You can tell he's no fool, and he seemed to be telling the truth about the train. It's a fact that they are going to take us to the east. We're not going to stay here forever. " He spoke to us as if we were grown men. I was proud to have a father who spoke to his son as if he were a big man, a comrade in arms, somebody who could be useful at the right time.

We came back to our place. The meat was all gone and my mother had tied a scarf around her neck to protect herself against the wind that had started up. The old man with the cough began to wheeze once again. He too had eaten some of the meat without protest, and I thought I saw a glimmer of friendship in his eyes. He nodded his head slowly and finally gave me a sweet smile. My father moved over and helped him button his jacket.

As if by magic Isaac comes back to us. He has some long loaves of bread with him. Nobody asks anything this time. We are beginning to understand his style. Elias comments in a low voice that he had been the same in the ghetto.

Isaac rubbed his hands, put them in his torn pocket, and said: "Expect the train in a couple of hours. The pigs don't want too many problems. I believe we're going to Umi, in Ukraine. That's where the troops of that traitor Vlasov are. He joined the Germans, and I don't hear anything good about his troops." That was all he said. He kept up that style of his, short and cutting, without too many details.

❖

Isaac's terse style drove us crazy, but it would have been foolish to ask for more. As it was, he had become a help we had not counted on. Despite his youth, Isaac was becoming a leader. His firm manner and confident words earned respect. He looked at the old man who coughed, searched in his pockets, and took out a small bottle of oil. It was unnecessary to ask where the oil came from. He went up to where the old man was sitting and tapped him lightly on the shoulder. "Rabbi, drink a bit, it will be good for you." Rabbi? It seemed odd to us that he would address the old man that way, but we kept quiet. "Do you remember when you used to talk to us about Solomon and David? It was interesting. But I think you had to pull my ear a few times to get my attention. I beg your forgiveness, Rabbi."

The old man, in the meantime, had swallowed the contents of the bottle. Isaac nodded. "At least it won't hurt so much when he coughs," he said, and he took off the scarf he had around his neck to give it to the old man, who was looking benignly at him. It was no secret that they already knew each other. When he came back he looked in the direction of the old man, who was coughing again, and said: "He has TB. I don't think the rabbi will survive the trip. A fellow who escaped from one of these trains told me that it is very uncomfortable inside the cars." I ventured to ask: "Isaac, why do you call him rabbi? Do you know him?" He slapped me on the back. "I thought you knew the story. Everyone in the ghetto knew it. Yes, he is a rabbi that came on foot to Czernowitz. He was carrying the scrolls of the Torah with him. The SS put him in jail for a while and then released him, sure that he would die in the street. But he's still here and clear as a whistle. It's a shame we can't listen

❖

to one of his sermons. He's a genius." Isaac looked at the old man with sympathy and sadness at the same time.

The minutes went by, slow and lazy, making us feel the time in all its fullness. The wind kept blowing, and the sky forecasted rain. With our scant belongings, we waited for the beasts to announce the arrival of the train. We did not have to wait long. The SS rounded us up again and a noncommissioned officer told us to form a line. We did as we were told. Nobody complained. Isaac and my father helped the rabbi stand up, and then, as ordered, we walked to the station. This time they made us walk fast, they did not want to waste any time.

After crossing a small forest we saw the tracks and at the end a dark locomotive with steam coming out between its smokestack and the wheels. It looked the same as the one that used to pass through my grandfather's farm. I used to enjoy seeing the train go by with its chug, chug, chug. It seemed to speak a language that only gnomes and mountain fairies understood.

But now I was frightened. Trips with the beasts were not very good. I knew this from experience. I walked along the tracks. My feet hurt and I held my mother's hand. At least she protects me with her slow-moving figure. With her I feel secure. There is something in mothers that makes one feel secure in the face of danger. In their weakness, they infuse us with strength.

They made us stand in line in front of the cars. They were huge boxes, with small openings for air. Boxes on metal wheels. Hitting us and firing their rifles into the air, the beasts drove us toward the cars. The doors opened with a dry, screeching noise. They pushed us inside in groups of five. They threw us in as if we were bales of hay. When I saw the darkness that awaited us, I was dis-

⚜

concerted for a few moments and in terror realized that I could not see my parents. I began to cry uncontrollably until a hand pulled me to one of the corners of the wagon. It was Isaac: "Wait for me. I'll go look for them. Don't move away from here." And he left me against a wet wooden wall that was secured with iron bars. Everything was happening so fast, it felt like a nightmare.

Finally Isaac came back with my parents. My mother rushed to me to hold me and feel me. She wanted to make sure I was alive. My father tried to crouch to my level, but there were so many people coming in that he couldn't. We would have to stand all the way, there was room for nothing else. He leaned against the wooden wall, near a window.

The rabbi was standing in the middle, coughing and with his head against his chest. People kept coming in. I couldn't see which car my uncles and cousins were taken to. They were not with us. The air was becoming heavy. Some of the odors made me dizzy, but slowly I got used to it. When the car was about to burst they closed the door and we had no more light than the dim rays that came in through the small windows.

Piled up like animals, almost unable to move, we felt the darkness and the lack of air. We were like this for quite some time. We could hear the orders the beasts were shouting outside. After a strange silence we felt the train starting to move. Chug, chug, chug, it pierced our ears. It was horrifying to hear this dry noise that came to life as the wheels moved along the rails. I closed my eyes to try to escape the asphyxiation I was starting to feel. For now nobody complained, probably thinking it would be a short ride. Certainly we hoped it would be short.

My father took me in his arms and held me close to the window so that I could breathe in a bit of fresh air. I

❖

could see that we were leaving the station, and with every minute the terrain got wider. The last remaining leaves were fluttering in the bare trees in a kind of farewell. I too said goodbye.

⚜

4

When the World Turned Dark

Three o'clock: it's dark here in the freight car. I don't know how many hours we've been traveling, but my muscles are starting to get numb. It is a harrowing situation, and it's hard to breathe. My father doesn't say a word. The silence has turned the atmosphere darker. I don't know if it's a premonition or fear. This cold silence doesn't bode well for us.

I can hear the wheels of the train screeching against the rails that are taking us to the east. I close my eyes to try to rest, but my efforts are in vain. The continuous movement of the train prevents me from concentrating, and ideas converge in my mind.

I see my grandfather's face with his red mustache, and immediately it turns into the drawn-out face of the rabbi. I can't put my thoughts in order and don't even know what I'm thinking. Pieces of recollections slap into my mind: the ghetto, our house in the city, sliding in the snow, my friends, my mother's pies, the Passover Haggadah. The images disappear fast to give way to others. Everything is chaos in my mind. I open my eyes. Everything is dark.

After a while I get used to the darkness. People around me seem to be nailed to the floor. They are standing up and barely look alive. No one looks at anyone else. There is no reason to look, I believe. The rabbi's cough has become stronger. It is a dry cough that breaks the silence and perhaps also the chest of the rabbi. A soft light comes in through the small window. I don't know whether it is raining. It is impossible to tell.

My father's arms are rigid, closed around me. I look at him and see that his eyes are closed. He is probably thinking and remembering, but his mind could also be blank. On the train we feel the need to escape from ourselves every moment. My mother is resting her head on my father's shoulder. I don't know where Isaac is. It is impossible to see him. There are so many people standing in the car that I can't see beyond the person next to me. I rub my hands over my face looking for a bit of fresh air. Nothing. A strange odor comes in through my nostrils. It could be garbage.

Yes, that must be it. The railroad car was dirty when we boarded. It is an acrid smell that comes up to my nose. The motion never stops. Everything seems to be turning around. It feels as if I'm going through a tunnel and I come back to my father's arms, but my nausea does not go away and now my stomach starts to churn. I need to throw up. I tap my father, who opens his eyes and I explain what I need to do. "Can you wait a bit? We'll be there soon." I breathe heavily. There is no place to put my head and I need to throw up!

It feels as if I'm going to drown. The tunnel becomes stronger and now I let myself be carried through it. I'm going fast now. Nobody can stop me. It feels as if I'm being yanked inside. My senses unite in a block and I'm a little ball rolling quickly through a tube. Later I rise to the sky only to come down again. The train no longer

⚜

exists, my mind is empty and my stomach contracts—then calm envelops me once again. I have vomited.

My father cleans my mouth with a handkerchief and does not reprimand me. It wasn't my fault. I couldn't help it. My mother strokes my hair. I have soiled their clothes, but they are not angry. The smell now mingles with the smell of the railroad car. Nobody complains.

I remember how a boy once vomited in a bus and everyone covered their noses. No one does that here. It's strange; they should. What if this is the madness Isaac talks so much about? How do you know when you're crazy? People are still standing up, without looking at me, their heads down. I hear a strange noise. I look and see that someone else has vomited. Evidently some have done it before. Now I understand why nobody protested. I close my eyes. The odor becomes stronger and I get stomach cramps. Darkness still surrounds me. I see silhouettes and shadows. I press my lids.

With my eyes closed, I try to eliminate the acrid smell coming through my nose, but I can't. You have to breathe this way, without complaining. The movement of the train increases. We're going down a slope. I seem to get used to the smell. I almost do not feel it. My nose starts to burn now. Later I feel the same burning itch in the soles of my feet, as if someone is tickling me. I try to contain myself and ask my father to put me down. Perhaps it will go away when I'm standing on the floor—but no, it only gets worse. Now I'm suffocating. Since I'm so small I only come up to other people's chests. I can only see belts and buttons. The odor of sweat and vomit overwhelms me. Here on the floor everything is worse.

I hit my thighs. I can barely move my arms. The space is very close. There is no place to sit down. I had not realized there were so many of us. The rabbi's cough comes

⚜

back. I hear a voice above me: "We're not getting out of this one, Miriam." The weeping of a woman goes through me. I take hold of my father's feet. He seems to understand and picks me up again. But up there the situation hasn't changed much. I don't see the light that was coming in through the small window. The whole car is in darkness. The beasts have closed us in like mice.

A blood-curdling scream makes my father open his eyes. We can't see where it's coming from, but people start to talk. Everybody is saying something else. "We knew it," a shrill voice says, "He was half-crazy when he came in, I don't understand how he held out so long." Another one, in a hoarse voice, is saying: "What craziness? We're all going to end this way, that's why they locked us up in here." He shut up suddenly as if a knife had gone through his throat.

Standing pressed up against the walls of the car, we didn't understand a thing and had all our senses alert to try to make sense of each phrase. What seemed like the voice of a woman said: "What did he do to be treated this way? Are we marked, do we carry the black plague? My God, how much longer?"

More panic. We don't understand anything. A man asks, "What happened, brothers?" From the other side of the railroad car someone answers: "A dead man." Those who had not bothered to ask start to squirm in their places. A dead man among us. This caught everyone's attention, and the movement of the train was now confused with the pushes and squeezes we gave each other. "A dead man," the idea went around in my mind, and what did these people who were moving around want?

My father pressed closer to the wall. He did not move a centimeter in the direction where they said the dead man was. I, on the other hand, opened my eyes wider to

❖

see if I could get a glimpse of what was going on, but I only saw shadows crowded like sardines. The rabbi's cough was barely audible because of the grumbling.

Suddenly a figure approached us from amidst the feet and bellies. It was Isaac. "I know where everyone is. I know the railroad car. It stinks. People faint but have to stay on their feet. The dead man is standing and oozing blood from his belly button. The madness—" My mother cut him short. "Come on, boy, tell us what happened?" We all listened closely. "Madam, it's very simple, the dead man was a doctor and had been crazy for a while. They arrested him but never took him to the ghetto because the SS needed him, but when a German doctor came in they fired him and put him here with us. His wife and children died in the ghetto, and from then on he never spoke. Except when we got to the station, he said he was planning to escape. That he would escape when least expected because he knew how to fly. That way, according to him, the shots would not hit him. His friends thought he was joking, of course, but he was already crazy. You can tell who the crazy ones are. Their eyes are big and dark because there is no light in their heads—" Someone took him by the hand and said: "Forget your explanations and say what you know, little philosopher." These last words seemed to bother Isaac. He stood silently, kicking the floor with his feet.

I got angry at the man who had tried to ridicule him. What was the big rush?—we had plenty of time on this train. What difference did it make if Isaac gave whatever explanations he wanted to. After all, none of us could go outside to see for ourselves, and we were all anxious for someone to tell us what was happening, to bring us out of this stinking mess.

❧

My father spoke gently to Isaac, encouraging him to go on with his story. He did so after some hesitation. "Whoever doesn't want to listen, let him cover his ears with his hands. It's quite simple; you just press your fingers against the holes in your ears, that's all. Anyway, the doctor opened up his own belly with a scalpel. He buried it inside real good and then screamed. The scalpel remained inside. Nobody could get it out. The whole thing went in. There he is with his lip torn and his eyes backwards. If he stays here he'll begin to stink." He swallowed. "This little trip is going to be a long one. Don't you understand? A man's watch said five o'clock. I couldn't tell whether it was morning or afternoon. In this darkness you can't tell anything. If you ask me whether I'm alive, I'll think twice before answering.

"I'll be back soon," he said, and lost himself again amidst the mess of bellies and legs in front of us.

Minutes went by. It was a macabre dance that did not stop its tick-tack. The air got thinner every minute. Even though we are used to bad odors we can't avoid breathing badly. The air is warm; we're breathing some kind of ammonia. We can't wait to get out. Where is the east? At the end of the world? I keep quiet. It is not worth asking where the east is. I feel that the tracks will have to end somewhere. The crying of the children makes the forced darkness even worse. The beasts do not want to open the windows and we have to make do with the dampness that seeps in through the cracks. I look at the floor and don't see anything. It must be night. I try to imagine the dead man at the other side of the car. I try to put it together like a puzzle. What else can I do? I don't know him. He could be a man of medium height with blond hair covering his ears, properly combed and with thick glasses.

⚜

That's what the doctors I knew looked like, and all doctors must look alike. I can't imagine that people could be different. But if that's the case, what the hell are we doing here, locked up like animals? No, the beasts are not people. They are beasts! My stomach hurts again.

I feel sleepy and close my eyes. But I can't sleep. The rabbi's cough and the children's cries come up to me, not to mention the rest of the noise. Everyone wants to rest, but there isn't enough room. You have to be content with the spot where you're standing. My head feels heavy. It must be the tiredness. I can't imagine what my father is thinking. He's been holding me for a long time and doesn't seem to be tired. And my mother, with her head on my father's shoulder, what can she be thinking about this darkness, these odors, the noise? Perhaps she is trying not to scream in desperation. Maybe this is the craziness Isaac talks about.

The man next to me is banging on the wall. He is cursing in a low voice, saying words I cannot understand. He breathes as if he wants to push his lungs through his mouth. I think about madness. I don't know what it is, but what Isaac says is enough for me. I walk through a thread of black light that I don't see. Why see it? That's what madness must be like, with your belly full of pencils and your hands swollen with blood.

My head hurts. I can barely breathe this strange thing that comes in through my lungs. I feel a strong urge to urinate. My bladder swells and the pain hits me like a bunch of needles. I think about the pencils in the belly button. I try to hold myself but it is impossible. I've been wanting to urinate for a while and cannot hold it any longer. I feel that my belly is about to burst in a thousand pieces that will fly through the car, hitting every one.

⚜

"Dad, I need to pee," I say in his ear. I squirm; I bring my legs together hoping not to burst.

I don't wait for an answer from my father to urinate in my pants. There was nothing I could do, locked in a place that disallowed any movement, no matter how small. I rest. I come back to life, whatever is left of it.

My father puts me down. He is not offended. It was something I had to do. On the floor nobody is bothered by my wetness. Others have already done it. I have felt that smell of ammonia around us. Down on the floor I see a bunch of legs shifting in search of a more comfortable position.

They're looking for a chair that does not exist, a bed that does not materialize. An acid smell makes me turn my face. Someone has defecated. We cannot escape our physical needs, and now we must do them standing up, without any preambles. I have even more understanding of what Isaac calls madness.

We are not ashamed of our needs. We all perform them out as well as we can, and period. Social norms disappear. We're in a box, in the darkness, feeling human amidst the putrefaction. The darkness shelters us from our misery. Yes, here in the box we are all equal, and the main thing is to endure, to survive inside these four pieces of wood on wheels that are going eastward. The beasts have embalmed us in their boxes!

I think with horror of the truck where they gassed the old people and the children. Could this be something similar? It is as if someone had taken me by the neck to make me say something I don't understand. I begin to cry in anguish. This darkness oppresses. I no longer care about the odors or the heavy air. I'm obsessed with the darkness, by my inability to move, by feeling trapped,

⚜

drowning in this box. My crying doesn't stop. My mother picks me up. Saddened by not knowing where her parents are, she tries to console me. "Israel, be patient, we'll get there soon, and then you'll be able to rest. Our journey will soon be over, yes, that's it." She sounded as if she was trying to convince herself.

I calmed down a bit when I felt my mother's warmth, this shelter that never left me alone in the darkness. Shadows, that's what we were. Something on our right begins to move. I peer into the blackness. It's a woman talking to the bundle in her arms. "Why don't you cry, love? Come on, baby, cry like the others, breathe, let me feel your body. Yes, leave that cold you have in your face, move your little hands. You were moving them a while ago, why not now?" I swallow when I hear one man tell another: "If they don't take us out of here, I'm going to kill myself like that other one. Do you hear that woman? She's been talking to that child for over an hour. She doesn't want to accept that he's dead, stiff, cold. I don't think we'll last very long in here." He talks in short sentences, obviously shaken; he too is nervous.

I tried to place the woman's voice but couldn't. My mother, who had heard the conversation, covered my ears, perhaps to keep me from hearing. But it was too late. How was the baby? Blue and with an enormous head like the one in Czernowitz? Death starts to look like a kind of madness.

In this box you talk to the dead as if they were alive. It's not like it used to be. Weeping, people offering condolences, like the employee at the funeral home. Moshe's father was buried in the usual way, and I don't think Moshe would have begun to talk to the dead man. Or perhaps in this box we are living in a different world. Yes,

❖

that must be it! How many times have I heard people talk about the other world? They always said it was a long and often dark trip.

I can't think. A horrible noise starts to spread through the car. Desperate people are pounding on the walls for the train to stop. It's the same in all the other cars. A noise that keeps getting louder. Tam, tam, tam. Strong, fearless, hoping to see something, to breathe fresh air. They shout, they cry, they pound until their knuckles are bloody. Nothing matters. Our fate is sealed.

I know there are a couple of dead people among us, but there could be more. This crowding, standing up without being able to move, leads to thoughts and dreams. But it is a kind of dreaming and a kind of thinking that only breeds misery and desperation. I can't breathe. Nobody can.

I too pound the wooden walls. I want to break a hole to breathe through, to see night or day. After a while, in the midst of the constant pounding, the windows open. I can't see anything. It's my first impression. My eyes are burning. I finally get used to the gray light of a rainy day. A cool breeze comes in and revives us.

The rabbi goes back to his dry coughing. I can't see him. I don't know where he is. I know he's alive because he's coughing. My father lifts me up to the window. The wind against my face is sweet, like a caress I have awaited for a long time. It is a pleasant feeling but does not last long. My lips burn, perhaps chapped by the fever. The breeze that caressed me so sweetly now begins to hurt. It's ironic. Nature seems to be against me. Everything seems suspicious and I doubt even what I see. Here in the box you can't tell what is true. We are citizens of desperation, members of a different world.

⚜

I fix my eyes outside. I look at the falling rain, making the bare trees cry. There's no one around. I only feel noise and anguish. I have no idea of the day or the time. It could be a Thursday or it could be Shabbat. We've been in the box so long that the notion of time is not indispensable for the normal development of our lives as humans turned into a mass that compacts as our anguish grows.

And, in spite of the fact that the four small windows have been opened, the banging does not stop. Everybody bangs on the wooden walls of the box; tiredness and the lack of oxygen have eroded our capacity to reason. We don't give a damn if we're scared, after all we can't descend any further. That's why we are banging and pounding. Some in protest, others half-crazy, still others pleading for mercy. Everyone has a reason to bang on the wall. There are some who do it out of hate.

The rabbi's coughs come at every shorter intervals. It is a hard cough that can be heard even above the noise we're making. My neighbor bangs the wall with both hands and challenges death as he cries. He is in bad shape, his eyes rolling in their sockets. Some fixation turns him into something he was not just moments before. His mouth oozes a thick liquid. The light comes in through the cracks and uncovers a muddy body that appears ashen because of the dirt. His fat hands are cracked and his knuckles are covered with blood. He's crazy; he acts like someone possessed. While banging, he takes little jumps and laughs, he has stopped crying to laugh. He has no reason to laugh, unless madness has taken hold of him. When he stops banging, I grasp my mother's apron. I'm afraid that the madman will turn his banging against me.

❖

Suddenly the train starts to slow down. I can't see anything that looks like a station. I begin to think that our "time has come"; a knot forms in my throat. We stop.

It is an empty field, without houses and only two or three bare trees. The banging stops. Silence. You can't hear anything except the rabbi's cough and a child's crying. The beasts have formed a line on either side of the cars. They are wearing long coats, and their machine guns point at the doors and windows of the trains. My father instinctively takes a step back; perhaps he is sorry to be standing against the wall. Others lunge out toward the windows to see what is happening. Had I not been holding on to my father, I would have been swept away by the human wave that rushed toward the small opening.

Suddenly the ones in front tried to turn back, but it was too late. The beasts began shooting, and the bullets went through the wooden walls. We heard the cries of the wounded. It was a fast but sure and sinister shooting.

Some men were squirming at our feet. Soon the beasts opened the doors of the car and we heard an officer announce: "We have orders to take you to Uman. But we also have orders to crush any attempt to revolt, which we have done just now. Anyone who tries to mutiny will be killed on the spot! Understood?" His mouth, thin as a scar, closed in a grimace. He ordered us to bring the dead and wounded out of the train.

The doctor who had killed himself was taken out, together with a couple of children and three of the five wounded. The two others had hidden among their friends. Everyone stood quietly. Nobody moved. The dead were placed next to the tracks. The one who had taken his own life had a sunken face and no glasses. He looked completely different from my image of him. Had he been alive, I never would have taken him for a doctor. By his side the two children looked like wax statues. They were pale and thin, and shriveled up like worms. The rain slid over their bodies and it looked as if they were crying or sweating. Their eyes were open and dull.

The mothers of the children were held back by the others to keep them from jumping off the car and holding on to the cold bodies of their children. They had even put gags on their mouths to keep them from crying. If the beasts found out, they would bring them down too, and we all knew the fate that would await them.

There was a movement in the center of the car. We all looked in that direction, and so did the beasts. The rabbi took a few tentative steps forward, then put his hand on his chest. A black liquid spouted from his mouth, and he fell head first on the floor. None of the beasts reacted. The rabbi turned a few times and ended face up on the floor. There was a sweet expression on his face. I had thought about this moment. Perhaps he did not want to die in the train without seeing creation once again, these fields of God.

With his eyes closed, his broken glasses and his torn coat, he had an imposing air that nobody had suspected. He died like what he was, a rabbi! His beard, stained by the blood from his mouth, looked like fire going up to heaven. His death was a sacrifice to the God of Israel.

The beasts pointed their guns at us once again. We stepped back, terrified. The door of the car was closed again and we were once more in darkness. The windows remained open, at least for now. Inside, next to the wall perforated by the bullets, was a puddle of blood. All in less than five minutes. The rabbi dead, the two children,

❖

the doctor—madness, like Isaac said! Nobody dared to speak. We were waiting for the train to start again, keeping away from the walls this time, in fear of being shot. You could expect anything from the beasts. We heard some shots. I thought about the wounded. They had given them the "hospital treatment."

Less than three minutes later we once again heard the chug, chug, chug of the train moving along the tracks. Once again the movement, the crowding, the foul smells. There were still too many people in the car. The two wounded who had stayed behind were now complaining. Somebody tore a piece of clothing to use as bandages. My neighbor, calmed down now after seeing the beasts in action, muttered: "These two will die also. The gangrene will eat them alive." I figured they would rot away like Moshe had.

The mothers were crying softly, and one of them began to cry hysterically. She was asking for her son, pleading for people to let her through to open the door. She hit everything in sight, saying it was time that they killed all of us. Her cries drilled through our ears, and my mother, like most of the other women, began to cry. A man went over to the woman and slapped her in the face twice. We all shut up. The man said: "She's hysterical, and this is the only thing that will calm her down." A grumble went around: "He's right, that's the treatment." My father smiled when he heard these words. To talk about reason in a place without any, inside a train to hell in the hands of madmen!

We were just as uncomfortable as before. And to top it off, rain was coming in through the windows, flooding the floor. My father picked me up in his arms once again. When I got close to his face I found his beard rough, but his skin was warm, not cold like that of the dead child whose mother had held him long after her warmth could bring him back to life.

Exhausted, with my head heavy, I closed my eyes and fell into a deep sleep on my father's shoulder, who leaned once again against the wall, not bothered by the rain falling on him.

I dreamed that I was flying next to the rabbi who had not stopped coughing and spitting blood. The two children drew close to my legs, and the doctor put his hand inside his belly and screamed for someone to pull it out. The beasts were behind us, laughing and pointing and throwing nets to catch us. Soon everything disappeared and I came back to the world where people lived crowded against each other. Bunches of people held together in an insufferable smell. All of them parading on a dead-end street, surrounded by black uniforms, listening to the black laughter of the machine guns and pointed at by millions of fingers that cried together: "Look at them, they're Jews!" And then they put us on a huge railroad train and lowered it into the ground, as they would a casket.

I woke up startled. I was suffocating and tried to get a bit of moisture through the opening. It felt horrible, as if someone had whipped me in the face. My father was sleeping standing up and I did not want to wake him. The wounded did not stop complaining. Their wailing went on and on, and rebounded slowly against themselves. In the intense cold, some people warmed up against each other, encased in the same coats. My mother, her hair falling on her face, had her eyes open, pensive and sighing every once in a while.

I again put my head on my father's shoulder. His breath warmed me up. The same questions came back to

❧

haunt me. What was all this? Packed like animals in this filthy car, what were we guilty of? Could Isaac have gone mad? The ominous wailing of a wounded man was my only answer.

The train kept moving and there was no way to get out and look or barter for anything. Could the beasts be planning to let us die of hunger? Yes, that was a possibility. As the officer had said, they had orders to take us to the east, but he had not specified whether it was dead or alive.

I tried to gather some saliva to freshen my throat, but then noticed the rain coming through the window and leaned over to catch some in my mouth

At first I felt like vomiting; my stomach, turning against the water, caused me a deep pain. I said nothing and looked at my mother. Her eyes were still fixed in space.

I counted seventy-two people in the car. The figure changes every time I count. My stomach does not hurt any more. Everything vanishes and I can barely see the window getting lighter. The rain keeps on. Hunger strikes again, opening a deep hole in my gut, where it burrows and pulls.

Dawn was coming for the people outside. The sun was coming up for everyone but us, the people on the train. Darkness, black pieces that sometimes light up weakly in order to silhouette people, giving them the shape of witches who can't find their brooms.

I had already listened when the women talked about superstitions. They used to say that the horrors were dark bulky objects whose faces it was difficult to see, and now I couldn't see anyone's face. I wait for my father to wake up. In the meantime, I count the shadows again. I don't know why I'm doing this. Something leads me to it.

⚜

In the back the children keep crying. They must be hungry and cold, or maybe they're sick. This is turning into an inferno. We cluster together like sardines in a can. The constant movement is now even more forceful. The train seems to be jumping. Maybe the rails are damaged. I don 't know anything, I can only sense and reason, and make a world of my own, a world I cannot share, a world that is lost and disappears among the darkness and the smells.

My mother realizes that I am awake. She draws close to me and takes me by the waist. My father opens his eyes. I can't be sure that he has slept at all. Everything seems strange. I can't be sure of anything. I don't know whether I am awake or still in my nightmare. I don't have to say that I'm hungry. My mother knows it ,and she takes a piece of bread from a bag she carries with her. She breaks it and gives a piece to me and another to my father. We eat slowly. My teeth hurt. They're weak. Maybe it's my gums. They're swollen. I'm scared to think that I'm sick. I don't want to rot like Moshe. A shudder goes through my spine. If I'm sick the beasts will send me to their "hospital" and take me out of my misery. Elias told me about the "treatment." I swallow with an effort. The bread is hard, but it's all we have to eat and I thank the Lord for it. When I finish my mother hands me a bottle of water. I take a swallow and it's sweet. I don't understand where my mother found sugar. Mothers know these things and you don't have to ask. You don't need to know. Facts give the answer. I look at her. She drinks a bit, but she hasn't touched the bread. Maybe she is saving it for later.

Hours go by. The screams increase. It is an everyday occurrence to hear people screaming and crying. Isaac

❖

finally shows up, scratching his nose. I notice that he's pale. I haven't seen him for a while. I sigh. My neighbor laughs by himself. He acts strange. He pulls his hair, but instead of crying in pain he laughs. His eyes are small and lackluster.

Isaac has been watching him. He scratches his cheek and says: "He's insane. So are many others. A few hours ago I was talking to a girl who gave me a lot of advice. She talked about hope, she told me to trust my strength, not to get carried away by my impulses. Suddenly she began to laugh and now she's crying. She too went mad. We're all going mad. Nothing is worth anything. We think, we try to dream; we try new ways of life. And what? Those who teach them go crazy and we remain alone, watching them screaming, melting like wax toys standing next to a fireplace." He was talking without looking me in the eye. My father watched him with interest, as his only possibility of knowing what was going on. "Do you know how long we've been stuck in here?" Isaac took his hands out of his pockets and contemplated his dirty nails for a while. He licked his dry lips with his tongue and said: "I don't know, but there's a man in the right corner who's been keeping score ever since we left. He calculates each hour and makes a mark in the wood. He figures it's been about five days."

My mother clutched her throat in a panic. How could we possibly have spent so much time in this box? My father, however, nodded. It was obvious that he too had been keeping score. I asked myself: "Five days standing in the dark, stuck in this box, dreaming, hitting the walls, screaming." It seemed impossible that the beasts could descend so low. They were killing us on the rails. They were aware of the days. They had calendars.

❖

Isaac took out a loaf of hard bread and offered us a piece. We told him we had already eaten. He shrugged and took a bite. With his mouth full of bread he said: "I told you that this was going to be a long trip. The Germans know it. They're pigs." And saying this he went back, squeezing among legs and bellies. We were confused, especially my mother.

I close my eyes. I don't know how many times I've done this. It's a way of not drowning in what I see, with this multitude of people that seems to squeeze even closer every time I look. I remember the gray color of the beasts' weapons, those machine guns that killed so many of us. I can see their metallic shine; I will see it until I die! How could I forget? I see Red's face saying: "When this is over, anyone who can should write about it." I remember. I piece together every detail. I don't leave anything behind. The cold penetrating my bones is now worth something. Everything is valuable in this box, so that I won't forget when I grow up, if I get there. In the box you learn to live with your hopes pinned on a doubt. We know we are locked in, and we scream, thinking that we will get out. The scream is worth something, and so is the hysteria, everything has its value. The life we are living costs something, and we quote it in the desperation of knowing that the values are not worth anything and that hope is the same as a bit of cold air. The breathing space is the life that cries out in the shape of bitter rain. My neighbor lives his insanity, laughing, standing up, and pulling at his hair in the hope of rising to the sky, going through the wood ceiling of the train. A vain attempt that also has its value. Here, squeezed in and drowning, I learn to value.

The piece of hard bread that I ate not long ago has its value in life. Because of this piece of bread I'm alive a few

❖

minutes more, perhaps a few hours more. I don't know if after the next one I eat I will be sane or mad. What's the difference? Isaac says that we're all crazy, and I think he's right. Who, if not a madman, would be standing up, suffocating, voiding in his pants, hitting the wood of the box, waiting for the time to get out and the time going by, marking even harder the enclosure? A madman. Period. I scream. I feel like screaming.

A bit of light comes through the holes left by the bullets. I don't care. Now everything is centered in my scream. In looking for a way out of the tunnel down which I'm sliding while I drown. I have a value, I know it, and I claim it, screaming. My screams are not alone, they get lost with the others. They're not alone; they go together, validating with more intensity our condition as unhappy human beings. I don't know about time and minutes. It could be a farce from the calendars. Time does not exist for us in the darkness. In this box, values are not measured in minutes. We have our own measure of screams. We get used to being on our feet, desperate, malodorous, our skin covered with sores. Alone in our misery. We go in by ourselves, and by ourselves we go out. It's a dance in which man subsists until he falls dead, but not vanquished. To subsist is worth screams and blows, cold and hunger. You transcend amid four walls when you scream at the top of your lungs, reaching history, sleeping when you faint, with an empty belly and a haggard face. Many have fainted without being able to fall down; they suffer the collapse standing up, without the right to fall on the floor, full of human waste.

Every passing moment things get worse. I don't know when I'm asleep, I could be dreaming that I'm awake and it would be the same thing. The nightmare is the same, with your eyes open or closed.

⚜

Every part of my body has a different ache, a different
smell, something that contributes to value each moment
of life, of this time that has stopped to run outside. Here
time has stopped. What should it go on for? What date
would we keep? Who's waiting at the station?

The man to my right has become quiet, with his nails
stuck in the wood of the box. He's very quiet, with his
teeth biting his upper lip. I'm afraid to touch him. He
could be dead or asleep. In that case I would wake him
up and he would start again with his laughter and his
narrow eyes. The man escapes through his eyes, he
denies the evidence. He does not see it. He lives within
himself and turns into himself, twisting like the thread
they use for fabric. There, quiet, without his laughter, he
seems to be measuring time from the outside. A long sob
takes me out of my reverie and I see my mother. A pair of
tears run down her pale cheeks. Perhaps she's thinking
that her last letter did not reach her parents. Or maybe
she's thinking about my father and me. We're like unde-
livered letters at her side, unable to give her joy. We are
together and apart, close and far away. The darkness
sets us apart, but we touch and we know that we are
there. My father, my mother. I also touch myself to see if
I'm there. Everything seems so unreal!

A girl sings a lullaby to a baby that is not there.
However, she cuddles some rags and talks to the baby.
Her hair is unkempt and falls all over, but she doesn't
care. I haven't heard her cry. She only sings and holds
the parcel. To her side an old woman chews on nothing.
Or perhaps she is praying. Her lack of teeth gives the
impression that she's chewing. Her eyes shine every once
in a while. It must be when she despairs. There are con-
spiratorial smiles between her and the girl. They have

❖

created their own world, and they don't share it with anyone. It is theirs, born here in the box.

My lids are swollen and feel like balloons. It is time for
another piece of bread and a sip of sweet water. I chew it,
thinking about a pit full of snakes twisting on the floor.
Of course I've never seen them. I know of them because I
once saw them in a book. Why couldn't there be snakes
in the train? Here everything happens. So then?

Everything darkens. I'm not afraid, I'm used to the
blackness. I can't be sure that it's night. I turn in the
darkness and the girl with the lullaby opens her mouth
to bite the sound that comes from her mouth. I don't see
her, but I feel her. In the box the five senses are one. We
live as we can. A woman raises her fist and screams: "So
what, doesn't it make sense that someone would faint of
hunger to start dying?" The collapsed body falls but does
not reach the floor. There's not enough room.

My neighbor comes back to life without uttering a
word. I see him turn around and face the people in the
front. He blows his nose, getting rid of the mucous. He
brings out something from his dirty coat and eats. He
swallows, making a strange noise. He keeps eating. He
finishes and blows his nose again. Then he throws up.
His hands look for support in the flat beams. He stands
against the wall with the vomit on his shirt. I can't distinguish the smell. I've been smelling so much that I'm
incapable of differentiating the odors. They're all acrid.
I'm used to them, we're accustomed to smelling bad.

The beasts have closed the opening again. We're in
total darkness. The bullet holes don't let in any light.
Night is still with us. Dawn does not come. Perhaps it will
never come.

A young boy starts to recite: "When the world turned

❖

dark, the ants ate the ashes. And they ate until they were sated. It was a day without sun, a day with many hours and no clocks, nor light. It was the day when the world turned dark!" He stops for a few minutes, then resumes: "This day lengthened to infinity, and the ants vomited the ashes to eat them again. How the ashes cried when they were eaten by the ants. It was a day when darkness was the world. And the ashes got up to eat the ants, and that day was a dark day, until the dark ashes ate the world to be sated with ants." He gave out a cry when he finished. It was the epilogue to madness, his admission test to the other side of the world of the living.

I looked at him without blinking, looking for his shape amid the suffocating darkness of the box. Isaac appeared once again, scurrying in between the legs of the people. He kept moving from one side of the car to the other. He was looking for a shape in the unshaped, he wanted to justify and accent his theory about madness: "Did you hear the poet? It's something you can only recite once in your life. He couldn't take it any longer and spoke in his own language. He believed that he was in a big theater. And did you see how we screamed to applaud him? This is crazy, what the world needs is not to go on like it does. Look, the man who keeps score tells me that we have broken a record. We have been in this box for eight days and the train still hasn't stopped. Are you thinking about graves? We could die here and it would be nothing for the Germans to throw the railroad car in the river. Come on, say something, I've been thinking about it for a long time."

The girl who was cuddling the rags looked at him surprised. "Boy, don't you know we have been dead for centuries? Look at my child; he was never born because people are not born among the dead. But I cuddle him and sing him songs, right, Ruth?" The old woman nodded, showing her toothless gums.

My mother hugged me to her bosom, horrified, and trying to keep me from hearing and seeing what was happening around us. But it was useless. The girl kept talking. "We were on this earth and were uprooted, like you pull up the vegetables on a farm. They changed our life for death and—"

She seems unable to think of anything else to say. Her words are suspended, floating, intermingled with the cries and the screams that come from everywhere. Isaac argues: "What you're saying is false. I'm alive, I just looked through the holes in the wood, and the world outside is in the middle of autumn. I felt the wetness of the rain on my face. I am sure that it's raining outside." The toothless old lady said in her trembling voice: "It has always rained. And when it doesn't rain, you cry, it's the same thing. We shouldn't think about the rain. We are the rain. Can't you see that her child is rain? Touch him and you'll see that he's wet."

My neighbor, with a superhuman effort, let out another one of his laughs. That was all he did. He remained the way he was. Isaac took out another piece of rock-hard bread, bit into it, and made himself comfortable next to me, looking for a space between the neighbor and myself. He made himself comfortable. It was his style. That's how he wandered up and down the car and found out how many days had gone by.

Fantasies increased as misery escalated. I stopped thinking. I did not care to do so. Whatever went through my head was okay. I saw forms that bore no relation to anything.

⚜

Huge faces and fangs tried to get me. The black uniforms of the beasts covered my face to smother me, and
I would sneak through the buttonholes gasping for air.
The image of my grandparents was vanishing, and I
could barely hold on to the image of the sleigh. I would
repeat the word "snow" and mix it up with "flowers." All
my ideas were upside down, but I was alive.

Isaac, however, kept on about insanity. "Yes sir, their
eyes turn big and yellow, trying to fly away. All the crazy
people fly and talk to birds. The birds tell them many
things. So many that the madman doesn't have words
enough to repeat them, or numbers to classify them.
Crazy things we'll never be able to understand as long as
there is a barrier of reason between the madman and us.
But what is reason? Members of the jury, the accused
has committed the crime of being sane, and I plead for
him, in the name of the people and the state, to let him
stay sane. He cannot live among us madmen." He would
often keep quiet, but sometimes he would repeat the
same thing or something similar.

Meanwhile, I watched my neighbors in order to find in
them a trace of something that would not be madness.
But they would cry and scream without letting anybody
know in advance. They would do it suddenly, with a piece
of bread in their hands, talking about homes and plenty
of food, of streets and of people who walked on the sidewalks without being forced to get on trains. They all had
a story, something to tell, a collection of phrases that
recalled a past. No one spoke about a future. This kind
of present ripped that apart. Taking refuge in vague
memories was a way out, a way of not being here.

A mature man, who spoke very little, talked about his
office. "If you could see the desk, all carved wood with a

❖

marble top and a pair Bavarian crystal inkwells. And the chair—"

The neighbor who laughed let one out in his face. The other man, who needed an excuse to explode, lunged at him, taking him by the neck and strangling him. "You're responsible for what's happening to us. I saw you fly out at night and steal a star. Stars cannot be touched. Because of you they have killed us and now you must die." He made no sense whatsoever.

My father and two other men quickly jumped in to keep our neighbor from being strangled by the financier. With a great deal of effort, they managed to separate them. My neighbor kept laughing as if nothing would have happened. Yes, he kept laughing as if the whole thing was a big joke.

Isaac stuck his hands in his pockets and began to whistle a song called "Hatikvah"—"The Hope." My father patted him on the back. "Well done," he said. Apparently the song had an effect on many people. Some faces looked at Isaac as he whistled in the dark.

Hours keep going by of this time that has stopped in this train. I eat my ration again. It keeps getting harder, and the water has taken on a vinegary taste. My thighs are burning. I move and it feels like they are tearing my flesh apart. Isaac tells me that it is due to defecation. The smells are part of the trip that doesn't end. I don't feel the shut, shut, shut of the wheels over the rails. But the train doesn't stop. The swaying doesn't end, a sign that we are moving. I believe that we have gone around the world. The east must be outside, in space, near the moon or a star. I feel a bit calmer. Must be because of the way I've been sleeping lately. I fall asleep without dreaming. Of course it could also be that I'm already dead. I look at

⚜

the girl with the rags and try to understand her lullaby—that sound that does not stop while we scream and bang at the wooden planks.

I hadn't realized that the breathing holes have been opened again. It is night, or else darkness covers everything. I know they are open because of the wet, rainy air that comes in. But outside it is also dark. I look to the side and see nothing but my neighbor starting to pull his hair again. Isaac is not there any more. He left without saying goodbye. He has immersed himself again in the crazy dark world of the railroad car. He could be with the man who counts the days, figuring the hours.

My mother's eyes are shut. I get close to her and rest. She is breathing steadily. I have felt the warmth of her breathing against my forehead, or could it be that dead people also breathe? My head hurts with every thought I try to put together. I can't seem to remember things. Everything gets confused. I don't know if I'm making things up or remembering. Darkness and desperation have had an effect on me.

I still don't know the madness that Isaac talks so much about. A strange noise comes in from the side of the box; a gust of wind hits our feet. Mine hurt. Some of the nauseating smell goes away. I look and see they have made an opening. Some of the people are going to escape. The idea goes around in my head and my stomach as if I had swallowed a stone. On the other side of the car people are knocking loudly, trying to distract the beasts. The opening on the left is pretty big. Two people can get through easily. A new hope is reborn. We know we can't all leave, but we unconsciously protect those who are going to try.

The crazy ones, for in one car there is a large group of crazy people, keep wailing and screaming. Isaac comes

❖

back. His face is beaming. He gets closer elbowing his way in. "Some of them are planning to escape this hell. They need people who still have some agility. Are you in?" My mother grips my arm. She doesn't want to let me go. My father seems frightened. He doesn't know which way to go. Isaac pulls me by one arm, but my mother holds me by the other. "I'm not going," I say, without an explanation.

Some light comes in through the opening. It must be morning. It is a gray light that comes in with a wet breeze. Just enough for me to begin to see some boys standing next to the opening. They will be the first to jump. You can see that the train is going at a low speed.

The first one jumps, and then the second and the third. There is not much time. The fourth and the fifth jump, and when the sixth jumps we hear the sound of the machine guns. The beasts have seen them and shoot at their bodies which fall on the side of the rails and roll down. I see the boys squirming when they feel the impact of the bullets on their flesh. They turn. A voice inside the train screams: "They're killing them." The banging gets louder.

We are almost insane. We cry and we bang against the wood. We unconsciously wish to be shot to finish this nightmare. My neighbor keeps laughing. I can see his face better. It looks muddy, with his red eyes nestled in a nest of wrinkles. He has pulled a lot of his hair out and there are bloodstains on his forehead. His lips are cracked, dry, and a thick drool falls from the sides. But he laughs, and a foul, nauseating odor comes out of his mouth. The shots have not stopped. The beasts want the fugitives dead, totally destroyed. This brings us into despair. The attempt to escape was a failure, and we lose all hope of getting off this train that never stops. Several

⚜

people, completely insane, elbow their way to the opening. They jump through the open space, ignoring the bullets that rain down from the top of the train. One of them is stuck on a piece of wood and I see how his head starts to fall apart into little pieces. Pieces of brain jump out at us as the man opens up his arms in a vain attempt to embrace the rainy landscape extending before him.

We go back. We keep away from the opening. It is a forced retreat. The instinct to survive is born again in us. I suffocate. The ones who are retreating almost flatten us against the wall. My mother has difficulty breathing. I cry, scream, kick. My father hits everyone around him until he has enough room for my mother to breathe.

Something similar happens at the back of the car. There they fight even more desperately for space. The opening that before was a dream of freedom has become a door to death. The beasts can go to the opening and open fire with their eyes closed. They can always justify the genocide with our intent to escape.

This thought creates a void in my stomach, the fear of seeing my body full of bullet holes. But the beasts wait until we get out to shoot at us. Nobody gets out.

In our despair we give positive value to life once again. We wish to conserve the doubt of the future. Those of us who thought we were dead now know that we are alive. You can't kill a dead man. Yes, the fugitives were alive. I breathe deep, filling my lungs until I feel them almost explode. I want to fill myself with air, with moisture. Life is reborn in me.

The girl of the lullaby looks around disconcerted. It starts to rain and it's windy. Water comes into the car. The floor, full of feces, turns slippery. My father goes into a corner. He takes me in his arms and pulls my mother

⚜

toward him. The body of my neighbor gets wet. The drops of water drip down his emaciated face. He looks horrible, but he keeps laughing and banging the wall. He won't give up. He is in his own world, and he plans to defend it to the end. The crying of the children gets louder. The cold coming in through the opening is bothering them.

I shudder. And so do my mother and father. We are lost. We don't go out because we know what awaits us, and if we remain inside we are going to die because of the water flooding the car and the endless cold. This time we cry to keep warm. We are afraid. Misery covers our bodies, as well as dirt. The light that comes in through the opening bothers my eyes.

Everybody squirms and cries. The banging must be felt for several meters around us. It is hard and constant. It doesn't stop. We have seen two days go by. The opening has turned dark and light twice. Nature can hardly be perceived in its gray autumnal garb.

I believe the landscape is laughing at our condition, or perhaps takes pity on us. We feel the need to abandon our own skins, to get lost in the cumulus clouds that we see in the distance. Many have jumped out to their death.

My neighbor emits a strange sound. He must have died. I don't say anything. I only wish to bang and cry so hard that my hands will explode. We don't care about anything. We know we are lost. We are hungry. I haven't eaten for two days. My stomach distends when I drink a bit of water. We all drink rainwater. It's the only thing we have. It is a slower process of death.

My mother is no longer whimpering. She looks without seeing. My father has not tired of holding me in his arms. Around me people clump together. There are fights all the time. It is a way to vent out anger.

❖

Decay is visible on some bodies. The face of the old lady next to me is covered by a green crust that goes down to her neck, and her eyes are full of a slimy discharge. I can't see her mouth. My stomach hurts to look at her.

Isaac came in and then left again without saying anything. He's everywhere, looking, elbowing his way in. I don't like his looks. There's something strange in the light of his eyes. But then, I may look just the same; I haven't seen myself in a mirror! Time goes by very slowly. In the darkness, at least, we weren't able to keep track of the days very well. But now we see them and everything seems darker. Yes, like the poet said: "When the world was dark, it turned dark, dressed in black." I feel my head big, the size of a box. My bones hurt, and strange red spots appear on my skin. When I scratch them blood comes out. I do it violently, screaming, hitting the boards of the railroad car.

Everything is dark. Our gaze is dark. Isaac comes back. "We are going to start dying. The man who keeps track of the time has counted twelve days." He says so with his face transformed by anguish—or madness!

Six hours or a year must have gone by, what's the difference? The opening has turned dark again. Shadows cover us and the cold increases. My neighbor is rigid, with his eyes open but dimmed. There is no doubt that he's dead. A boy covers his face with his torn jacket.

My throat hurts from screaming so much. Perhaps I don't even have a throat. My vision blurs. We get even closer to each other. We are worms.

The thought of the machine guns curdles my blood. The valor of knowing how to survive, to endure, comes back to me. My father holds me closer against his chest.

⚜

Some boys, I can't determine how many, take a chance at jumping out. They are fueled by despair. We wait for the shots. Nothing. Those who were going to jump have stopped. The machine guns don't rattle. Isaac sticks out his head through the opening. He raises his arms and cries: "The station." We can't believe it. It must be a trick of the beasts to kill us all. We wait with tense muscles. We hear a voice from a loudspeaker:

"Everybody get off the train!" The door opens. It is night, and our journey has ended.

They are giving us orders to get down, to touch land. It seems unreal, incredible. Who knows? Perhaps now they will shoot us.

❖

5

The Devil's Whip

They made us come down onto the muddy ground. My extremities and my head hurt. Everything was so strange, so full of questions, so dark. My mother was weeping, perhaps expecting the end. I looked at her askance, trying to make out a shape. After this journey I could no longer detect shapes very well. My father put his arms on our shoulders and waited for the beasts to start executing people. However, the moment still had not come for us.

We were in a halfway camp, a hole that led to the sewer. The people around us were just like us, bewildered, touching themselves to make sure they were alive. But our reconnaissance did not last long. The beasts made us line up and we could see the black muzzles of the machine guns in front of our faces. No one shuddered, and no one reacted. We were feeling dead already! I entertained myself by looking at the guns, waiting for them to start vomiting their death rattle. It was not that we were resigned to die. None of us were. Who can resign himself to die when death has become a daily occurrence, akin to the coming of night? Death was not a stranger. Many had died in front of us. I used to dream about enormous lakes of blood where the beasts used to go to take a bath. Blood was red. Routine. It was blood that would mingle with the earth when you least expected it. What guarantee was there that I would be alive in a half hour? There was no assurance, no future. The line of waiting people hardly moved.

It began to rain, but we kept quiet. One of the SS officers jumped up angrily: "Come on, let one of you start moving! I need you to cry, to ask for mercy. Come on, Jews, let one of you kneel in front of me!" Nothing. All quiet. It was strange. Several minutes before we had all been banging against the walls of the train, we had been screaming, we had been going mad, begging for a bit of fresh air, and now, quiet, as if we were asleep, not ready to pierce the silence of the night. We wanted nature to witness our murder, not our desperation.

The officer, obviously drunk, kept screaming. He turned red and foamed at the mouth. Nothing. Not even one scream, not a murmur. Even the children were quiet. I could see that some of the beasts were impressed by our determination. If they killed us they would have to do it in cold blood, without a reason. The officer shook his whip. It was a dead noise. Nothing. We were still in our places, awaiting the barrage of bullets that would end with what was still hanging on our bones. Like someone possessed, the man began to count, and every time he got to ten, one of us was taken out of the line. Many people were moved to the front, among them several old men and some children. The officer took a small boy of about five. put a gun to his head, told his men, "This is how you do it," and then fired. The boy fell without uttering a sound. His eyes were open, looking at the last night of his life. He remained quiet, with his brains around him and a thin thread of blood coming out from the corner of his mouth. But the mother couldn't help it. She came out of the line and grabbed the body of her son. She was screaming, begging them to kill her. The officer, laughing, began kicking her and whipped her in the face, making her right eye jump out. They took her away from her son. With her face destroyed and a hole oozing blood where her eye had been, she was left alive. A shudder went through my spine. We were coming back to life, acknowledging that we needed to live. We woke up from the strange lethargy and began to value things. I was afraid but did not scream. We could not give the hangman the price he exacted to kill us. My mother trembled, and I saw how she bit her lips in order not to cry.

The men who had been pointed out had to undress. The beasts made them kneel and executed them with a shot to the back of their heads. They fell in silence. Then they pointed to others at random. Among them was my father. A quiet scream almost exploded in my throat. My mother was petrified, her face transfigured. She waited for the empty sound of the rifles. Nothing. The men they had pointed out had to carry the dead men several meters beyond where we were. They were lost in the shadows, escorted by the beasts. We heard some more shots in the back. My mother fainted, but the man behind her in the line propped her up. We had to keep her from falling. Any sign of weakness was a sentence of death. My legs were trembling. I was thinking, "He must be there with his neck broken. His eyes would be open, looking at the sky, looking for us to say good bye." I repeated these words over and over, looking for a chance to pounce on the officer and kill him. They were forcing me to think about killing. I was thirsting for vengeance. Instead of feeling sad, I wanted to destroy. I got goose bumps, my skin felt like a sort of armor. I waited for the right moment. My eyes keyed in on the beast and I began to turn my fingers into claws. When he got closer, I would take him by the neck and not let go until his eyes popped out.

I gritted my teeth. I couldn't see anything but the officer and his whip. Everything else had disappeared for me. It was as if I were looking through a tube and at the end could see the figure of the assassin, the pointing beast dressed in black. I breathed deeply, trying to find in the air the approval for my vengeance. The officer was turning toward me. I waited like a shadow, ready to jump as soon as he was in front of me. Each step was slow. He did not come close fast enough. He was walking slowly, perhaps feeling my hatred. I made a fist.

He drew closer and closer. It seemed as if I was floating on air. My body had no weight. Thousands of lights went off inside my brain.

It was time. Five more steps and I would grab him by the neck, pressing my fingers into his dirty throat. He stopped. He burrowed his whip into the protruding belly of a pregnant woman. She bent and vomited a whitish liquid. Somebody jumped out of the line and grabbed the officer's face. I dug my nails into the palm of my hands. He had gotten there ahead of me. That man had taken something away that was mine! I closed my eyes, trying to avoid the feeling of loss. The officer was mine, mine!

When I opened my eyes again they almost jumped out of their sockets. The officer was standing up. The man who had attacked him was at his feet, oozing blood from his nose. The SS officer punished him with his whip, hit him in the ribs, broke his face, opened his stomach. The whip came and went on the man's flesh. When nothing

❖

was left but a mass of flesh that moved reflexively when struck by the whip, the officer took a shovel and brought it down on the leg of the wounded man. He cried in agony. It had sliced off his leg. I shuddered. Another blow with the shovel and an arm flew off almost at my feet. The third blow opened up his head from ear to ear. This time the women could not contain themselves, and holding their children, those small bags of bones that refused to die, they cried out in despair. The beasts pointed at us. The officer was laughing. "That's it, Jews, scream, cry!" At gunpoint they took us to a kind of corral.

The crying increased. With my head bent, I tried to hide my anger. Impotent, unable to do anything, quiet, bound but not with ropes, I felt a prisoner in my own shell. After a while another group was taken to the corral. They came more beaten, but alive. I wasn't sure what was happening. I was taking care of my mother, who was now on the ground, breathing with difficulty and covered with sweat. I began to cry. There was nothing else I could do, and I had to let out my anger I did it by crying and digging my boots into the mud.

The camp seemed just like the train. We were locked in, dying slowly. Isaac showed up. He came with my father. At first I thought it was my imagination. My father had been killed in the dark. I had heard the shots. There was no doubt. But when I felt his body next to my mother's, I could see that his eyes showed the light of life. He wasn't dead! The dead had big, open eyes, but dimmed. My father's were shining. I shook my mother so that she too would see him. She half-opened her eyes and gave out a little cry. She hugged my father. She did not doubt. She felt him alive from the beginning. Isaac bent down. "It's not our turn yet," he said and got up again. He left

❧

quickly before I could say anything. That was his style, always the same. My father looked at us. His face was bruised, as were his legs and arms. "We're in hell," he said. "Over there is a pit full of decomposing bodies. They told us that tomorrow we have to dig a new one. They are murdering us." He was gesticulating desperately, trying to make us understand the magnitude of the picture he had seen. My mother took his head to her bosom. His eyes were red, but brilliant. The brilliance took on an enormous value, it was life.

In a few minutes he fell asleep. My mother began to doze off, and soon she too fell asleep. The last few hours had taken a toll on my parents. Many slept. Nature was giving us a break that surely would not last long. I could not sleep. My imagination was working overtime. I couldn't concentrate. Thousands of shadows came in and out with no specific direction. I imagined some things and tried to remember others. I got up, wanting to move around a little, burrow in the mud, find out what was happening.

I began to walk among the sobbing and the crying. Children were biting into rags, trying to find a taste in the filth. Women looking into the void, unthinking, were trying to disintegrate into the falling rain.

An old man took a tattered book out from his clothes, kept at the risk of his life, and began to read aloud. I went on. Everything was the same. Crying, hunger, madness, a dream turned into a nightmare, bowed heads. A man was biting his nails until they bled. Tears streaming down, he kept saying that it was time to go out to the avenue. I stared at him for a while. He bit his fingers furiously, he cried and slobbered, trying to heal his self-inflicted pain. He kept on talking about his avenue. I

❖

thought about the streets of my own city. The man was talking about his, and I had a right to remember mine. It was the only thing the beasts had not taken away from us yet. We could still find sanctuary in our memories. These were values we still kept intact, away from the claws of the executioners. Someone put a hand on my shoulder. I turned around startled, the beasts had simple ways to single us out. I relaxed when I saw Isaac's face. We looked at each other for a few minutes without saying anything. The man who was biting his fingernails gave out a loud, shrill scream. He had just broken his index finger and was looking at the piece of flesh that was hanging down like an idiot, moving from side to side.

Isaac swallowed. "He's crazy, lots of people are. They'll kill him soon. The Germans don't want crazy people."

His voice was hoarse. My belly hurt. Crazy? How come I hadn't realized it? Yes, he was crazy and I hadn't caught on. I looked again and felt nauseous. The man was chewing on a piece of finger. He was cannibalizing himself. Isaac lunged at him and pulled his arm behind his back to hold him immobile. The man twisted and turned without making a sound. A few people approached us. A woman pointed at the man, saying, "It's Meitek!" and then fainted.

Isaac pushed him to the side. Meitek was crying like a child. The onlookers said in unison: "He's crazy." A big man pulled us out of the circle. "Go away, you ruffians, this is not for your eyes." He probably meant well. He didn't want us to see a such a sight. But hadn't we seen enough? The question worked its way into my brain. It hurt me to swallow. "Was there more?" Isaac didn't understand and took me by my arm. As we tramped through the fields, it began to rain harder.

⚜

The last rains of autumn kept on and on. I began to believe that the sky was crying. Yes, it was crying like the women, like us, tonight the sky was in despair! It suffered in silence, just like the mothers, pouring out its tears over the blood-soaked earth. Isaac stood silently at my side, trying to tell me something. I saw him swallow with difficulty. His words were stuck in his throat, refusing to come out. As time went on we got used to the unspoken language of gestures and signs. There was no need to ask. The answers could be seen in our faces. This daily walking between life and death, not knowing when you're going to get a bullet in the back of your head, turns you into an owl. There is no fear of death, I can't see the difference between life and death. It is important to exist, to see, to be aware of the smallest sign. I'm adapting to the environment that the beasts have created for us. The executioners are torturing us psychologically, trying to destroy us with uncertainty and guesswork. In reality, no one can be sure of waking up alive. Time does not exist for us. It is an irony to see a ticking watch. Its cycle is not ours. To be aware of time you have to be living, not just existing. And we exist, we move, trying to conserve at each step the feeling you get when you put one foot in front of another. We begin to understand eternity.

Isaac speaks to me. "Israel, let's make a treaty. To live together from now on, aware of everything, looking for a way out. We must tell the others what's going on. Can't you see that they are murdering us? Maybe some of the men will understand. Not all of them are crazy like Meitek. Did you see him? Who would believe that boy was almost a mechanical engineer! Nobody! Nobody believes crazy people. That's why we must pledge to each other

❖

not to go crazy! We must endure standing up. Cry to let everything out, look ahead. We must not let them cut our heads off." He talked slowly, calculating every word. I listened attentively. Something told me that I could trust Isaac. I had to hold on to any spark of light, and my friend's ideas were the only bit of brightness to be seen.

Dawn found us standing up, without having closed our eyes all night. My head hurt. Isaac was asking questions that he himself answered. He would lift his index finger and point to the sky. "Is it possible to forget the dead in time? Those eyes, those bodies, and the illusions they nurtured? No!" He looked at me with bulging eyes. "Do you see that pit? The bodies inside are rotting away. They don't smell because they're covered with lime, but they're there. Ask your father. There, one on top of the other, nearby, waiting for us to join them." I shuddered. I had never heard Isaac talking so vehemently. His words were cold, cutting, calculated. He never said anything in vain. Those hazel eyes did not lie.

The sun hurt us with its dim light, uncovering the misery around us. Suddenly we saw a group of soldiers running toward us; they were not dressed like the SS. They looked strange, it was the first time I had ever seen them. They were carrying the terrible machine guns. I ran over to my parents. Isaac followed. There was nowhere else to go. We stuck together like a mass standing ready to defend itself, only we knew that defense was useless.

My mother began to tremble. My father stroked her hair with shaking hands. We waited for the final moment, the shot in the back of the head. They made us stand in line. The man who spoke was a Romanian officer, and the soldiers were Romanian. Later on I found out that they

❖

were collaborators, willing to do anything to ingratiate themselves with their new Nazi masters. They were slaves with a permit to relieve themselves on us. Slaves with power. Slaves who believed in Nazism. Horrible, with stony faces and the terribly executed goose step. Rats trying to assimilate the new invader and doing whatever they were told. Men dulled by war and alcohol, their eyes red with remorse. Many of them would have turned in their brothers. Maybe even their own parents.

The soldiers stopped in front of us and the slave officer spoke with a trembling voice: "Jews, behave yourselves. Anyone who violates the regulations will be executed immediately!" His last words were a dull cry. They showed that he was afraid of us! The slaves were revealing their weak side. They were afraid of us, a defenseless group that could be massacred in an hour. I burned his face into my mind. His fearful expression gave me strength to keep on living. I think Isaac understood, because he poked me with his elbow, that we could use the fear of the slaves. The officer barked some more about regulations. It was another psychological game of the beasts. What regulations? What laws were we supposed to obey? From now on the law was intuition, cleverness. They were forcing us to exist with all our senses in full working order. The troops got closer to us. The Romanian officer saluted and a beast officer turned up by his side. The SS hangman with the whip, his uniform pressed and boots shined. He was stroking his whip in his hand and looked at us with a vicious smile that broke the squareness of his face. He strutted in before us, displaying his power.

Many of us watched fearfully, expecting the worst. After the night before, anything was possible for this wild

⚜

beast with a whip. Gesturing effeminately, he stepped
toward us, covering his nose with his handkerchief. "You
stink, Jews! You smell of shit, which is what you are." He
made gestures of smelling something horrible. He made
us understand that we smelled worse than the carcasses
of his victims in the pit beyond. "Jews, many of you will
have to be treated. Don't you know you are an expense to
the Reich?" He turned around for a moment. When he
faced us again his face was congested. He pointed men
out with his whip. "Step forward, Jew!" He savored the
word —"and stand up, idiot!" The people he designated
turned white. Most of them were old men or sick children
who were still able to stand up. The beast smoothed his
hair with his fingers and said something to the Romanian
officer. The order was gleefully passed on to the slaves.
They began to urinate on the people in front of them. As
the urine ran over their faces, the SS officer shouted hysterically: "Drink, drink, aren't you thirsty?" The soldiers
laughed. The earth opened up under my feet. They were
humiliating us in the crudest manner, they were making
fun of our misery. They were performing these atrocities
with the support of their machine guns. When they finished, the Romanians ordered their victims to undress.
My hair stood on end. It was easy to imagine what would
come next.

When they were completely naked, the SS officer separated the old men from the children. The slaves took the
old men and ordered them to dance in the mud. Those
who refused were shot in the feet. The old men gave
everything they had left. They didn't want to die. At the
last minute they held on to the last remaining miserable
bit of life. The slaves and the beasts laughed, hitting
those who didn't want to dance, or didn't jump high

⚜

enough, with the butts of their rifles. The first one to fall was an old man with a full head of hair. They immediately shot him in the legs. His body writhed in pain. One of the slaves began hitting him with the butt of his rifle and crushed his head. The others, seeing this, began to dance frenetically, calling upon their last strength. But they did not have any more and fell like flies. The rifle-butt treatment followed until only a red mass remained on the ground. The slaves massacred thirteen old men as we looked on impotently, terrified, nailed to our spots. Nobody even dared to breathe. The slaves and the beast might have taken the sound of our breath as a protest, and that was against the "rules."

The beast, as if nothing had happened, began to strut before us again, careful not to dirty his boots with the blood of those he had massacred. "Don't be frightened. Old men and children have no value for the Thousand Year Reich. Don't worry, you have nothing to fear. Jews may stink, but they are useful for work in the east. " He began to laugh when he said "work in the east," cracking his whip in the air. The sick children watched in terror. There were five of them, crying soundlessly. Silent tears that accepted their fate. Then a man began to scream

It was Meitek the madman. He got out of the line and began to crawl toward the officer. The beast raised his arm and ordered the slaves not to shoot. He wanted to enjoy the show. Meitek dug his hands into the flesh of the massacred old men. He smiled at the SS man, who signaled him to approach. When Meitek reached his feet, the officer began to caress his messed up hair with the butt of his whip: "You're a good little Jew. This is how we need you, docile, conscious of the inferiority of your race. You see?" he said, looking at us and smiling, "it's easy to

⚜

crawl. All of you, down on your knees!" We obeyed. We were terrified by what we had just seen. The sick children, watching us, did the same. The beast was satisfied. "That's it, Jews, we're beginning to understand each other and to realize that the one who gives orders here is me! We supermen are destined to win!" The slaves turned serious. The offense included them and the SS officer knew it. He glared at them with his whip ready to tear the face of anyone who made a move. The slaves straightened up, accepting their status. I felt how filthy they were. The beast made the five children stand up; he cracked his whip, and they shuddered when they felt the iron tip on their flesh. And he did it again and again, brandishing his whip at skinny arms and bony faces. The slaves kept their guns pointed at us, ready to fire at the least provocation. The beast concentrated on the sick ones. When they fell he gave orders to shoot. I saw how their lives escaped through the bullet holes. I felt terror and anger and an absolute need to live! I looked at the beast. I tried not to miss any of his features. I burned them into my brain, I sculpted his face in my mind, never to be forgotten. If I survived this hell, I would look for him until I found him. I would hunt him and make him remember, plead, cry. I imagined his capture. There would be no trial. I would put him in a cage and take him from town to town so that people would get to know a beast, a murderous monster.

My head was turning with amazing speed. The back of my knees began to hurt. The cold got through to my bones, and I had to swallow the suffering, the anguish of seeing this genocide. The beast quieted down a bit, coming down from the weird sadistic pleasure he felt when killing, and he smiled, shrugging, as if what he had just

❖

done was no more than a naughty prank. He rubbed his face. "On your feet!" It was a cutting order. We got up in pain, feeling that we were lifting a piece of ground with us. Many were sweating, with big, open eyes.

I felt slightly dizzy when I got up. It was weakness, hunger, lack of sleep, insecurity. My mother was cold. I felt it when I took her hand. We waited for whatever would come next. Completely disoriented, we again waited for the order to start killing us. The beast took his whip and tapped it lightly on his boots. And then happily said: "Nothing has happened. Nothing happens here, it all has to do with following orders. Isn't it so, Jew?" Meitek smiled like an idiot. The beast took out his gun and pointed it at the madman's head, who did not stop smiling, looking at the torn index finger that he had bitten off with his own teeth. The German turned slightly and fired. The madman rocked for a moment and fell to the ground, his smile turning into a grimace of pain. The beast addressed us again, as if he had to justify everything he did in front of us and the slaves. "You can die in many different ways. Sometimes fast, without sweat, like those old men. Do you know that death is sweet? My mother used to tell me that after you die a door opens in the sky and the angels come out, singing to the glory of God and to those who have just ceased to exist. Pardon me for telling you this. I forgot you were Jews and have no right to go to heaven." He said this with such seemingly simplicity that the slaves couldn't keep themselves from laughing.

The SS officer felt important. He was the leader of the trash! He crossed his arms and I saw him as effeminate, just like a girl being praised. He went away taking small little jumps while hitting his hips with his whip. When he

⚜

disappeared, the Romanian officer turned to us. "Some of you, take the bodies to the pit over there. The rest of you, wait here for the recruiter. Don't try anything. You know what will happen." The slave went back to his soldiers, and they pointed their guns at us. This business about recruiting hammered in my head. What kind of trap where they now setting for us? Who was the recruiter, and what was his mission? I put my hands in my pocket and waited.

It kept raining. The blood of the dead men mixed in with the mud. I drank some of the rain to quench my thirst and sank deeper into the mud. I drank sticking out my tongue and trying to get some water into my throat. One of the slaves, who had been watching me for some time, came over and slapped me in the face. I thought I had lost my teeth. The blood ran copiously from my lips. The slave left without saying a word.

His slap had been explicit. It was forbidden to drink unless ordered to do so. Anger made me want to run after him, but Isaac held me by my belt. I stopped. I knew that I couldn't do anything. If an SS beast had seen me drinking, I would no longer be alive. I quieted down, crying bitter tears because drinking too was forbidden. The tears ran down my cheeks, mixed with the unending rain.

We heard the sound of footsteps. Looking up, we saw a group of Nazi beasts approaching with their guns ready. Behind them, with the whip-happy SS officer, was a chubby little man, with round glasses and a huge mustache. He seemed to be limping on his right leg. Judging by the number of black-uniformed men around him, he must have been important. He drew closer and adjusted his glasses. There was no expression on his round, well-shaved face. "Jews, this is Dr. Floss. He has the noble duty of selecting from you garbage the ones who are capable of doing some kind of work." The little man went down the line, looking us over. At the end of the inspection he nodded. "I can get something out of this shipment. Take them to my office," and he walked away.

After a while they took us to the little man's office. We had to walk fast, urged on by threats and rifle butts. The slaves were doing their job well. We walked in columns of five. Everyone tried to end up in the middle to avoid the blows, which never stopped, even for a moment. We did our best to walk fast. We knew something. At the office they would decide who was going to live. The little man with the round glasses had our lives in his hands. He was the one who would decide with a yes or a no. We walked fast, anxious to know our fate.

There at the office they would let us live or simply execute us. Everything seemed so easy. The little man with the glasses separating us left or right, pointing with a tired gesture.

We got to the door of a stable that the SS beasts had reconditioned for contract labor. They made us stand straight. I looked up and saw the swastika. The Nazi flag was wet and limp, not imposing the way it had been when the soldiers who occupied Czernowitz had raised it. I felt like laughing when I saw that rag hanging like a piece of cloth one no longer has any use for.

However, the beasts guarding the door, with their dogs beside them, intimidated me a bit. I still remembered that morning when we had to go to the commissariat to be assigned our place in the ghetto. Those dogs were the same as these. They were just waiting for someone to get out of line so that their masters would let them loose. They were trained to kill. But nobody moved. At

⚜

the door the dogs growled and the beasts holding their leashes looked as impassive as statues.

We waited to get to the desk. Waiting had become a routine part of our existence. We were used to waiting, not thinking about tomorrow, living while waiting through each second of the present. We were going on a par with the time, that is why time did not exist for us. We existed in the wait!

When my father's turn came, I hesitated to follow him. But they pushed me, together with my mother and Isaac, who came after me. The little man at the desk looked at us above his glasses and jotted down on a piece of paper: "Name?" My father told him his name, my mother's, and mine. The man looked at Isaac: "And you're not planning to register him?" My father looked at Isaac. The boy's eyes zeroed in on his. "Yes, yes, his name is Isaac" The man with the small glasses looked up in suspicion. "Age of the boys." Before my father had a chance to answer, Isaac said: "Israel is eleven and I am twelve."

"Good. They can work." My mother, understanding, looked gratefully at Isaac. They asked my father another question. "What kind of work do you do?" He looked at Isaac. "My wife and I are housepainters." My mother nodded. The man kept writing. Later he made us stand in front of him. "What's wrong with this boy, is he sick?" He had noticed the swelling that the slave's blow had left on me. My stomach turned—I was being sentenced. Isaac went to work again. "He fell down, he's clumsy, can't you see?"

"Let your parents answer!" Isaac got a little closer. "I beg your pardon, general, but I pushed him and my parents don't know it." The man, a sergeant who made peo-

❧

ple call him doctor, was pleased to be addressed as "general." Isaac had won his bet. The man sent us out toward the left. The walkway was cold and wet. We had no idea what awaited us at the other end. My mother took Isaac and me by the shoulders. She was starting to consider him a son, and he was eager to show what he could do as long as he was my mother's protégé. My father walked in front, carrying our meager possessions. A group of people who had already been selected was waiting for us at the end. We were going to work. We were winning against the beasts and against death. We were still alive!

When the contracting formalities were over, a little more than half of the people from the train were held with us outside the office.

My father looked everywhere for his brothers and cousins. But the guards marched us over to the barracks of an old ammunition factory occupied by the Soviet troops before their retreat. They drove us ahead with curses and threats. The slaves were in a hurry. We were assigned ten to a barracks. Space was limited and the walls were wet and covered by mold. Some of us immediately lay down on the floor to rest.

We saw slaves going by in the hallway, but this time they were not Romanians. Later on I found out they were the Ukrainian troops of General Vlasov, a collaborator. Isaac went to a corner. My father followed to thank him. "You're a big man, my boy." My father's eyes filled with tears. Isaac shrugged: "Anybody would have done the same thing. Last night, talking to one of the old prisoners, I found out that everyone under ten is being killed on the other side of the Bug River because they are useless for work." My mother and I looked at each other. "When talking to one of the old prisoners?" We didn't ask what

❖

he meant. We were beginning to adapt to his style. He knew how to obtain information, food, everything. For Isaac there was a way out of every situation.

I sat on the floor, tired, hungry, and cold. I was beginning to fall asleep when the shots from the other side of the Bug woke me up. They were killing those they considered not fit for work. As tired as I was, I began to conjure macabre shapes in my imagination. The dead in the pits were getting up to greet the fresh bodies that fell in with holes in the back of their heads. The children the beast had massacred raised their little heads and made way for their newly executed friends. The images of the dead did not leave me for a moment. I saw them in every color, with their eyes dulled, chewing on their own bones, like Meitek who had eaten his own index finger. Mad, crying, hitting the sides of the tomb, and letting out howls that mingled with the lime that covered them. I woke up in a sweat. Without realizing it, I had fallen asleep in the midst of the noise of the nonstop shooting on the other side of the river. I felt a bit guilty at being alive, at lying down in the barracks while others my age were being given "the treatment." In order not to cry, I bit at the sleeves of my jacket. I bit on them until my teeth hurt. I felt my head explode. At times I saw the walls of the barracks coming toward me. They wanted to flatten me out, to make my brain explode, to turn me into a shapeless mass like the bodies of the old men they had made dance before killing them like strange, dangerous insects. My mother dried the sweat that ran down my forehead and kept asking if I felt sick.

I shook my head. I wasn't sick—it was the anguish, the impotence, this cruel confinement that made me exist without differentiating between life and death.

⚜

I looked at Isaac and saw him sleeping soundly, or at least so it seemed.

The Ukrainians did not stop their damn rounds. They went by laughing and pointed at us. This upset those who noticed the mockery of these slaves, no less dangerous than the beasts themselves.

For a glass of vodka, I learned later, they were ready to spend a whole night killing people. Bloody and cowardly, they were always drunk and ready to perform all sorts of sadistic acts. The beasts had found in the Ukrainians their most loyal and bloody slaves. First-class people for the application of the "treatments" demanded by the promoters of the so-called Final Solution to the Jewish problem in Europe.

It was a terrible night, and I did not see the light of dawn again. In the morning they woke us up by hitting us with their whips. The Ukrainians were doing their job. Once again we had to form a line. All on our feet, with swollen eyelids and skin covered by insect bites. A new day, gray and rainy. I looked toward the trenches. I could still hear the shots. I swallowed some saliva and it tasted bitter. The new slaves shouted, gesticulated, did everything in their power to please their masters. They were as dirty as lice. With their machine guns at the ready, they moved from side to side.

When they finally had all of us in line, the SS officer with the whip showed up. He was neatly groomed. He yawned, bringing his gloved hand to his mouth. After a deep sigh he began to walk along the front of the line. He squeezed his whip. In the silence, we listened to the sound of the cold wind running through the naked branches of the trees. But the calm did not last long. The whip cracked in the air and I heard a whimper. Another

❖

round. The crack of the whip and the corresponding whimper.

The cracking and the whimpers did not stop. I believe the beast slashed about twenty of our people with his whip. I could see some of them from the corner of my eye. They shivered. Blood ran down their faces. I shuddered when I realized that the whip was striking their faces. When his round was finished, the SS officer placed his whip under his arm and began to rub his hands. He spoke: "This is another day, Jews. Obviously some of you did not wake up with a good attitude as the rules require. Those people needed to be marked. They weren't ready for work." He talked slowly, enunciating each word.

He referred to us as people. There was no gesture of displeasure on his face. He was trying to inspire some confidence in us. Smiling, he spoke again: "Today you will begin to work for the Reich. No conversations. Talking is forbidden. Our scientists have found out that Jews work better when they don't talk. And it is an honor for you to work for the good of Germany!" He really believed what he was saying. He accompanied his words with gestures, as if he were an employer giving instructions to new workers. He stepped over to one of the men marked by his whip and gently drew him out of the line. "This will be the boss of the other marked ones," he said. And ordered the others to step forward. Many of us relaxed. They were not going to kill them, as we had supposed. The marked ones stood to the right. The rest of us were told to line with our plates ready for our daily ration. A woman wanted to go back for a plate, but the attitude of the Ukrainians made her desist. We were going to be given our food in our hands! Nobody had thought of bringing a plate when we woke up. It was our first day in the camp and we didn't know the routine. The marked ones were taken somewhere else. Before "breakfast" we heard machine-run fire. They had shot them. Surely in front of the trenches and after making them undress. I was beginning to learn the rules. It was important not to be marked, that was a death sentence. You had to wake up ready to go to work.

We got to the big pot filled with our morning ration . The man in charge, a Romanian with a dry face, motioned for me to put my hands together. When I did, the bastard poured in a burning liquid. I reacted reflexively. When I felt the heat I pulled my hands apart, and my ration spilled on the ground. I was left without breakfast. The same thing happened to everyone. I can still hear the laughter of the slaves when we screamed and parted our hands. We existed, we moved. That was all. The gunshots we had just heard did not affect us as much as the hot soup spilling on the muddy floor. The beasts were "treating" us. They were looking to throw us into despair, and sometimes they succeeded. They ordered us to stand still without getting out of line. The "doctor" showed up. The recruiter with the round glasses.

He took some papers and began to read out the names and professions. Upon being called, my father, my mother, Isaac, and I went to where they told us. We had to paint some fences and the walls of the beasts' houses. They gave us the brushes and the cans of paint. We began to work just as the SS man of the whip told us, in silence.

A week went by. Every morning the SS man came out and pointed with his whip at those who were to die for not being "fit." He gave us a sermon, and then we quick-

❖

ly marched off for the dirty soup they gave us in the morning and the evening. We nicknamed the beast the Devil's Whip." The name went around the camp in a flash. He was the killer, the one in charge of "treating" us. The slaves all feared him and readily did whatever he wished. The last few days of fall began. My father finished the fence and the walls. Later on we were separated. Isaac and I were sent to crush stones. The beasts needed crushed stones.

The number of dead increased. Many dropped from exhaustion, due to the poor diet. Whenever this happened the Ukrainians went into a frenzy, hitting the fallen ones with the butts of their rifles. Later they were taken to a special department, and from there were dispatched to the other side of the Bug. Some graves had been dug on the other shore. We knew that whoever went across the river wouldn't come back. The shooting never stopped for a minute. One afternoon, while crushing stones, we saw all the people who had just arrived in a train taken to the other side of the Bug. Some of them asked where they were going, and were told in loud voices: "To work!" That night the shooting did not stop.

The shots ceased just as we were receiving our evening ration. They were all gone! No trace of those women who had crossed the river, counting on a piece of bread for their hungry, crying children. No trace of the old men, the men, or the girls who had looked at us hopefully as they passed us. If we were alive, there was hope for them too, the poor people probably thought.

My parents kept painting. The Germans loved things to look clean and neat. In the meantime, Isaac crushed stones, and I picked them up in a wheelbarrow. I walked fast with my load, not raising my head, avoiding the

❖

tricks of the slaves. If I looked at them they would immediately mark me, and the next day I would be crossing the Bug.

I existed, according to the circumstances. I was silent during the day, dulling myself looking at the stones in my cart. I went back and forth. I had to work. The Devil's Whip was marking the weak and the sick. Every day the number of marked ones increased. Those marked by the whip, as well as those marked by the butts of rifles, went to the other side of the Bug. The executions continued day and night. At dusk they would look for those marked during the day and take them to section B: "Special Treatment." In the morning the sick ones would be marked and later taken to Section A: "Hospital." Those who were sent to these sections met on the other side of the river, in the graves. Within a week suicides began. A man lifted a huge stone and hit himself in the head with it in such a way that his eyes flattened out and were left like two lines that oozed out blood on the sides. When the slaves came in it was too late to do anything, but they shot his dead flesh! Maybe they were relieving themselves of the daily sting of remorse in their consciences, if they had any.

At first they shot some of our group right in front of us. The beasts were furious about the continuous wave of suicides. Not that they minded their deaths, only that some of the suicides were still strong and had done good work. The beasts and their slaves urged us to inform on anyone who was thinking of killing himself. But this didn't accomplish anything. There was nothing to tell. Those who were contemplating suicide did not divulge their plans, except perhaps to one or two who were very close to them.

⚜

Suicide became very valuable to us. It was something sacred, and no one could take away this right, which rose out of the conditions in the camp. Although we did not accept it, we did not prevent it either. The only obstacle we placed, especially at night, was the spoken word. The men argued the reasons, exposing what they were about to do, trying to persuading the suicide not to do it. But no one lifted a finger to prevent it. Deep inside we understood conscious that the suicides wanted to rejoin their loved ones and hoped for a quick death without complications. Suicide was better than falling into the hands of the slaves or the beasts. Many wished to die but avoided the "pleasure" of torture at the hands of their executioners. They simply killed themselves, and they did it in many ways.

In the midst of the misery that surrounded us, the despair and the daily filth, those who wanted to kill themselves tried ways that sometimes defied the imagination. A girl began to eat dirt compulsively. She ate it without stopping, swallowing the mud and the filth together, chewing on the stones and the pointed objects that she found in it. That night they found out. Some held her arms to keep her from killing herself. It was too late. Within a half hour the girl began to shake and then to wriggle. She was vomiting something black and smelly. Her face contracted and a strange foam began to come from her nostrils She had reached the end, and we watched in terror as her life ended without us being able to do anything. The girl got up somehow and went over to the wall of the barracks. She seemed agitated, moving her hands over the bricks. A hoarse sound and she fell on her face, with her mouth open and the vomit covering part of her face. I came closer, to help accommodate the body. We placed it to one side. I could see that her fingers were bleeding and that her nails were destroyed. When we looked at the wall we saw that the girl, in her agony, had written a message. A man read it. It was in Yiddish: "The doors are opening. Here's to our assassins, dressed in black, on their filthy hands they have white gloves. They take us out of synagogues in twos, with our hands over our heads. Dear brothers and sisters, it is very hard to say goodbye to such a beautiful life. Those of you who are left alive, never forget our sacred Hebrew way. Brothers and sisters, take revenge on our assassins!" She signed it Esther Srul. We had difficulty understanding. In her agony she was remembering her synagogue and her murderers. The message, written in blood on the cold bricks of the barracks, shook us. It was a voice clamoring for vengeance in the very bosom of the executioners, in their noses, at the gates of death.

My father took my by the arm. "Israel, from now on, stay at my side every night." They were hoarse, pleading words. It was not out of order for him to think that seeing so many suicides would be a stimulus for me. And he had a right to do so, since a boy of my age took his life that midnight. He hung himself with his belt. He climbed on top of a box and tied the belt to a rafter. When he called out "Push," a friend kicked the box away. The suicide let out a dry sigh and dropped his head against his chest. His thin body rocked for a while. Then his friend, who had pushed the box, lowered the body and placed it next to Esther's.

At night I would listen to that "push" followed by a kind of snoring that is produced when somebody's neck is broken by a belt. I shivered, trying to sleep, and ended up in a strange dream. They were pushing me with force

⚜

from an undetermined point. It was as if my whole life up to that moment was erased in a single blow. But, seeing I was still alive, the phantoms who populated the graves on the other side of the Bug began to haunt me. I trembled, wrapping myself up like a worm. I tried to forget by every means, but it was impossible. I unconsciously began to form the idea of killing my brain, of handing over all my ideas and abandoning the capacity to think. The only thing that was important was to exist. They were long nights, full of bugs, cries, curses, and prayers.

For the last fifteen days I had been living in a gray, nebulous world, where each of us would take advantage of his own established values and enjoy them, since nobody could guarantee we wouldn't be singled out that very same day and taken to the other side of the river.

We looked for ways to exist among the beasts and the slaves. Nobody wanted to cross the Bug, but somebody had to do it every day, and this is where doubt haunted us, closing in almost to the point of suffocating us. Who would be next? we asked ourselves, and everyone would answer that question in his own way, always hoping to be last. As the mornings went on, we saw ourselves closer to the "treatment" sections. The camp, the quarries, the barracks, were turning into another version of the railroad car that had transported us to the domain of the Devil's Whip. We were moving about in a trap, walking on a floor that could collapse any moment. A face that greeted us affably in the morning could turn into blue and congested, hanging from a belt, that same evening.

We did not trust ourselves. I didn't know how I would react a bit later. Terror was our daily bread. The abyss could open at the smallest provocation. As Isaac used to say, we were all crazy, but some of us would get a sick

⚜

craziness and call out "Push!" Every moment that went by was engraved in our brains, pointing the way to the "treatment" section. The beasts wanted to psychologically destroy those of us who survived their inferno. It was their way of handling those of us who existed without being marked.

More trains came in, and with every wave of new people we saw our end getting nearer. It was only logical; we couldn't all fit in the barracks, and the "doctor" kept choosing those fit to work. And the new ones generally were in better physical shape. They were coming from places closer to the camp and had not suffered as much as we did. With their arrival our fight for survival was more difficult. It was hard to face reality. The barracks were full, but their occupants were being replaced by the new arrivals. The shots from the other side rang in our ears. They came to us calling us by our first names. In my nightmares I would hear the machine guns repeating my name with their rat-a-tat-tat. The black mouths said: "Israel, Israel, Israel!" I communicated my fears to Isaac, and he, who had been thinking the same thing, became quiet before answering. He scratched his head and took me to a corner of the barracks. "Israel, be brave." He wanted to tell me something, but he couldn't say a word. Finally his tongue loosened: "Your uncles Elias and Reuben were treated." I didn't need to hear anything else. I understood. A terrible knot formed in my throat. I wanted to cry, to hit myself against the walls, to jump on the Ukrainians, hang by my belt. Isaac tried to console me: "They're better off than we are. At least they've been delivered from this hell." I got up without a word. I hadn't seen them since before we were put on the train, and now they were in the grave. I went to my father. Looking

❖

at his face and the tears rolling down his cheeks, I knew that he knew.

He took me by the shoulders and drew me toward him: "Israel, this is getting complicated. It's possible that we won't all survive, but you must, it is an obligation I'm imposing on you. You must endure, live! Do you understand?" He shook my hand, signaling that we had a pact. My mother watched as if in a trance. The work she had to do had left her pale and weak. Maybe it wasn't her anymore. In this new world, in this miserable hell, people did not exist, they moved but were no longer the same. The beasts exacted the price of existence by dulling us. Seeing my mother looking into space drove me crazy. I didn't want them to catch her like that and marked her to be "treated." I fell down, not thinking of anything, as if my head were full of rocks, the same rocks I had to haul from morning to night.

For the first time in many days I slept until the Ukrainians woke us up. It was an empty sleep, without nightmares. I thought about death. That's how it must be, an empty dream! I ate the soup and then went with Isaac to begin our work. I couldn't let them win. I had to overcome, for my people! And even though I was thin and weak, I gathered strength from the depths of my being. The beasts were not going to destroy me so easily. Isaac, circumventing the watching slaves, passed me some cookies. I gulped them down. If they saw me chewing, they would flatten me. I knew it because I had seen it. The Ukrainians had caught a man chewing a piece of bread. They had lunged at him and held him by his hands and feet. One of the slaves took out a bayonet and ripped open his belly, while yelling for the rest of us to hear: "It is forbidden to digest that, you swine! Don't you

❖

have enough with what we feed you ?" The man screamed in pain, writhing in the arms of his torturers, trying to get himself free. When they released him with all his guts hanging out, he was destroyed, dead. That evening there was no ration for anyone, and five men were executed on the charge of being fatter than the rest of us, which indicated that they were eating more than we were

They made the victims take their clothes off and lower their heads, then began beating them with branches. At that moment the Devil's Whip showed up and began to use his weapon. He was screaming hysterically. His whip took their eyes out, broke their backs and necks. Later, somewhat more calm, he gave the order to execute them. The slaves dug their bayonets into the ribs of the accused. They fell down like sacks of sand. The Devil's Whip, who took every opportunity to give one of his speeches, stood at attention in front of us and began: "These food thefts do nothing but discredit the good diet we feed you. We're even giving you more than you deserve, because the work you do does not compensate the food you receive from the Reich. It is not good to steal food, Jews. Whoever breaks this rule will be sentenced to death, and his accomplices with him. From now on, for each guilty one, we will execute five accomplices." His last words were very forceful, indicating that he would do as he said.

And now I was swallowing whole the cookie Isaac had just given me. I swallowed fast, so that bit of nourishment that would allow me to live a bit longer would reach my gut. When I finished the two cookies, always with my head bent down and looking at the stones I carried in my cart, I thought about the words of the Devil's Whip, of that rat who was the master of the Ukrainian slaves.

❖

What could he be thinking? That we were so stupid as to believe him? He talks about food, and every morning, when I receive my hunger ration, I ask myself, "What food? This isn't fit for a dog!" But I don't say anything. One word and I go to the other side of the Bug. When I got back to Isaac to pick up a new load, he motioned for me to come closer. He talked without raising his voice: "Tonight, are you game for a little job? In a few days winter will start and we have to survive!" Grunting my agreement, I took my load and went back to work, to the constant dragging of that wheelbarrow that sometimes pulled me into despair and took all the strength I needed to survive. But I did not give up. The thought of taking some kind of action, of doing something, as we had in the ghetto, gave me renewed strength to go on. Isaac had become a sort of link between life and survival. I knew that as long as he was with us, things could not be entirely wrong. He knew too much and he kept quiet, not to compromise himself or others. He worked his own way, with that peculiar style he had demonstrated way before they packed us onto that train.

I let the day go by, ignoring the rain on my back, not letting out a whimper when one of the slaves hit me with the butt of his rifle. My body was already covered by black-and-blue marks, full of welts, but my face was clean. They had not marked me, and I was not going to allow that to happen today. I had to go to the meeting. I had to be present, without being marked. It was something important. Isaac was not in the habit of talking nonsense. I had never heard him complain. He had gotten used to the pain, and I knew that he ate on the sly, probably stealing the food from the beasts. I waited for the day to end.

⚜

I was soaked when I returned to the barracks. My parents were surprised at my vivacity. That night, although hungry and cold, I felt alive. I was ceasing to exist in order to start living. In this crazy world, values changed from one moment to the next. What before had been a pattern of stability could stop being so in a few hours. We adapted to circumstances and took advantage to the maximum. Who could be sure that tomorrow we would all be there? Every moment counted, and tonight I would meet with a group that wanted to survive the rigors of winter. I waited an hour, and when darkness filled the barracks, I went to where Isaac and the others were. I tried to orient myself with my memory. The last days of fall had turned into gray that turned into pitch black at night. Feeling my way around, I got to the place.

I heard Isaac's hoarse voice: "We've been waiting for you for a while." I excused myself as best I could. They paid no attention to my explanation. Isaac began to talk: "I have found a way out. Not all the wires are electrified. Under the watchtowers, there is no current in the wires, and the searchlights don't reach there either. But that's not my idea, as you may be thinking. Last night I went out and got these cigarettes." He took a pack out from his clothes and displayed them like a trophy. "I got them from some farmers. They're willing to sell if we have money or valuables. They sell and don't ask questions. Of course you must do a benediction and greet them in the name of Our Father Jesus Christ. If they find out you're Jewish, you're finished. The Germans pay for every Jew they turn in. They give them bread and sugar." I felt like I was in the ghetto again. It was like listening to Red. Isaac rubbed his hands: "Are you willing to gamble on the escape?" he asked. We all said yes.

❖

"Well," he said , "everything depends on memorizing the plan I am going to explain. We'll go out one by one. We'll maintain the intervals by counting to one hundred. At the end of the barracks there is a trench that is going to be used as a latrine; we can crawl through it, always with your body pressed down. Don't raise your heads. Each movement must be slow, so the dogs won't notice. Do not worry about them. I know how to get a bottle of gasoline. If we rub some on our legs, the dogs will lose the scent. I tried it yesterday. When you get to the tower, where the wires meet, crouch and crawl underneath. The guard will be sleeping. They don't believe we are capable of getting out. The slaves need their rest. They're not as big as we think they are. Once past the wires, we keep crawling north, in the opposite direction from the river. About fifty meters on there is some tall grass. Wait there for the group to get together. You understand?" We nodded again. Isaac brought out a knife with a shining blade. He put away the pack of cigarettes and said, "Anyone who talks is dead," holding the knife in front of us. Before the meeting broke up he gave us some final instructions: "Don't forget to get some bills or valuables. The farmers won't give anything away and we'll have to bribe some guards. Sometimes they are not completely asleep. They'll shut up for a few cigarettes. And they'll keep quiet if we give them a few bottles of vodka."

He lay down on the floor and turned his body over on the wet straw that served as our mattress. Suddenly he got up again and gestured: "Hurry up; we start tomorrow night. You have all day to familiarize yourselves with the terrain."

I half-slept, waking up startled. I could hear the shots from the other side of the Bug. The graves kept filling up

❖

without a moment's letup. Dawn came up slowly and cold. The winds from Siberia began to whip the region where the camp was. The day went by endlessly, with constant rain, but my senses were on alert.

I looked at the route Isaac had explained and tried to engrave the details in my memory. That morning I learned the path from our barracks to the watchtower where a Ukrainian soldier stood guard at night. When night fell, I took some gold coins I had obtained from my mother. The others also brought money, gold coins, and jewelry. Everyone had something, ready to exchange life for these objects.

At Isaac's signal, we began to slip out of the barracks. The first one to go was a thin boy with black hair. I didn't know him very well, but Isaac stood behind him. He did the job with no problem. Then the second one went. I was the third. I soaked my pants with gasoline before leaving, as Isaac had instructed.

How had he gotten it? Where did he find it? That was his style. Nobody asked questions. They gave me the order to go out. My stomach turned. I felt fear. If the slaves caught us, there was no need to imagine what would happen. My legs trembled, my knees knocked against each other. I got to the end of the barracks. There was the trench. I jumped into it and began to crawl. I felt as if the searchlights were beaming on me and remained quiet, waiting for the "halt." After a few minutes, I began to move again. The wet earth soaked my belly and smeared me with mud. Even my face was muddy. But I had to go on, and every moment the place where the wires were not electrified seemed farther away. I finally got to the crossroads. I crawled under the wires and began to move faster. My entire body trembled when I moved. Suddenly I saw the beam of the searchlight above. I moved ahead fast, but my right foot was completely illuminated. I felt lost, massacred, sentenced to a slow torture in which they would draw the last drop of blood from my body. I turned white, but the light went on without stopping. The mud had saved me. I was camouflaged by the mud that covered my entire body.

For a few moments I was part of the field, part of the nature that looked on, without protest, at the massacre to which we were being submitted. I got to the shrubs and found the two boys who had preceded me. They were shaking, I don't know whether it was the cold or the fear. The hollow noise of shooting reached us. The executions continued, and we could see a train leaving the camp, probably loaded with the belongings and gold teeth of the executed. They did not leave us anything. Even the mouths were checked by the SS beasts. This I knew because Isaac had a contact who worked on the other side of the river, a fellow who swam to the other side every fortnight, passed on a few coins and things, and then came back. He was another of the boys who worked like Isaac, in silence, risking his life every instant, sure that any moment he would end up in the ditch. I don't know what agreement he and Isaac had made, but whatever it was, it was honored. Isaac had more money than all of us together. Isaac's contact got to where we were waiting. He was covered in sweat, trembling, pale. He hugged us when he found us waiting for him in the grass, then began to cry. He probably thought he was not going to find us. Nobody paid any attention. We were alive and that was enough. The rest was part of the terror to which we were being subjected, and it was not strange that our happiness had to be manifested as fear. We were waiting for Isaac. He had stayed behind, just in case.

⚜

Isaac arrived and, without a word, indicated that we were to follow him. We went deep into the fields, following him. When we got to a small elevation he stopped, pointing to a hill. "Behind that small hill there are three houses. Go there, and don't tremble when you ask what's for sale. Say you need food, and don't forget the salute. They're Christians, and you must act like Christians. Do you understand?" We nodded and he gave us the last instructions. "Bargain with them. If we pay what they ask, they may be suspicious. It's best not to let them know we have money. That way they will believe you are sons of Russians soldiers who are hiding around here."

The rest we knew, and we had all night to finish the operation. We were safe as long as it was dark. At dawn, when it got lighter, our silhouettes could be seen from the watchtowers. Isaac asked me to go with him. I was the youngest and he was going to protect me.

We went along a narrow path. At the end we could see a small, rather ramshackle house. We knocked on the door. Isaac did the talking. "Good evening, in the name of the Lord Jesus Christ." The man who opened the door stared at us for a while. Finally he grunted: "What are you looking for, kid?"

Isaac did not flinch. "I have some money and I want to buy bread and butter. And also salt, if you have any." The man let out a howl that got mixed up with a cough that did not cease even for a minute.

"And you really have money?"

Isaac answered: "I have enough to pay for what I buy. No more." The man, a bit more confident, let us in, stroking his thick mustache. The house was warm. I had not felt warmth in a long time. Although patched and tattered, the house was full of life. I waited for Isaac to

❖

speak. I did not utter a word. My accent would have made them suspicious.

"How much money do you have?"

Isaac answered fast: "I have to see the things first, then I'll make an offer."

The man with the mustache smiled: "Ah, a little scoundrel!

"Very well, we have bread and butter. I can sell you half a pound of salt, I can't sell you any more."

Isaac gave him a malicious look. "Let me see what you're talking about." The man went into the house. A woman was watching curiously through some curtains. I was frightened by her penetrating stare. I felt as if she was looking for a signal to turn us in. Isaac saw what was bothering me, and, to build my confidence, said hello to the old woman. She greeted him back. The man returned with four loaves of bread and two cans of butter. The salt was on top of the bread. Isaac inspected the merchandise, set it down, and put his hands on it. The man with the mustache looked at him, blinking. Isaac had what he wanted. The old man thought him an expert, so the price would not be too high. However, the man asked: "How much are you willing to pay for this?" Isaac answered: "Two gold coins are enough for you." The man took the merchandise as if he was going to take back it to the pantry. Isaac played his last card. "The Russian fighters are not gonna like this at all." The man stopped right away. He was white and his hands were trembling. That round was won.

"They're yours for the price we agreed. Two coins are enough."

Isaac smiled. "We'll be back soon. Don't make a mistake. We pay a fair price." And he took the bread, the butter, and the salt.

❖

We said goodbye and went back to the fields, toward the meadows. When I felt the wind against my cheeks my body filled with a strange happiness. I was free, away from the barbed wire of the camp. For a moment I wanted to keep on running, to enjoy my freedom and not go back to the quarry, to the Stone Cross, as it was called.

But the image of my parents made me feel guilty for feeling happy. As long as they were trapped, I couldn't escape. I had to follow them to the end. Perhaps it wouldn't be the same as our recent exit. Luck is a moment that does not last forever.

Isaac was walking at my side. He didn't say a word and was barely breathing. He took a different route back to the meeting place and on the way stopped at a hole he had dug under a tree. He took out two bottles of vodka and several packs of cigarettes. Without looking at me he said: "This is what I stole the other day. They'll come in handy in hell and winter." By then the other three had joined us. I sat on the wet grass. It began to rain again, with a strong wind. It was raining hard. Our faces were stung by hail. It was a strong, hollow blow. I put two loaves of bread, the salt, and a can of butter under my clothes. Isaac put three packs of cigarettes in my pockets. I was shivering from the cold. Isaac said: "This is good for us. In this weather the Ukrainians and the dogs won't bother us. Thank you, Mother Nature." Finally the others joined us. They were loaded down with bread, vodka, and sugar. The thin boy with the black hair gave Isaac a satisfied look. "It wasn't much, five gold coins." I exclaimed: "Five!" Isaac told him: "In the barracks we'll straighten out accounts. You have a lot to learn, boy," and we headed toward the fields once again.

We returned in the same order as we left. Just as Isaac said, there was not much of a problem. The rain

❧

was protecting us. I too said to myself: "Thank you, Mother Nature, thank you very much." We came back victorious from our first incursion. Luck had been with us. I didn't think about the future. A mark on the face and then—the other side of the Bug.

When we got to our barracks, Isaac made us give everything we had brought with us. He indicated that we should cover him while he hid everything. We couldn't be sure of anyone. A rat might blow the whistle on us for a double ration of soup. We understood and lay down next to Isaac, pretending we were asleep. My wet clothes were uncomfortable, but I was happy, fulfilled at having served again, of being older, a capable person who had acted and might survive in this winter. I began to lose my fear of being replaced by those who came in now. I knew how to get out of the camp and therefore I would live.

Isaac pushed aside the straw, lifted up the planks in the corner of the barracks, and put in our purchases. We had never noticed him digging the hole or what he had done with the dirt. That was Isaac's style. Nobody said a word. He was the boss, and we had no business questioning his way of doing things. He took out his knife again. "Anyone who talks is dead. A dead Jew in the middle of the camp is nothing strange. The Germans will blame it on the Ukrainians." It was a warning, and we all accepted the deal. I went over to my parents.

My father was awake, and when he saw me, he took my arm, squeezing it hard. "Where were you, Isaac?" I didn't say anything. He seemed to understand that I wouldn't talk. He gave up, but I could see a glimmer of anger in his eyes. I understood. What is a father to think when he wakes up and his son is not there, especially in a situation like ours. That the executioners killed him! I

⚜

put my head on his chest and cried. Before long I fell into a dreamless sleep. The emotions of the night had left me completely exhausted.

Winter began. The first snowflakes came into the barracks. We worked like animals, dragging our feet, which turned blue from the ice covering the camp. The ration was still the same soup. The beasts had their own methods. They left us alone but rationed our sustenance. They allowed us to live, in that they left us at the mercy of the weather, of that biting wind. And as the snow increased, so did the deaths from malnutrition, cold and suicide. Many of us could not endure. By the hundreds they would wake up, completely blue, looking for a bit of warmth in their misery.

Isaac wanted us to meet every three days. He spoke slowly, to make sure we understood every word. "We've made it a few times and you know how it works. But things are getting complicated. From now on we must be ready to go at any time. And we must go while it's snowing. That way the tracks will be erased. Otherwise, they'll kill us." That's how it was. We began to go while it snowed, risking death in the snow, with our lungs full of ice.

I still did not say anything to my parents. If I had, they would have stopped me and Isaac's plans would have been ruined. I could not fail him, I was part of the machinery he had put together in order to survive this winter that was getting worse every day. Whenever I went out, terror gripped me. I thought I wouldn't be able to get back, that it was my last escapade. But we always made it. The story of the Russian soldiers had its effect on the farmers. They sold at reasonable prices. They feared retaliation from the People's Army. Some of the

Ukrainians could be bought with a bottle of vodka and a few cigarettes. Of course, there were only a few. Only a few of the slaves still harbored a bit of mercy. And they were the ones you could bribe. But their help consisted in looking the other way when we chewed as we worked. They didn't know about our escapades. We couldn't tell them that there was gold inside the camp. They would fall on us like dogs. They probably thought that we were chewing on roots or something like that. Isaac kept his contact on the other side of the Bug.

One night I went with him to meet his contact. We crawled through the camp in the middle of a snowstorm. My knees ached and the palms of my hands burned when they touched the snow. Sometimes my hair would stand on end, especially when I heard the howls of the wolves. I had already seen them prowling around the camp during these winter days. They were as hungry as we were. We reached the agreed spot. Isaac whistled like an animal and immediately a man with a dry, blue face came out of some shrubs. He was the one who lived on the other side of the Bug. I looked at him, surprised. It seemed impossible that someone could live on the other shore, where the shooting never stopped. He pointed at me with a finger. My eyes popped out in terror. Isaac calmed him down. "He's one of us," he said. The man breathed a bit easier. He opened his shirt and brought out a bag. Without even looking at it, Isaac put it inside his jacket, already torn at the elbows. The man with the blue face, taking Isaac by the shoulders, said: "Comrade, this is the last time we talk. I can't stand it any more. Tomorrow I'm going to kill myself."

I swallowed hard. I dared to ask. "Why don't you escape?" The man smiled sadly: "Over there they know

❧

exactly how many of us there are. And if someone goes missing, they have sworn to kill a hundred. How could I live knowing that one hundred innocent people have died because of me? And anyhow, if I escape, I'll most probably soon be back. In my state," he said, looking at his thin body, "they would send me to the special section for a treatment." Isaac looked at him without blinking.

"Have you thought about it seriously?"

He nodded.

"Are you going to kill yourself?" The man with the blue face nodded and walked away. Any sound and the guards would be on top of us.

In the barracks Isaac stretched his legs and asked me: "Boy, have you ever met a philosopher? Yitzhak was one. Yes, that guy you just saw is a philosopher, and he is going in search of a new life, with the help of a cord around his neck. All philosophers are crazy!" He shut up and took out the package his contact had given him. There was money, some items of food. and a note. He put everything under the floorboards and looked at the paper. With his feet he nudged his neighbor, a thin man with vivacious eyes. "I need you to read me this." The man woke up. "Are you crazy, kid?" Isaac answered very quietly: "The Germans would like to know that you buy some of the food that the Ukrainians steal from the camp kitchen." The man turned as white as the snow that was falling outside. His face began to tremble, and the muscles of his forehead contracted. Isaac knew everything. His neighbor had his own way of surviving. He used to buy the fruit and the food the slaves managed to steal from their masters' table. But he thought that nobody knew, and, learning that Isaac knew about his dealings, he thought himself lost.

❧

"Don't be afraid, I'm not a rat," said Isaac, handing him the piece of paper. The man, petrified by Isaac's comments, had no alternative but to read. He read slowly, as he had been told to do. "We are the last Jews to have worked for the Gestapo in Chelmo, which is between Debica and Kolo. These are our last days. We inform you of that. Perhaps some relatives and friends are still alive. Let it be known that all the Jews deported from Litzmannstadt [Lodz] were murdered in a horrible way, tortured and burned. We salute you, and if you survive, avenge us!" The paper was signed by eleven people, with first and last names and place of birth.

The man who read the letter shivered. Isaac explained that the letter came from the other side of the Bug, the place where some prisoners were assigned to collect the clothes of the people who were killed. The reader had difficulty breathing: "How is such evil possible!" he said between sobs.

We went over to the corner were Isaac slept. He said to me: "Obviously they are killing quite a few tonight. No, they aren't killing them, they were already dead." He began talking to himself. "Yes, Yitzhak was a body that refused to be buried. But he has given in. The Germans were stronger. May God take pity on him." I saw him cry silently, not making a single sound, letting his tears roll down over his cheeks, red with the cold. I left him alone with his reveries.

That morning the Devil's Whip was furious; he swung his whip from side to side, marking people without discrimination. If it had been up to him, he would have marked us all for death, but his Reich needed our labor. He marked more than a hundred, among them Isaac, who received a whiplash on his neck.

⚜

The SS man stopped, a bit tired, and barked: "Jews, you are all cowards. Last night a bunch of your people committed suicide. Yes, they killed themselves in protest against us. Dogs! They were treated like kings. And then they kill themselves—" His words made no sense, it was difficult to understand him. He talked as if possessed by a strange illness. When he finished his speech, during which he yelled until hoarse, he made the marked ones stand in line. The line began to move. I lost sight of Isaac as they headed for the other shore. He was walking with his head up, a firm step, and a terrible light in his eyes. My stomach began to hurt and an acrid taste filled my mouth.

I was losing my friend, the only one I had in the camp and in life. I began to cry. I spent the whole day hauling stones. We were dispirited. Each day things got worse and worse.

Every morning the Devil's Whip kept marking people. And the shooting never stopped. My whole body began to hurt. I didn't give a hoot if they marked me. At night, after eating the garbage they fed us, I went to my spot and stayed there with my eyes open, trying to find a logical explanation for what was happening. What had I done to be punished with a future set in a common grave? I cried with rage, with uncertainty, with fear. My mother caressed me, trying to offer some consolation. But to no avail. I was not resentful, nor did anything hurt me. My pain came from living without understanding what was happening. I gritted my teeth and made a fist, turned on the straw, and opened my mouth to fill it with it. I wanted to let out a cry that was trying to come out of me any way it could. It never entered my mind that Isaac was lying in a pit, with his neck broken and his body cov-

⚜

ered with lime. While these thoughts were going around in my head, I felt someone pulling me by the shoulders. I ignored it. But then he pulled me even harder. When I turned around someone covered my mouth. My eyes almost popped out. It was Isaac!

For a moment I thought his image was part of my imagination, of my memories. I shook my head and again I saw my friend's face looking quietly at me. My father's figure helped me to believe in what I was seeing. Yes, it was Isaac. He had come back. I got up and hugged that wet body that had been born again.

I couldn't sleep the rest of the night. The next morning he told me how he had escaped. "They took us to the other side. We were in formation, and some Ukrainian friends of mine were escorting us. One of them noticed me. I told him to make sure his shot was on target, not to miss. He laughed. Soon afterward an officer made me step aside. I played my last card. After all, I had nothing to lose.

"The Ukrainian looked sideways at me and said: 'What do you mean, you want us to shoot you on target? And how do you know that we do any shooting here?'

"I told him that we always heard the shots from this side and that none of the people who crossed the river ever came back. He laughed. I closed my eyes a bit and lowered my chin. I didn't want him to recognize me. I smoothed my hair over my forehead and lowered my head. The officer asked once again:

" 'Well, wise guy, where do you want us to shoot you?'

" I pointed to the back of my neck, near the ear. They didn't say anything and told me to get back on line. When we got near the pit, they took me aside once more. Twelve of us were set aside, and they made all the others take off

❖

their clothes. They made us pick up their clothes and sort them according to the garment. On one side the shoes, on the other the jackets, there the caps, here the underwear. The naked people were standing alongside a huge pit. They made them kneel and began to shoot them. My plan worked. The slaves wanted me to suffer, to die alive, before giving me the last shot. I had played my cards and won. We worked all day. Those who have been working there for a while don't talk, they simply go from one side to the other, following orders. When it got dark and it began to snow, I decided to come back here. I crawled toward the river and jumped into the water. I thought I might drown, but I made it here. I played my last card and won." He was back to his old self, his usual style.

Isaac was not someone who let himself be cornered. He always looked for a way out and, as he said, he took his chances. He was not one for concocting plans. "It's silly, " he used to say, "while you're thinking, you can act and then you'll have time to spare!" The wound on his neck was covered with mud. "They'll think it's dirt or shit. They can't demand hygiene from us." And we went back to the stone quarry and our escapades in the snow-storms. We had money and food put away.

Every once in a while I took a piece of bread and butter to my parents. They were surprised, but didn't ask where it came from. They simply ate it. Every night I brought them something to eat. I didn't want them to wake up blue and quiet like those corpses we had to carry out to the pit every morning. These were hard times, and every one had to survive as best he could.

It was not yet time to share what we managed to get. The reason was simple. First, we knew there were

❦

informers among us. Second, there wasn't enough for everyone, and if we all ate only a little bit, we'd still die of cold and hunger. The best way, and we agreed on this, was to survive by our own means. You couldn't succumb to sensitivity, since the luxury of such feelings might hasten the end. The executioners punished by death anyone who showed compassion. They were trying to turn us into animals, and to a great extent they were succeeding.

It was terrible to see the hunger and misery and to know that those pale children might wake up dead tomorrow. But what could we do? If we gave them a few crumbs, we would only be delaying their death by a day. That was it. We would be giving them an artificial life. Many times I had to close my eyes and cry silently, knowing that I had drunk hot tea in the home of one of the farmers. It hurt me to see my mother shivering, rubbing her cheeks every morning, so that the Devil's Whip would not mark her. She rubbed them hoping to give them some color, to achieve a look of health.

By the middle of winter the situation became unbearable. We barely had a few crumbs put away, and the salt and the butter were gone. Our escapades were becoming more difficult. The surveillance had been reinforced. Probably an informer had let them know that some of us were getting out, because one morning the Ukrainians stormed into the barracks and made us get up with out hands on our heads. One of the slaves, a lieutenant, shouted: "We know that you are keeping food here and we're going to find it. Everyone stay put. Anyone who has something on him will pay with his life." They began to search. A man was found with a few dried potatoes inside his jacket. They took him out, hitting him with the butts

❖

of their rifles. They looked everywhere. A few pieces of fruit, lumps of sugar, breadcrumbs, and a few bottles of vodka fell from the roof. The Ukrainians screamed joyously whenever they found something. I didn't look at Isaac, but I was imagining him under the rifle butts of the slaves, his head broken, rolling on the floor like a ball. When they got to him they searched him thoroughly, they made him turn over the straw where he slept, they looked in the crevices of the walls, they dug their bayonets into the floor. But nothing. After the search, the slaves left, with us confined to our barracks.

We were not allowed out for three days as punishment. Those on whom they had found something were killed right at the door, and when we were allowed out again, we had to take their bodies to the pit. Eighteen bloody corpses lay there for three long days, during which we did nothing but look at each other, afraid to speak. The beasts might have taken conversation as an excuse to kill us. At the end of that time, the Devil's Whip broke his marking record. At least four hundred people were marked and sent to the other side of the river. The dead, already bloated and malodorous, were taken to the pit. That day they made us work harder than ever and denied us our ration. That night I fell asleep right away, without hearing the howling of the wolves or the shooting on the other side of the Bug.

As the days went by, more Kafkaesque scenes unfolded. A woman threw herself to the hungry wolves. The animals devoured her, together with her small son, whom she held onto until her last breath. A wave of suicides began. People would go crazy and throw themselves to the packs of hungry wolves in the fields. The beasts and the slaves watched the spectacle with pleasure. The

❖

wolves were saving them work. However, the Devil's Whip never stopped. Marking prisoners for death each morning seemed to have become a daily need for him.

It was part of his routine, and he was never a minute late. One day the wolves were haunting us, I felt an urge to stop and let them catch me. But something made me keep on running toward the barracks. I needed to live any way I could. My father kept repeating it for a minute. I knew that my mother and he were enduring for me. I couldn't let them down.

Every day the number of survivors dwindled. The shots on the other side of the Bug never stopped, as if the pits were crying out for blood. There was a thirst for victims, and the Ukrainians, the Romanian slaves, and the beasts were quick to satisfy their destructive urges, the compelling need to end human lives.

One afternoon there was hardly any work left, but we managed to find something to do and thus avoid being sent to the other side, that feared shore. I saw a train arrive with I don't know how many gypsies. They made them line up. The Devil's Whip gave them one of his speeches He said that the Jews were responsible for the war—that we should die and they, the gypsies, should help the Reich with this job. Many of the people on the line hailed Hitler. My insides turned cold. Would they turn into new slaves? Would they treat us worse than the Ukrainians? I didn't have time to talk to Isaac about my fears.

The gypsies, more confident after listening to the SS man, allowed themselves to be taken to a "special treatment" section. Fifteen minutes later we could hear the shots. The Devil's Whip had tricked them and didn't even have to mark them. They killed the whole trainload.

⚜

One night a rumor went around that the old men and children under fourteen were going to be taken to the camp at Uman. Isaac shivered. It was the first time that I saw him truly scared. It must have been something terrible if he was opening his eyes so wide.

"Things go fast at Uman. The ones who go there are sentenced to death. They're going to kill us once and for all. And they're doing it because there isn't any more room here for the ones they kill." He was almost screaming, his features distorted. I didn't say anything to my parents, but I saw the anguish in their eyes. They too knew. The rumor was real. Old men and children under fourteen would be sent to Uman because they were unfit for further work at the Ladyzhin camp. A bitter knot began to form in my throat. It was impossible to escape now. There were too many slaves, and there was a guard posted every five meters along the wire fence.

The summer was starting and every shape could be detected immediately, even at night. Now nature turned against us. The sun was becoming our enemy. It burned our backs and our faces during the day. And the night, illuminated by moonlight, guarded us as if the beasts had ordered it to do so.

Everything became terribly complicated. Our parents tried to hide us, to dig holes to put us in, so that when the time came to leave, the beasts and the slaves could not find us. But it was all in vain. Where the devil were they going to put us? And on top of that, the beasts, probably suspecting something, made the slaves watch us continually.

I felt lost, trapped, stuck in a manhole full of excrement. With the seasonal heat, a terrible smell began to come from the pits. The slaves moved around nervously, smelling their genocide, with their crime stuck to their noses. Every day I saw them more drunk than usual.

Finally the feared deportations of people unfit to work began. They began with the lower barracks. In one single day they loaded more than six trucks, and we saw them leave for Uman. Isaac was no longer doing anything. He spent most of the time brooding, regurgitating his thoughts, and talking about madness and death. My mother cried desperately, trying to find a way to keep me by her side until the end.

The day after the first deportation, a general roundup began in the camp. They were playing cat and mouse with us. They tormented us with psychological traps. There was no security of any kind. They took away all hope of order. I always thought they would take a long while to get to my barracks. But everything went to hell. I might be caught at any time. All that was needed was for one of the slaves to grab me and period, trapped like a mouse. We witnessed the most horrible scenes. A mother, seeing her son taken, began screaming to be taken also. The slaves took the boy and shot him in the side. He twisted in pain. They shot him on the other side. Then in one leg, and so on. They killed him slowly, calculating each wound they inflicted on him. They had to be precise, so that none of the shots would bring a fast death. The woman cried hysterically, while three slaves held her by her arms. She watched her son die. Then the Ukrainians let her go. She held on to the body and cried out to be killed. The slaves laughed out loud, and the more she pleaded the louder they got. They grabbed her by her arms and took her back to the barracks. They didn't want her to kill herself. It was a common tactic the beasts used in order to kill people while they were still alive.

My turn came a week later. One night the slaves came into our barracks. They took us by surprise, while we were trying to sleep in that suffocating heat and the horrible smell of the decomposing bodies in the open graves. My mother let out a scream when she saw a Ukrainian lifting me up as if I were a toy. My father stood petrified, not knowing what to do. Any move could be the cause of a slow death for me. He knew it and had seen it. They took us all out.

Isaac let himself be dragged out. He went with his head down and his arms by his side. I did not know exactly what was happening. I felt like I was in a dream. Yes, the end shouldn't be like this. I was trying to convince myself that it was a nightmare, a bad dream. But the pale faces of those around me, those shining eyes that meant life, let me know that it was real.

Kicking us unmercifully they took us to the trucks that were waiting for us. They didn't even give us time to look at our people, those who were awaiting even worse tortures. I began to cry. Everything was happening so fast.

The beasts were in a hurry. They put seventy boys in one truck. When it began to move I felt the weight of death on me. I began getting used to the idea that I was already dead. I had no alternative. But it was a cruel death, one in which my mother did not even have time to say goodbye to me.

They took me away from her as if I were a pesky insect. I knew that she would have given her life to be able to at least touch my hair in a gesture of impotence

❖

that turned into hope and trust in the God of Israel. I smelled the odor of the bodies and lifted my eyes to mingle with that stinking voice from the graves. I was already a corpse like them. As the trucks started up, the earth seemed to open beneath my feet. I cried until I fainted.

⚜

6

A Desperate Leap

Ladyzhin was behind us. I lost all sense of myself. Everything was mixed in a sea of shadows. Thousands of ghosts visited my brain. The dead in the graves rose up and opened their dry, yellow arms, attempting to embrace me with their stink. Nausea mixed with tears, and I burrowed in like a worm, with my head bowed, ready to drown once and for all in the mouth of death that the beasts had prepared for us. I fainted. It was a way out for a few moments. I went though the silent tunnel of the path followed by those who had gone to the other side of the Bug River. I must have walked. I was being pushed, with my neck tight, breathing with difficulty. I only half awoke, barely aware of the movement of the truck. I didn't care about anything; everything had lost its value from one moment to the next as I thought about Moshe and his mutilated father. I too had lost my parents; the beasts had taken them from me, and who knew if I would ever see them again? I shuddered, imagining my mother and father traversing the narrow bridge that went to the other side. My brain did not respond to my thoughts. In my confusion I imagined the most horrendous things.

All my past memories joined together and took the shape of a huge monster that opened its jaws to devour me. When I opened my eyes, everything was different. My ideas took on a more normal shape. I quieted down when I remembered that the graves in the stone quarry had been closed. For now it was a relief to know that my parents wouldn't be forced to cross to the other side.

I fainted again. I was weak, terrified, lost. All my strength left me and I turned into a bag of anguish clamoring for understanding, a distant caress, something with a motherly taste. I was going to die alone, without my mother's eyes giving me strength to come to the end. I shook my head and began to cry desperately, ready to melt like a candle. I fell again, totally vanquished and apart. There was no room for ideas in my brain. It hurt to think, to imagine anything. I was a phantom, a shadow that scurried with the unconscious intention of protecting itself. As the truck rolled on toward Uman, my insides quivered. That was the most horrible torture I had suffered so far. Away from my parents, possibly lost forever, what value had an existence to which every possibility of life had been denied? I don't know when I woke up again.

When I looked around, all I saw was the pale faces of boys who had accepted the fate the beasts had decreed for them. Almost all were staring at the floor. They were drilling with their eyes, thinking perhaps to be opening the grave they would occupy as soon as they got to the camp. I too fixed my eyes on the floorboards. I put my elbows on my knees and let the ghosts inhabit my head once again. A long shadow signaled for me to get closer. It was laughing, indicating a place in my neck. Later other shadows joined the first one and made a chorus. They were singing the symphony of the dead.

It was a hoarse singsong that did not stop for a minute. I got closer to the sinister figures and let them embrace me. They were frozen, malodorous, toothless. I wanted to go back but I couldn't. I couldn't move. The ghostly shrouds pinned me down, unable to move. I screamed and the floor opened under my feet. I felt that I was falling into an abyss. I was falling fast, dragged forward by a rope around my waist. I was running through a black hallway, through the cold fog of the world of the dead. Moshe's father was waiting for me at the end, always looking at the wall, showing his mutilated leg. Next to him Moshe was rotting away. The hair fell in bunches over his toothless grin. The mother, insane, was eating stones and sparks were coming from her eyes. Behind her Meitek was chewing on his remaining fingers. He chewed contentedly and showed his bleeding hand, while his bleeding stumps pointed toward the mark left by the SS. I was rushing toward that horror scene, pushed by an invisible force.

I wanted to talk, but my throat did not utter a word. It felt as if choked by rags, by yellow sand, by pieces of executed people. I wanted to put my hands in my mouth to destroy them, but I didn't have any hands! I was a bundle that was coming down, something without legs or arms. Anguish opened up my stomach, and my intestines fell all around me. But there was no blood. Everything was a greenish liquid that smelled bad and tasted bitter. The shadow forced me to drink it. Suddenly everything disappeared and I saw myself in front of a huge grave where there were no dead people. I was going to be the first to be executed. The shadows had become black uniforms that laughed and laughed without stopping to scream at me: Jew, Jew!

Isaac woke me up. I didn't believe in anything. To be awake was the same as being in a nightmare. I didn't know whether what was in front of me was reality or part of another dream. I couldn't differentiate fiction from reality. My eyes met the Russian fields. I saw the trees go by, moving their branches in an attempt to say goodbye, but I ignored them. I was dulled and far away. My head was hard as a stone. I wouldn't have given a damn if one of the beasts had put a machine gun in my mouth and pulled the trigger. I was already dead. Isaac shook me again by my shoulders. "Israel!" he said, shaking me violently.

He had to slap me to bring me back to reality. I looked at him with my eyes full of tears. I cried and cried. And this was an indication that I was still alive, that I still had not gotten the bullet in the back of my neck to fall face down on the bodies already occupying the common grave. Isaac's eyes were shining, furious, full of a desperation that was turning into determination: "Israel, we've got to jump out of the truck. Better a shot in the back, breathing a bit of freedom, than to bow your head in front of a grave surrounded by barbed wire!" He talked softly, but it seemed as if he was screaming. For a few moments I couldn't understand what he was saying. My brain was still buzzing. The nightmares still resounded like the arid blows of the SS whip. I didn't understand. I saw shapes distorted. Isaac seemed to be talking from far away, screaming, sending me a message I couldn't understand.

I looked at him stupidly, feeling a sharp pain that dug viciously into my ears. Isaac repeated what he had said about escape and I nodded without realizing what I had just accepted. I shrugged and kept my eyes open. I was trying hard not to faint again. Outside the fields lay open; the trees stood proudly, some farmers watched us without knowing our destiny. And if they knew they kept quiet and turned away, so they could tell their consciences they had not seen anything suspicious. In time of war it's so easy to wash one's hands! Little by little I became aware of things again. I felt the humming of the trucks' motors, the pungent smell of gas, the bumping when we passed along an unpaved part of the road. Once again I met Isaac's shining stare. He was squeezing his hands and moving his feet constantly. "Do the same thing. If you jump with frozen feet you'll be done for. Come on, start moving." I tried to smile but couldn't. The image of my terrorized parents pierced my brain. I started to move my feet and my ankles. My whole spirit surged. I had to survive, save myself from the shot at the back of the neck, gamble everything. It was a dire need. The beasts had to pay for what they had done! I became aware of my existence, of the present moment. I needed to jump, to lose myself in that field that extended toward the horizon, embraced by the sun. Everything depended on a gamble. We had nothing to lose. If we stayed in the truck, our cards had already been dealt. I felt a terrible hatred for the beasts. Yes, escaping was imperative, a pressing need, the only way to avenge the fallen. Something told me that my parents would have been proud of my jump to freedom. But I couldn't keep my body from shaking fearfully.

I listened to Isaac to give myself a bit more courage. "We jump when I count to forty-five. We run toward the meadow and lie down there for a few minutes. We have to dodge the bullets. I can't guarantee that we'll get there alive, but—" He didn't finish and instead started counting. My stomach turned to jelly. I couldn't think. My eyes were pinned on the road. Everything was riding on that jump. It was what was needed and the decision had been made. Jump, the word filled my brain. Jump and run.

⚜

Run with everything I had, zigzagging with my eyes on the meadow and not looking back. Isaac was already at thirty-two. All my muscles were tense. My head, my eyes, and my belly were burning. But we had to jump. "Forty-two," Isaac said and got close to the edge of the truck. "Forty-three." All of us, five in total, pinned our eyes on the floor. "Forty-four." We stood up and got ready to propel ourselves. The other boys watched with dulled eyes. I prayed to the God of my ancestors. "Forty-five!" It felt like someone had whipped me on the back.

I saw myself in the air, I landed on my heels and started to run with everything I had. I was going fast, not looking at anything but the tall grass that lay a few meters beyond. I hadn't gone more than five steps when I heard the machine guns. The shots went buzzing over my head. I ran crazily, trying to outrun the bullets. The beasts and the slaves were shooting in a rage. I couldn't see, my body was moving of its own volition. I heard a scream. For a moment I thought I had been hit. But I kept on. I didn't see anything. There was no goal, it was all in the running, jumping, moving from side to side in an effort not to be hit by the endless gunfire. I slipped. I felt lost, but something stronger than myself made me get up and keep on with my crazy running toward the meadow. A second scream pierced my ears. It was a dull sound, a definite goodbye to this life. I wasn't tired. I didn't give a hoot about breathing. All I cared about was running, keeping the pace, trying to increase my speed. And the more I ran, the farther away seemed the meadow where I was supposed to stop and rest in order to start again.

And again, in the middle of the insanity, fast and desperate. Fast, they're going to get you, this bullet grazed past you, you must be dead already and in your agony

❖

you think you're still running. For each shot an idea, a way of interpreting, a new sense. Finally, close at hand, the meadow. Fast, now or never! A jump, the bullets perforating the leaves of some plants nearby.

I fall heavily, like a sack, I'm a bag. Only two seconds and I have to get on my feet again. Below, a hundred meters away, the forest, the protecting trees, Mother Nature ready to give us sanctuary. I get up, once again the bullets, and a third cry that fades into a groan—deep, anguished, frustrated. But I can't stop. My life is hanging on this run, on these legs that are starting to weaken. I don't know who is at my side. Maybe I'm alone. Perhaps I'm dead and dreaming that I'm escaping. I can only respond to my instincts, reason is of no value now. I hit myself, the sharp pain makes me let out a whimper, but I don't stop. I flee, run, I let the rocks hit my flesh. I suffer, but I miss the bullets that keep coming. They keep me company, alongside me, over my head, bouncing against the rocks, digging into the ground, breaking the trunks of young trees.

Over there, in front of my eyes burning from terror, the big trees, the labyrinth, and the protecting wood. I enter the woods without stopping. My chest hurts, but the fear is stronger and I keep running. I don't dare look back for fear of finding out that I'm alone.

A stream. I jump into the water. It's harder to walk this way, but I do it. Without fear, I put my feet in the water. A branch. I grab it. I gather momentum and jump. I'm on top of a big tree. I quickly climb to the top. There it ends. I've played my hand, and now I wait, trembling, for the results. I look toward the blue sky. If they kill me, at least I'll die free. Only free men die looking at the sky. I wait with a terrible knot in my throat. I don't see any of the others who jumped with me. In my weakness I grasp the branches. I might fall—I'm already dizzy. I tie myself to a branch with my belt, but I don't dare close my eyes.

I feel nauseous, thank God I have nothing in me to vomit. That would be the end. I bite my lips to keep from screaming. I'm alone. I hear footsteps. Coming fast. The boots of the beasts and the slaves have come into the woods. I can see their helmets. They're yelling, egging on their dogs. But the animals don't respond. They don't have a clue. There are no tracks on the ground. Whatever tracks I left ended at the stream and the slaves are looking for them. They don't find any. They can't figure out how I disappeared from one moment to the next. I'm shaking up in the tree. I'm afraid. I feel like they're looking at me, pointing. I bite my lips. I'm afraid that the chattering of my teeth will give me away. Some of them are leaning against the tree. That's it, they've found you, and you're finished. They're going to open your mouth and fill it with sand. Yes, they'll pull out my teeth and my eyes and smash my head with the butts of their rifles. You're done, trapped, with no one to save you. Lost in a hole, together with the bodies in the grave. Your escape was a failure. Any time now one of the beasts will look up and see you there huddled up, tied to the branch and will go up to get you. Or they will open fire . You're gonna be tortured, kid.

I swallow. All kinds of ideas jump in my head. I don't dare look down. The smallest move could give me away. There's no wind. If there was a breeze of some kind it would be easier. If the branches were moving, I could move also. My legs are cramped. I can see myself in the clutches of the beasts and I can't begin to imagine the

❖

tortures they have in store if they find me. It would be so easy to look up and see a boy hiding on top of the tree! But now I hear footsteps again; this time they are leaving. I wait a while and look down at the spot where the beasts and the slaves were leaning. They're not there.

Saved by a hair! I rest. I can allow myself to breathe! God was with me. I wait a bit longer. An hour goes by, two, who knows how many? It was a while. I wanted to wait for dusk, but I couldn't. All my muscles are tense, hurt. I feel the pins and needles produced by bad circulation, so I let myself down to lie on the grass. I wanted to rest a bit, touch the ground, and kiss the free soil. I came down slowly, afraid of seeing the beasts, the slaves, and their dogs again. When I touched ground, a feeling I had not appreciated until now filled me. I was free! I could walk, roll on the ground, and lie down where I pleased. I lay on the grass and fell into a dreamless sleep, stuck in an infinite white with no images of any kind. When I woke up it was night. The stars were shining above and a huge moon softly illuminated the pathway through the woods. I felt frightened and anguished once again. I smoothed down my hair with my fingers and put my head between my knees. I remembered the last moments. They took you away from your mother's arms, they shoved you into a truck, and there you began to die, as if they had put you out to dry in the sun.

The inferno, and then Isaac talking about the escape. And you escaped, kid, you ran with the wind, through the grass, the stream, and then the tree. Up there, numb, watching the beasts who were looking for you with their hound dogs. They almost found you Israel, it was a miracle they didn't. And now here, awake, alone, looking

❖

fearfully at the moon and the stars. Was it worth it to escape? People get lost in the woods and then end up eaten alive by wolves.

The thought of the wolves' jaw made me shiver. It was impossible for it all to end that way. I shook my head and started to cry. I needed to let out my pent-up anguish, the huge amount of seemingly endless emotion. I was hysterical. I pounded my fists on the ground, pulled up the grass, writhed in anguish. I wanted to dig a hole and get in, disintegrate with the soil, with the warm soil of summer. Freedom meant being alone? Did it make sense to risk your skin to prove that loneliness was the prize for a desperate run? No, I didn't agree with Isaac. This time he had failed. He had figured things out all wrong. I screamed at the top of my lungs: "Isaac, you screwed me!"

After a while something moved among the shrubs. I tensed up. The beasts were spying on me. Had they left me alone just to nab me later? I didn't even try to run away. I was ready to see the face of my last card. I waited quietly, not moving, listening to the noise from the small trees. A figure approached and let out a shout: "How did I screw you?" I opened my eyes until they hurt. It was Isaac—Isaac was still alive, keeping his own style! I got up as if they had shot me and ran to him. We hugged.

He looked the same, only his face was a little more tired and his eyes less bright. We started to laugh without knowing why. We could just as easily have cried. It was a way to express what was inside us. Internal impulses looking for a way out. "You're a sleepy head. When I found you, you were snoring like an old man and I didn't want to wake you. It's sad to wake up an old

❖

man." He said this jokingly. "I think we should get going. Getting around at night is easier; they ask fewer questions and it's less dangerous. But we'll have to keep away from each other at night. You never know when you ask someone a question if they're going to answer with a machine gun. Let's go." We began walking, quickly moving away from the main road. I felt more confident. There were two of us. Things would work out.

We walked all night and at dawn saw a barn. Isaac pointed it out. I followed without a word. The whole time he hadn't said anything. I didn't want to question him. We got to the door of the barn. We heard voices from the farmhouse. They were about to start their daily chores. I felt scared again. The Germans would pay these people a few pounds of sugar for a Jew. I looked at Isaac with despair ripping my guts. He didn't say anything. He was looking for a way into the barn. He finally found it and went in without thinking twice. He gestured for me to follow. I went inside. There was no alternative. In the darkness we touched every object we came in contact with. Finally a ladder. We went up and found ourselves in a loft with some bales of hay. There was plenty of hay, and behind it a wooden wall. Isaac made a hole in the hay and helped me inside. Then he got in and put something over our heads. The air was heavy, but at least we were protected against any intrusion. Of course we had to endure some insects, but by now we were used to that.

I fell asleep and dreamed about a huge lake. I was riding on a goose like the ones on my grandparents' farm. The goose and I were swimming, sliding easily over the blue surface of the water, watching the fish. Suddenly everything disappeared and I woke up sweating. It was terribly hot and there wasn't enough air. I shook myself

⚜

awake and almost fainted when I realized that Isaac wasn't there. I stuck my head out from under the hay. The brilliant light of daylight hit me full force and for a few minutes I couldn't see anything. I smiled. Nearby, stretched out on top of the bales of hay, was Isaac. At first sight he looked like a tourist taking the sun on a beach. He had a huge loaf of bread in his hands and at least half a dozen tomatoes. When he saw me he raised his head and invited me to join him. Without any preamble I took a tomato and devoured it. I was hungry. He offered me a chunk of bread. I bit into it even breaking off a piece. Rubbing his eyes and yawning, he watched me. After a long belch he said: "We can't leave anything. A crumb and we're lost. By now the lady of the house must be looking for the bread she set aside for lunch." He was laughing. "At times like this, things don't belong to their owners, but to those who need them." I nodded, swallowing, filling up my belly, chewing without stopping. I quenched my thirst by squeezing a red meaty tomato that stood out from the others. After about ten minutes of nonstop eating I paused. It felt as if everything was stuck in my throat. I picked up the crumbs and put them in my pockets. Isaac did the same. We put the remaining tomatoes and bread inside our shirts and went back to our hideout.

The heat was still unbearable. Memories of the train came to me like pistol shots. Now I was looking for the breathing hole but couldn't find one. Every once in a while a hot wind hit my face. I felt like vomiting what I had eaten. Isaac opened the air hole a bit more. I was able to breathe easier, but the heat was just as bad. I had to take my shirt off. My hair, like Isaac's, was wet from sweat. I closed my eyes, trying to relieve the choking that

❖

gripped my throat like a cord. I could hear the noise out-side. A woman was screaming and the chickens respond-ed in a choir. The shrill barking of a dog led me to believe that he was not too big, probably a domestic kind. I could hear the mooing of the cows and the calves. The whole farm was in motion and the sun was strong.

Suddenly the image of my mother appeared in my mind. I saw her crying without me, covered by tears that swelled her eyes until they were huge red balls. And the impotent gesture of my father, trying to hide me, cover-ing me with his hands so that the slaves would not take me to the truck. It seemed like this had happened many years ago. The notion of time did not apply to me. Everything happened in the midst of a slogan that I kept hearing again and again. We had to survive! Hold on, walk, don't let yourself be caught. I was committed to do it for them: for those who were in Ladyzhin—those in the graves; for myself and for Isaac's trust in me. We had to go on, existing, escaping until we could escape no more. Everything had a goal, and the beasts were not going to the take over the whole world, massacring and killing without pity. I knew that the slaves obeyed, but maybe they would rise against their masters. They would devour each other like the wolves.

I felt guilty that my thoughts were so cold and emo-tionless. The vanquished were done for from the begin-ning and I didn't consider myself one of them. I opened my eyes and saw Isaac asleep. While he slept he scratched his face and made some comic gestures. Nobody looking at him would have imagined he was one of those people who knew how to come and go, to get around without being caught. The light dimmed, signal-ing the coming of night.

❖

Isaac woke up: "The sun is setting. Good, that's what we needed. When it's completely dark, we leave. Let's get out a bit." We stood up and stretched. I put on my shirt and ate some more bread. I looked at Isaac. How had he escaped from the beasts? Had he run as much as I did? Did he lose them by climbing up a tree? I was going to ask him that night. And what about the others? Those groans? He must know. Everything was possible with Isaac. He would have the answers. I watched the red sunset. It was a light slowly sinking in the fields. I thought about a big pit. It was logical. The only people who went down covered by red were the ones they killed with a shot to the back of their necks. Looking at the sunset I felt that I was listening to the shots from the other side of the Bug. Tears rolled down my cheeks. It was my offering to those who had been massacred.

Isaac looked out a small window that faced the farmyard. He moved so quickly I barely noticed. He was still acting his own way. He turned his pale face. "We'll have to steal a bottle. You don't think the tomatoes are going to last forever. We'll need water." Without giving me a chance to answer, I saw him go down the ladder and out the hole from which we had come in that morning.

I had my doubts from the very beginning. What if they caught us? In order to survive we had to gamble from minute to minute. A step in the wrong direction and we were done for. Every moment had a value. I waited fearfully. I ate another piece of bread, not from hunger but to pass the time. I needed to do something, to act. I counted the pieces of hay in each bale. I was insane, but I had been living in a world of insanity from the moment that I realized my duty was to survive any way I could. I got tired of counting the hay and decided to chew it instead.

✦

The palms of my hands were wet from nervousness, and I began to see ghosts watching me without expression, waiting for me to blend into the shadows. The barn turned into a prison. The heat was getting heavier, even though there was no sun. I could see the stars again through the window. But to hell with them, I was worried about Isaac. He finally returned with a liter-sized canteen. I was struck dumb when I saw that he also had a bag full of eggs and a huge chunk of cheese that was still oozing moisture. I was speechless.

The heat invaded my body. Night fell completely, but we still did not dare go out. It was too risky, for the people in the house might have seen our silhouettes. Many farmers, on hot summer nights, used to sit outdoors and smoke a pipe or play a guitar or the violin. Outside a young man was playing a balalaika. The sound came clearly. Isaac smiled. "We have a musical background for our exit. Just like in a puppet show; have you ever see one, Israel? People in love don't notice anything. They're like idiots, looking for a smile from the girl they like. If we get out of this one you'll understand." I shrugged.

I knew that love was for grownups. Isaac was boasting. How much could he know about love if he was only six months older than me? Well, that was up to him. He probably had to pretend to be a man in order to do the things he did. We had to survive, and you could only survive disguised as more than you really were. These were the rules of the game, and we had to follow them. We went down the ladder. The cow watched with its huge eyes but said nothing. She became our accomplice. I wanted to pet her, but I couldn't. If we stopped, things might go wrong. Every second counted. I went out first. Isaac followed. We got to a stone wall and crouched. We

❖

crawled for a good while, very close to the stones. The sound of the balalaika was behind us. The night gave me confidence. We could move ahead without much danger, even though there was always a chance that we might be stopped and questioned. When we got to the open fields we got up and ran for our lives. We needed the woods, the protection of the trees.

In the distance we could hear the barking of the dogs, that constant howling to a distant moon, up there, out of reach. When we got to the woods we stopped to rest. I sat on a huge root. "Isaac, how did you escape from the beasts?" He stretched his legs and rubbed his hands for a while. He finally answered.

"I don't know. Like you and the others, I ran. Our number wasn't up—theirs was. I saw two boys who were running with me fall down. I heard the other one scream. He must have been hit. In a situation like this, you don't scream unless you're hit. Because you know what it means to be wounded and fall into the hands of the Germans or the Ukrainians. Lost, done for, all your bones broken. Of course I got scared when they came with their dogs. I had to get into the water. I was ready to drown rather than to fall into their hands and the jaws of their dogs. There was a cave under the water with some air. I stayed there until I figured they were gone. I went out, wandered for a while, and then saw you asleep on the ground. How come I'm telling you this story? I don't know. This kind of thing makes you think about the existence of God. My number wasn't up. I took a chance, and once again I won."

He was silent for a few minutes. "And what about you, Israel, how did you end up here with me?" I told him my story. When I finished he looked at me with satisfaction. "I knew it. You're someone I can count on. You're not

❖

totally retarded. If I had known you in the ghetto the way I know you now, well—" He pulled up some grass and threw it in my face. "We're going to survive, Israel; we'll resist the Germans, you and I." We laughed. It didn't cost anything to dream, to make plans, to feel victorious. It was a way to escape the terrible reality that was stuck to our heels. We got moving again.

We walked fast, with determined steps. Isaac was talking about his future plans, for when he grew up. "Everyone has to get married. It's the only way to make sure the human race goes on. And I'm going to have so many children! More than the Germans ever dreamed of. Lots of them. That will make the SS run to the pits, and once there they'll be buried alive. That will be my revenge." A sob cut through what he wanted to say. We knew that we could only dream to a point. How could we ignore our condition as fugitives? It was impossible. We had to survive, swallow the bitter taste of memories. How could I make plans knowing that my parents were still at the quarry, walking a thin line without any assurance that they would be alive the next day? We looked at each other and lowered our heads. The truth was that we had to walk a hard path made of stone. That's why we walked only at night. Daylight was our enemy. The sun that everyone else could see and feel was forbidden to Jews. The beasts had even taken away even that which belonged to all men without distinction of race or creed. They made us fall into the pits with our necks broken, hide in basements, flee under the cover of night. We walked quite a distance without saying anything. Sometimes I was in front, other times Isaac. We took turns, shadows escaping to live a few minutes longer, a unit of time that could end up in a common grave.

⚜

I asked Isaac. "Why don't you talk about insanity? I think we're insane." I said this partly just to talk about something, but also because I had a feeling that our behavior was not completely normal. I didn't have to ask twice.

He began talking as if addressing a huge assembly. The trees listened quietly.

"Are we insane? Of course. Who wouldn't be after what we've seen? Haven't you cried and kicked, haven't you tried to escape knowing that behind you there's a bullet ready to rip into your back? That's insanity, Israel! And the insane survive. They gamble their lives every minute. Pain gives us life, urges us to keep living. We trust something we don't know, keeping our faith in the unknown. Insanity is beautiful when you are aware of it and don't let yourself be carried away by your emotions. You saw crazy people who couldn't take being crazy. They killed themselves, or put themselves in a position where someone killed them, they threw themselves into the claws of the SS and didn't want to know that they had a chance to live in their insanity. Despair is only for the sane. That's why they let themselves be killed. If they were totally mad, do you think they would have allowed themselves to be killed in such a vile manner? No way! The crazy man risks everything, not minding if he loses what he has already lost. For that, you need to be crazy like you and me, like the other three who escaped with us. To lie in this hell you need to be crazy, otherwise you can't take it!"

His last words were almost a scream. I noticed a slight shudder in his body. He rubbed his face and began whistling. He improvised. They were tunes that came from the deepest part of his heart. "Israel, don't you think

❖

it's crazy to not know where we're going? Haven't you noticed that we're not going anywhere in particular?" My stomach turned. It was true. Where were we going? It seemed as if the trees were asking the same question. I didn't want to answer. I had nothing to say. The truth manifested itself. Where were we going? What was our goal? I felt anguished again. My vision blurred and I fell on the grass. Isaac turned around, frightened by the sight of me on the ground.

My mind was a blank. If someone had shot me at that moment, I wouldn't have felt it. "Israel, don't give up. As soon as we find a house, we'll make believe we're the children of underground fighters. The people around here must know where to go. Come on, you can't give up now. " While saying this, he rubbed my forehead with a wet rag. Then he made me drink a few sips of water. Soon I was able to get up and keep walking.

Sometimes I fell into despair—being alone in the woods, going nowhere, was drilling my brain. Now I followed Isaac. That was all. I walked just to walk, without any special interest. That morning, our feet aching, we reached a railroad line. We sat there for a while. Isaac said that tracks always led somewhere. "If we follow them, we'll soon be able to find a house." He was trying to console me. He made up stories to make me laugh, but in his eyes I could see the same despair. He was talking for himself as well as for me. He was trying to infuse me with confidence in order to become confident himself. It was a game. I looked into the distance where the tracks seemed to meet, but it only was a visual trick. I imagined that the rest of the world was the same; it went by our side, without lending us a helping hand. It separated a bit at certain points, so as not to see the graves and the

❖

mass deportations that were taking place in all the cities of Europe. I felt anguish looking at the track. It was long, cold, heavy. I felt my parents' absence stronger than ever. I cried. I wanted to cry, and in this dark freedom I could cry, at least it was a right nobody could deny me now. When I was through, I looked at Isaac in an attempt to excuse myself for my weakness, but he, like me, was drying his eyes. He was thinking about his loved ones, his things. He motioned for us to get going.

We walked alongside the rails. The horizon was becoming clear. The faint light of a sun that would soon be biting our backs like a bunch of wasps. We kept walking and about an hour later met some farmers starting their work. They looked at us with curiosity. A youth with a round face and a flat nose approached us with a menacing grin: "Thieves, at this hour?" Isaac, looking him straight in the eye, asked me: "Igor, what do you think?" I could hardly understand the language, so I shrugged. Isaac kept talking. "Comrade, my name is Ivan, and this is my friend Igor. We've been walking for about a month, ever since the village was bombed. Nobody was left. Only a few of us boys were able to survive and we're scattered from farm to farm. We're looking for a roof and a bit of food. We're ready to offer our humble work in return." The others listened attentively.

The youth with the round face whistled, deferring to an older man who came over and said to Isaac: "Ivan, are you by any chance hiding from the Germans?" Isaac was a brilliant improviser. "Germans, what are Germans? Excuse my ignorance, but I don't know what Germans are. All I know is that some soldiers are bombing the villages."

The man let out a howl of laughter. The others joined in. It seemed impossible that anyone wouldn't know who

❖

the beasts were, but Isaac's innocent face and my look of surprise convinced them we were telling the truth. The man came over to me. A shiver went though my spine. If I said anything he would find out that my Russian was not that of a boy from the area. I swallowed. Just as he was about to speak to me, Isaac said: "Comrade, don't make fun of Igor. He's very sensitive, and you'll upset him if you laugh. Igor stutters and can hardly put two words together. They say a witch pinched his tongue when he was born." I nodded. Someone said: "We'll call him Igor Igor."

The others applauded and went on their way, laughing and talking about us. The man and the youth with the round face looked us over for a while. Finally the younger one said: "Do you know what Jews are?" Without missing a beat, Isaac confidently answered: "Father Nikarchos says that the Apostles were Jews, no? The Jews are the apostles." Both men laughed. The older one said: "Ivan, you need some education. Can you handle a sickle?" He nodded without hesitation. "And my friend Igor will help me." The one with the round face and flat nose agreed. "Well, if you can produce, you'll have food and you can sleep in the stable. I suppose you won't be bothered by the cows." They had swallowed the line.

That day we worked steadily, without resting, until afternoon. Isaac cut slowly, picked up slowly, but worked, and I behind him piled up the cut wheat. We had lunch with the Russians, who made some fun of us but accepted us. At the end of the workday I was totally exhausted. Isaac was sweating profusely but kept going. We walked with them toward the farm, a big old house that stood in the middle of the steppe like a lighthouse. As soon as we got there the women crowded around. Questions flew fast and furious. They wanted to know

❖

everything. Isaac answered them all, making things up, his imagination working overtime. He told them about my stuttering. Some of them gave me a compassionate look. Others waited for me to say something. Finally, between questions and answers, they sat us down on a bench and I ate the first hot soup I'd had in a long time.

At first it hurt a bit to swallow. The soup burned my tongue, I had completely forgotten how normal people ate. The old men talked about the harvest and how much they had to give the landowner so that he in turn could give to the Germans. The girls never stopped talking about us. One of the men, a young fellow with a thick head of red hair, came over to me in an effort to impress one of the girls and said: "Wouldn't it be fun to take off the pants of the one who stutters? The Jews can pinch their tongues to talk badly." When he was about to put his hands on me, Isaac jumped up with a sickle in his hand. "I'll cut you if you try anything. Are you a fag like Vladimir? He used to say that we had to pull the boys' pants down to see if they were fags, and you know what? He used to enjoy them himself!"

The old men let out a howl, applauding Isaac. The older one, who had brought us into the work group, exploded: "This Ivan needs some religious education. But he knows a lot about other things, isn't it true, kid?" The laughter increased. The redhead turned beet-red. Isaac's words had stopped him. He turned away, smacking his hip. The women were chattering and laughing. He left like a scolded dog, with his tail between his legs. I relaxed. My hands were cold, and I wasn't shivering just from fear at what had nearly happened. I was thinking that from now on we would have to be very careful with the redhead. Later, after we had eaten a dish of cabbage,

⚜

the guy with the red face took us to the stable. "You can sleep here. I'll wake you up in the morning. Have a good night and don't forget your prayers like good Christians." He went away singing a love song. We made ourselves comfortable on some hay in a corner. "Don't you think it's dangerous to stay here? Did you see that guy who wanted to check out if I was circumcised?"

Isaac took off his boots and answered: "Well, to survive you have to take chances. These are good people, but ignorant. To avoid trouble we should go everywhere together. And be careful with conversations. Use whatever Russian you know, otherwise we're finished. And don't dare speak to me in Yiddish. Always speak to me in Russian and always stuttering, that way they won't notice your accent. People who stutter don't have an accent. Come on, say something. The first thing that comes to mind."

I smiled. I didn't know what to say, how to start. Finally I loosened my tongue and said the first thing that occurred to me. It was a deficient Russian, full of errors, with a funny pronunciation. And I didn't have to fake the stuttering. My pronunciation was so bad that I couldn't help stuttering. Isaac laughed. "You're doing fine, pal."

Well, I resolved to be the farm's stutterer. I lay down in the place I had chosen and fell asleep in a few minutes, haunted by nightmares. Once again the image of my parents behind a thick barbed wire fence. My mother tried to touch my face but couldn't reach me, and I couldn't reach her because my feet were stuck in the mud. Then everything started to go around. I was turning at a fantastic speed, I left through the center of a green whirlwind and came back suddenly. Scene after scene went by without any rational sequence. Once again the pits, the yellow arms trying in vain to go back to a life that had been taken away from them by machine gun fire. I woke up shivering, even though it was unbearably hot. I looked around and quieted down when I saw Isaac still cuddled up in the hay. I heard his rhythmic breathing, signaling to a life always ready to risk everything. I closed my eyes again, but the image of the redhead haunted me. I couldn't fall asleep, I saw him menacingly coming toward me, ready to pull down my pants to scream jubilantly: "You see? Like I said, he's a Jew. Only Jews are cut down there!"

I despaired at the thought. It made me nervous thinking that tomorrow I was going to run into him again, maybe without any protection, without being able to do anything. I thought for quite a while, weaving ideas, and thinking about a way out. Finally I fell asleep once again.

It was still dark when the man with the round face woke us up. "Get up, lazy bums. It's time to wake up!" I saw his silhouette moving about the stable. Isaac got up growling, as if taken away from a wonderful dream. We went to the well and put our heads under the water for a long time. The coolness of the water made us wake up completely. I laughed when I felt the liquid running down my cheeks. It had been quite a while since I felt so much water.

Isaac, seeing me laugh, did the same thing and threw some water at me. The older man, seeing us play, reprimanded us: "What are you doing, kids, don't you know that around here we don't give water away? Come on, hurry over to the kitchen because we have to go to work in a few minutes." And he pointed the way. We went in, and I greeted everyone as well as I could. I noticed that the cook could hardly contain her laughter. Obviously

⚜

people who stuttered were not too common around there. We sat down at a rough wood table and were given a bowl of hot cereal. It tasted good. Too good. It was the food of kings for us. I ate fast, without looking up, like the beasts had taught us. I was almost free, yet I still could not get rid of the vices of the concentration camp.

But no one was paying attention to anyone else. The farmers had their own way of eating. They gulped the food down, licking their dirty fingers. When I finished, and was calm and ready to start working, I saw the redhead. He gave me a look. I looked back and he diverted his eyes. I became uncertain again, the night terror. I kicked Isaac under the table. He looked at me in surprise, but when he saw the redheaded guy he understood. "Don't worry," he murmured in my ear and got up to where the tools where hanging on the wall. He took the sickle and ran his fingers along the edge. He took a bag and gave it to me. We joined the other workers and got ready to leave. We were just walking out when a woman began shouting: "Ivan, Igor!" My stomach turned. It seemed as if every new situation spelled disaster. Maybe they suspected something and were going to turn us over to the Germans. The woman shouted again. We stopped. She came over and gave me two warm bags. "You were about to leave without your lunch, boys. May God be with you," and she turned away. I relaxed. Ivan had not known about the lunch either. We followed the line of men going deep into the fields. The ones in front were whistling a tune. After about an hour the sun began to shine. At first it had a pink cast, then it began to shine, and then the light. We worked all day, hardly stopping to eat what the woman had packed in our bags: a piece of cheese, a chunk of bread, and a few slices of onion and

❖

tomatoes. We drank from a huge canteen that served everyone and was carried by a little man with a nose full of pimples. We set out for the house at dusk. On the way, the man with the round face and the redheaded guy began walking alongside me. "You're dead," I thought. "You gambled and lost. They figured it out." I looked at Isaac in terror. He gripped the handle of the sickle. The man with the round face said: "Igor, we work in teams and the boss doesn't like anyone to be upset. Nikita wants to make peace with you. Come on, shake hands and be good comrades." I didn't understand very well at first. Things were turning around. I extended my skinny hand and the boy gripped it forcefully. He smiled idiotically, and I did the same. Isaac whistled to relieve the tension that had him on edge ever since the redhead came into view. He touched my shoulder to give reassure me. The flat-nosed man made Isaac shake hands with the redhead also. Isaac did it halfheartedly: "And you're not going to bother Igor any more. It's a mortal sin to make fun of someone with a physical defect, and he stutters." Nikita smiled and nodded his huge, sunburned face.

Days passed at the farm. It was a harrowing routine. In the mornings we cut wheat and at night slept in the stable. I was worried all the time. I didn't trust anyone and expected the beasts to turn up at any time. They would have made us drop our pants. Before going to sleep I would talk to Isaac. There was no place safer, he said. Most of the farm folk never even talked about the fate of our people. Either they didn't know, or made believe they didn't.

One Sunday the boss invited us to go into town, a village a couple of hours away. At first I was terrified. It would be dangerous. If someone recognized us, we'd be

⚜

done for, especially in times like these, when every accusation was taken seriously. Isaac persuaded me to go. "We'll gamble one more time," he said, pushing me into the cart. Throughout the journey I had a bitter, painful knot in my throat. The palms of my hands were sweating and my body felt uncomfortable in the clothes they had given me. I felt it floating inside the outfit I was wearing, which was big on me, but I had no choice. I watched the roadside, certain that the beasts were going to jump at us from the shrubs. My persecution complex was in full swing. Finally we got to the village.

There were several houses hovering one next to the other as if seeking warmth. One street led to the square, crowned by a little church with cracked walls. We got off and waited for the boss to tell us where to go. Suddenly the doors of the church opened up and a priest with a big black beard and a huge hat raised his hand to bless us all. Everybody kneeled, including Isaac and me. Later they began to pray out loud. Isaac was whispering something in between sobs, and I tried to imitate him. A few minutes later the ceremony finished and we had to go to the altar to receive the priest's blessing. Isaac and I received the benediction from the priest, while the good man patted our heads: "The spiritual future of our dear country is in you," he said, looking at the ceiling, asking God for his prayers to be answered. Our boss, hearing this, began to beam. He was a religious man and was proud to have among his workers people who were well regarded by the priest, since most of the field hands were drunkards who only came into town to fill their bellies with vodka. He smiled and gave us a few coins: "Go buy yourselves something," he said, and then began chatting with the priest.

⚜

Isaac and I walked around the square. There wasn't much. Just a few stores and dozens of women in kerchiefs talking to one another. The animals— horses, mules, and dogs—walked about untethered on the cobblestones. The men laughed out loud as they raised their cups to toast or curse. I saw a huge man chew up a vodka glass and spit the pieces onto the table while his friends cheered him on. On one side, someone began playing an accordion. Music filled the place and everyone began to dance. It was a fast dance with long steps. The men formed circles and jumped in the air. We looked on, enjoying the show. It was something new, and the accordion music was a spiritual stimulus that forced us to keep the beat with our hands. We looked on and clapped. We were letting go of our past anguish. I felt like I was born again, that I was that boy who used to visit his grandparents and enjoyed sleigh rides seeing the snow swirl under the horses' feet. Suddenly some German beasts showed up on the other side of the square. Isaac pointed them out to me.

All my happiness vanished. My spirit melted and gave way to terror. I began to sweat. There were about twenty of them, and they had their weapons at the ready. Not wanting to take any chances, I lost myself among the dancers. Isaac followed. We came and went with the rhythm of the accordion, jumped up in the air and kicked our legs. We were desperately trying not to be noticed. The Germans went on to the commissariat through a narrow door and disappeared in twos. Before long I was very tired. The dancing and the fright had affected me, and I had no choice but to sit down on one of the benches next to the vodka drinkers The redheaded guy screamed out: "Igor." My blood curdled. He and his

❖

friends leaned over. "Good comrades, you dance better than we did when we were your age." The others, a bit drunk, nodded in agreement. Later he addressed Isaac: "Ivan, you never told us"—pointing at me—"that this guy knew how to dance. Were you jealous that a guy with a stutter could dance better than you?" Isaac nodded. Why get into an argument with a drunk? One of the redhead's friends treated everyone to a toast. They brought the bottle and served a couple of glasses. I had to drink one and Isaac the other. I closed my eyes and drank. It felt like I had swallowed a flaming piece of carbon. The others laughed when they saw my tears and heard me coughing. It was the first drink of my life and I almost couldn't get it down. I did it to show the redhead that I wasn't afraid of him. Then they made us have another. From one moment to the next they had made us part of their group and were treating us as equals. One of the men at the table said: "Do you know there's a home for Jewish orphans up north? My brother, who travels that way, told me. What do you think, taking care of Jews?" Another answered: "Those Romanians. They can do what they want. What do we care? Our Jews are at the commissariat and the Germans are about to take them away." Isaac and I looked at each other. We would have to walk on eggshells. If one of these men suspected anything they would give us away in a second. I had another drink, trying to appease my fear. In the background, the music and the dancers carried on.

The boss, who had been looking for us, came to our table. "Ivan," he said, addressing Isaac, "come see the Jews. They're going to take them away now." Isaac got up and I followed. The others didn't even notice when we got up. We crossed the square and mingled with the people

⚜

waiting at the door of the commissariat. "You'll see. They're the last ones. We have no more Jews." I was angry. How could a man who seemed so good, a God-fearing religious man, join a crowd to watch so tragic and barbaric a spectacle as the exodus of helpless, frightened people sentenced to death for the crime of believing in something different—but nonetheless in the same and only God?

Isaac held my arm so that I wouldn't try something foolish. I was repeating in my mind. "You have to survive, survive. For them, for your parents, for the ones in the pit." I repeated this a thousand times without pausing. Otherwise I would have exploded and shouted "Murderers!" at the crowd. Yes, they were accomplices.

They were justifying the fact that the Germans were systematically exterminating us. In their subconscious, the spirit of the slave was boiling. After a while the door opened. The first ones out were Ukrainians. You didn't have to be very observant to notice that they had a few bottles of vodka in them. Next came our people. There must have been ten or fifteen, most of them women and old men. Only one boy. I was sure they had given them away. They walked with their heads down, dragging some torn bags with their miserly belongings. I was holding myself not to cry out. The words were turning in my throat. I wanted to warn them about the pits, to tell them to try the impossible—to escape. But nothing. I had to shut up, to swallow my wishes, see them parade impotently to their deaths. The slaves forced them to march fast, using the butts of their guns. I cried silently, wiping my tears with the sleeve of my jacket. I felt like I was drowning in the middle of that crowd that was enjoying itself watching the pale, faint faces of our people. Isaac

❖

gave me a bottle of vodka and I took a long swallow. I wanted to swallow it and chew it. It would mean to die in a moment, without anyone being able to do anything about it. I was burning to scream: "I am a Jew, so what?" But Isaac kept his eyes on me. He knew the state I was in and was not going to let me do anything. He had one arm around my neck, and I knew he would put his fist in my mouth if I made even the slightest effort to speak. His eyes were shining and the path of his tears was still visible on his face. He too swallowed the words.

I was choking in the middle of that crowd. The onlookers craned their necks to see the last traces of our condemned people, who were fading like melting candles. I was choking among the red faces of the women pointing at the condemned Jews while clutching prayer books in their hands. A thirst for vengeance filled every space within me once again. My hands had to do something. I felt my fingers clawing, ready to close on one of the beasts to strangle him slowly, screaming in his face each one of his crimes. Finally the poor victims vanished and the square went back to normal. The boss looked at us in satisfaction. He was sure he had shown us something important. "You see, those were the Jews! They say the Germans treat them a certain way. But we're not interested in knowing what they do with them. Yes, those are the Jews!" He was talking about them as if they were animals that it was good to get rid of.

I spent the rest of the afternoon with my head down. The field hands were making fun of me, telling me that the hangover would soon go away. But the truth is that my soul hurt. I imagined my parents on the way to the pit, dragging their misery, leaving behind the world they had helped to build, with their hands and their intelli-

⚜

gence. It hurt me to breathe air that those they had executed could no longer breathe. I felt like someone con-
victed of living while my people were being massacred.
But I held on to a thought that did not leave my brain for
a minute. I had to survive. I couldn't let myself be killed.
I had a duty to live, to endure, to go on. We arrived at the
farm well into the night. I didn't utter a single word on
the way. I simply looked, again seeing those that had left
the commissariat never to come back. Some of the field
hands, like sacks of potatoes, slept off their drunkenness
next to me, sometimes hallucinating. That evening I did
not want to eat. I went to the stable right away, I was
looking to relieve myself by crying, no longer needing to
hold back my tears. I cried until my eyes closed to
immerse me once again in my world of nightmares, memories, and ghosts. I woke up several times, trembling. It
was the fever. On my left Isaac kept chewing on bits of
hay. He didn't sleep all night. A couple of days went by.
We worked as a routine, trying to escape our interior
world. The Wednesday after that terrible Sunday Isaac
spoke to me about leaving. I had been thinking the same
thing and asked his reasons. "Do you remember that
man who mentioned the home for Jewish orphans in the
north? Well, two days from now, on Friday night, we're
leaving. We need to get some clothes and some food. Do
you understand?" I nodded. It was all right to leave
again, without letting anybody know. When the man with
the round face came for us, we would be far away. And
we had to take advantage of these last days of summer.
Pretty soon the rains of autumn would come and things
would be more difficult.

We woke up on Thursday before the man with the
round face came for us. He was surprised to see us

❖

already with our faces washed and ready to go to the kitchen. "This is very good, you're turning into good workers. Waking up early is a good sign." We followed him to the table. There we ate slowly, carefully chewing everything. We needed strength. It was our next-to-last day on the farm and we could not make any excuses. That day we worked hard. Isaac gleaned and put the kernels in his shirt pocket. I did the same thing. Thus we finished the hot workday. At dinner, before we went to the stable, the boss gathered us in the living room of the farm. "Tonight we will celebrate my daughter Masha's birthday. You're all invited!" We had to stay. But first we said we had to go back to the stable to change. The redhead laughed: "They're clean, these kids, eh?" A woman answered, "And you should follow their example." He raised his hand, making a face. When we got to the stable Isaac took out a bag from under the hay and we put the kernels in it. The canteen we had brought from the previous farm was also in it, along with some clothes, four loaves of bread, and a package of sugar. Once again I hadn't known what Isaac was doing - that was his style, his things were his and there was no use raising any objections. We went back to the farm so as not to arouse any suspicion. They were already playing the balalaika and the accordion. Inside things were very animated. For them life was going on as usual. They slept, they ate, and they partied. War was something far away about which they barely had any news. Seeing us at the door the boss's wife, a fat woman with a red face and a round nose like a potato, made us come in. The house was brimming with that distinctive Russian gaiety. The odor of vodka bounced from the walls, burning our nostrils. A girl of about eleven came to me. "What's wrong that you have

such a sad face?" she asked. I smiled and she immediately sat by my side and started to talk about the cows
her father owned, the new cart they were going to buy,
and the enormous amount of fruit they had harvested.
She talked fast, without stopping. I hardly understood
her. Even though I had improved my Russian during the
last few days, it was still difficult for me to follow a conversation. Someone said to her: "Alexandra, don't talk so
fast, Igor may not be able to follow you. He has a defect
on his tongue that does not allow him to court with his
voice." There was some irony in those words, but I didn't
care, there was a certain advantage in being known as a
stutterer. It was a shield against suspicion. The girl
looked at me for a few moments. "They got your tongue?
Were you such a liar?" I shrugged. "No," I said slowly,
repeating the syllables, as I had taught myself with so
much repetition, "what happens is that words don't come
out whole like with everybody else." Becoming aware of
my handicap, she started to laugh. "Oh, you stutter. I
know someone else who does and he's almost cured. He
puts stones in his mouth and repeats the words until
they're almost all right. You should try that." We looked
at each other. Alexandra was not bad looking. Her blonde
braids fell becomingly over her ears. She had light blue
eyes and a small, pink mouth. She took me by the hand,
and without knowing why, I felt a terrible heat all over my
face. She smiled, showing her teeth, which were white as
snow. "Igor, you have turned beet- red. Is this the first
time you have talked to a girl?" It was the first time that
I had talked to a girl like her. The others I had met were
now in the pits, stuck among the yellow bones. They were
girls who did not have time to smile, who had rotted in
life, eaten away by the bugs and the filth. But how could

❖

I tell her that the girls I had met were Jewesses from the ghetto, girls who had to act like men in order to survive one more day. The need to scream once again gripped my throat. I held back my urge. "Yes, it is the first time."

What else could I say? I was Igor now, and this really was the first girl Igor had spoken to. Smiling, she offered me a piece of bread and butter. "We're going to eat it between the two of us. That way we can be good friends." I bit into it, again feeling that heat on my face. And Alexandra, who never took her eyes off me, laughed with the laugh of a girl who knew nothing about the horrors of the war. It would not be strange if she too hated Jews. She asked me to dance. I declined, but the redhead, who had seen me dancing like a maniac in town, without knowing that it had been due to the presence of the beasts, came over and said. "Come on, my friend, you can't say no to the boss's daughter." I was being pressured, and after giving me a huge shot of vodka, they pushed me into the center. I started to jump keeping the rhythm of the accordion. I did it in a rage, thinking about the old men the Germans had forced to dance before massacring them like dangerous bugs. I danced propelled by a deep desire that screamed from within: Endure, carry on, you're leaving tomorrow. You have nothing to lose. It is your chance to gain these people's confidence. That way you'll be able to take one of the cheeses that are in the kitchen. It will be handy on the way. Think about yourself. I danced three songs until I fell onto the floor tired, vanquished, bathed in sweat and tears. I felt like a puppet. If they only knew that the kid dancing for them was a Jew, their applause would probably have turned into accusing fingers and shouts of "Dance Jew, dance!" Alexandra was exultant. She came

❖

to me with a glass of juice. I drank it fast, trying to calm the fire within. "You're very good Igor. Very good!" I wanted to scream out that I was not dancing, that what I was doing was relieving myself, letting out a silent scream that translated into frantic movement. But I said nothing and instead dried off the sweat and the tears that covered my face.

I talked for a long time, improvising. The party ended around two in the morning and I went back to my place in the stable, not without promising Alexandra that I would meet her the following Sunday after mass. That same night we packed everything we were going to take along. Isaac kept quiet, looking for space in the bag, Barely breathing. He lay down without a word. I paid no attention. He was not one to talk while doing. His style was still his very own.

On Friday we woke up around seven. The red-faced man had red, swollen eyes. A thick odor of vodka came from his mouth. "Let's go to work, and work hard," he said, holding his belly, which was probably hurting. He looked like he had been beaten up, but it was the effect of the drinks. I ate everything they put in front of me. As the workday progressed, the moment to go back to the farm seemed far off. Tonight would be the escape, and I wanted to leave now, without any further waiting. The desire to leave came up to my throat, making me so nervous that I almost knocked over the bag where I had to put the sprigs of wheat. That day I worked slowly, keeping my strength for the evening. When I went out I did not stop to look at anything. If we aroused even a tiny suspicion, the beasts would be inquiring about us.

While I worked I thought about my people. In the orphanage I wouldn't have to pretend, calling myself Igor

❧

*Israel, Age 4,
Belz, Romania,
1936*

*Israel and Parents
Karlsbad,
Czechoslovakia, 1947*

Lapciuc Family, Miami Beach, Florida, 2002

Israel Lapciuc

and passing as someone who stuttered. It was the only way to find out about my people, to know what was happened. Anxiety gripped me. I could see myself walking in the field, going fast, in search of my people. I had to gamble again, but it was worth it. From the beginning we had been rolling the dice, and we knew all along that in order to exist we had to take the chance of winning or losing. The ability to risk everything was the only thing the beasts had not been able to take away from us.

After dinner we went directly to the stable. The others stayed behind, talking about the party the night before.

Isaac put a hand on my shoulders: "Tonight we leave, Israel. Don't be nervous, everything will come out all right," he said. But I think that he said it to reassure himself. The truth is that the beginning of the game was always difficult.

He took out the bag from under the hay and looked it over for a few minutes. "Everything is in order. Let's wait until it gets dark, and then shalom! If we wait too long, we'll end up staying until they catch us, and in that case it would not have been worth it to escape from the SS." He took a few rubles from his pockets. I looked at him a bit frightened. "Where in hell did you get rubles, Isaac?" He smiled: "Yesterday at the party I found a chest that belonged to the boss. I took out what I figured he owes us. Nobody works for free, right?" Now I wanted to escape more than ever. If the man found out he would raise such hell that it would have been better never to have known him.

The hours went by slowly. The lights of the farm went out, and the dog, which already knew us well, lay down to one side of the stable door. Isaac spent a long time petting him. "That way when we leave he won't bother us.

❖

He'll wait quietly, thinking perhaps that we went out to pee." He scratched his head and got up. Zero hour was here. My hands were cold and sweaty. I took the bag and got ready to go out the door. But Isaac stopped me. It was better to lift a board. He did. He waited for me to go out and then put the board back. We circled the stable. When we got to the door once again, he closed it with a cross bar. He had done the same thing inside.

"That's to give them something to do in the morning," he said with a nervous giggle. We started walking fast, without looking back, putting our trust in God. We wanted to go northward, but we only knew the east and the west, and that because of the sunrise and sunset. We climbed the fence and ran for a good while. We reached a small forest. We were the guests of the trees again. We were free and were risking everything!

⚜

7

The Tunnel of Misery

I don't know how long we walked. The farm was behind us, lost in the shadows of the summer night. We walked among the roots that came up from the soil, getting tangled in the shrubbery. We stumbled against the stones. We advanced fast, without looking back, our eyes fixed on the horizon. Our advance through the forest is painful, full of ghosts that beckon to us from the other side of the path. My feet and my back hurt, but I go on. I can't stop. We've made a decision and we have to escape. If we fall into the hands of the people from the farm, we will certainly end up in the commissariat and from there be paraded past a crowd of curious onlookers who will point at us as the last surviving Jews. The thought makes me walk faster. It's a fear that breaks through me, filling every space in my guts with a dreaded sense of cold. It makes breathing difficult.

The bag I am carrying is heavy. I try to accommodate it, switching it to another hand, putting it on my head, but in the end it is still the same unbearable weight that cramps my muscles and hurts deeply. I want to scream, sit down, stop, and wait, once and for all, for death to come. But I continue. At times I despair, but then I gather strength again. It must be the terror of thinking that the others are behind me, at my heels, ready to take it out on me, to laugh and point at me as if I were an animal to be branded. And the branded ones are taken to the other shore. Later came the shots and the pit started to fill up, slowly and constantly, with people who fifteen minutes before still had hopes of living, of possessing a piece of life that was worth fighting for. And there they were, one on top of the other, their faces covered with lime and a hole in the back of their necks.

Should I stop? Wouldn't that be betraying the ones in the graves? For them I must keep walking, fleeing, making believe that I stammer. Let them call me Igor, Alexis, Dmitri, what's the difference? They live in me and I can't let them hunt me like a rabbit. I make a fist, breathe hard and go on. Sweat rolls down my forehead, it obscures my vision, holds on to my lashes. My whole body hurts, but I must continue, stay on my feet, sustain the dead in me.

In the distance I see the reddish glimmer of dawn. Isaac looks at me satisfied. We are a whole night ahead of them. Just now the man with the round face must be getting to the stable. Isaac smiles at the thought of his face when he doesn't find us. They will scream and carry on, the boss will be flustered. Alexandra will have to give up the idea that I was going to wait for her. But we are far away. A whole night away from them and their threats.

We have reached a clearing in the forest. From here dawn appears in all its splendor. I stop. Isaac does the same, as if he had been waiting for it. I lie down on the wet grass. I fall like a stone. My body unites with the soil, sticks to it. I feel the blood running in my veins. I breathe out, allowing the air in and out of my mouth and my nos-

⚜

trils. It feels like I have been running for ages, whole years, walking day and night. I look around: trees, light, fresh air. I wake up from a long dream: I am free! I don't have any problems.

Nobody is watching, I don't see any signs of the beasts and their slaves. I can talk without pretending. I don't have to be Igor any more, that Igor who ate in fear, who walked in fear, who was afraid of his own fear, that elf that danced in my throat, wishing to manifest its presence through screams and tears. But I didn't cry then. Now I can cry as a way of prayer, grateful to be able to live for those who crossed to the other side of the Bug.

Lost in these thoughts, with the night's walking finished, I fall asleep. It's a vast prairie covered with wheat. The spears stand tall, defiant, proudly showing their golden kernels. I walk, fly over the spears, and cut from one moment to the next. I jump from one stack to the other but don't touch them, I am not happy. It hurts me to see the cut-down spears. In the back, near a swampy lake, some are still standing. But they don't stand as proudly as the others. Their kernels are not golden, and the blowing wind makes them almost touch the ground. I try to get to them, but I can't. The North Wind hits me and I float like a marionette. But I feel something warm beside me. I look and see a huge track that sometimes breaks, later reappearing along the way. I start to hyperventilate. All my efforts are centered on reaching that track. I let out a scream and wake up with a terrible headache. Isaac grunts and hands me a piece of black bread. Surely he thought I was crying from hunger, or who knows what!

I shake my body, touch myself, and make sure it's still me. I chew on the piece of bread. I swallow with some difficulty and start to talk with my mouth full. I tell Isaac about my strange dream. He answers: "What, you mixed me up with Joseph in Egypt?" I finish my ration and drink a bit of water. "Doesn't it mean anything to you, that thing about the stalks and the tracks?" He opens his eyes, licks his lips, and says: "Well, we all dream about something. I just dreamed I was full of stones, full of sand, with my belly sewed up with thread. And what does that mean for me? That in order not to have your stomach sewed up you better not eat stones and sand!" He remains serious for a few moments and after a while breaks up in laughter. "I didn't mean that. With this life you start going crazy, and after a while you don't even know what you're saying. I just invented that dream. I was jealous of not having a dream to talk about. I can't remember what I dream, even if they threaten me to cut off both my ears. But seriously now, my neighbor, who was a very well read man, used to say that dreams are warnings. Sometimes he used to discuss this with the chazzan and the rabbi, and the neighbor used to win. Thanks to him I learned the story about Joseph in Egypt. Why don't you tell me your dream again? It could be useful."

I told him again what I had seen while I was sleeping. Everything seemed so real that I even doubted that it had been a dream. I talked about the wheat as if I had the kernels in my hand. And I told it in such a natural way that even Isaac grimaced as if he were seeing it too. When I finished he was pensive, perhaps looking for arguments and answers to the questions that were going through his mind. Suddenly he got up and started to walk on the grass. He turned around and faced me: "I don't understand it very well, but there is something. We must get to

❖

the tracks. Trains always go to cities and towns. If we walk along the tracks we will get somewhere. And you already know what you have to do." He didn't say anything else, took his bag, and disappeared through the trees.

I also got up. I walked with some difficulty, still feeling some pain in the waist and legs. It was cool in the forest. The sun's rays did not get down to the ground. They remained among the branches, stuck to the tree bark. Underneath, the dampness stuck to the bottom of our boots. We stepped on slippery moss, decaying leaves, and other plants that grow beneath the big trees. Isaac and I kept going, looking for the railroad tracks. My dream had indicated a goal and we marched toward it. Whether it was close or far didn't matter. The main thing was to find the tracks and go forward alongside them, hopefully toward the north.

Almost at dusk, after stopping a couple of times to rest and eat something, we saw the rails. We ran toward them. We wanted to touch them, to know that they were real and trains moved along them. Isaac looked at me with bright, bulging eyes. "Israel, don't ever forget your dreams. From now on, tell me all of them. If not for your dream, we would still be in the forest, eating moss and digging holes." He was excited by our discovery.

We sat by the tracks for a few moments. We spent a long time looking at the line, which faded in a deep angle, in the yellow background of a summer sunset. I felt animated. Without knowing why, my whole body felt lighter, without the weight I had been carrying for a long part of the walk. I felt light, with an enormous will to start walking along the railroad tracks. It was as if something was pulling me toward that deep angle that became a point

❖

on the horizon. This time I got up first and, without saying a word, started to walk. Isaac whistled, threw a few stones at an imaginary target, and picked up his bag to follow me.

A fresh breeze cooled our faces. Autumn was coming, that rainy season about which we still did not think. We walked with long strides, without even remembering the farm, thinking about only one thing: to arrive! Where? We didn't know, but the thing was to get somewhere, feel a presence, see the smoke from the chimneys, the round faces of the farmers, and smell the stables. On our escape, we needed to be human, to feel alive among others.

It must have been around midnight when we heard the sound of a locomotive. The first impression was one of terror. It was the beasts! Isaac did not have to think twice. He took me by the sleeve of my jacket and we ran into some nearby trees. We were trembling. The image of the train made us remember the one that had taken us to the stone quarry. Like two animals of prey, we waited for the train. It was surely full of human beings, all packed together, crazed by anguish and despair which translated into screams and banging against the walls of the cars, of the dark, infernal boxes that imprisoned them. Finally the huge black locomotive came into view. It was moving slowly, letting out some whistles that I interpreted as wails. The train was wailing and its passengers were surely crying. You didn't have to be an expert to recognize that transport of death.

A caravan of cars went by, each marked with a huge Magen David. In the moonlight the symbol was quite visible. You could also see the silhouettes of the slaves and the Nazi beasts on top of the boxes, with their guns ready to vomit their death message at any attempt to escape. We heard some faraway weak knocking. Isaac looked and squeezed his bag against his chest as he cursed: "Pigs, sons of bitches!" It was the first time I heard him talk that way, but circumstances made us react accordingly. I repeated his words and wished to have the power to engrave it on the forehead of each of the Nazis and their slaves.

We kept watching. It was a train with many cars. When it disappeared from view, lost in the darkness of the night, we came out of our hiding place. Isaac banged his head: "You realize that nothing changes? Trains do not stop. Cars upon cars wait to be filled up. If God exists, he is asleep. Yes, don't get scared if I indulge in blasphemy, how can you explain why we have to flee, why our people are forced to fill up the graves, to open their mouths so that the beasts can take their teeth out, to lower their heads so that they can put a bullet through them? Can you be sure your parents are still alive?" I shuddered, how could I know whether or not my parents were rotting at the bottom of a pit? A bitter knot gripped my throat and I fell to the ground. I cried out screams and curses. How could the rules of good conduct matter now if at every passing moment the beasts made me feel more like an animal? Isaac tried to console me, asking my forgiveness for having hurt my feelings by talking about my parents. But there was no reason to apologize. The memory of my family was always with me, it slept with me, it ate with me. What hurt was to stay alive without knowing about them, without thinking about the fact that any morning, if it had not already happened, they would have to look at the grave and feel the impact of a bullet tearing every fiber of their necks. I cried from impotence, for not being able to escape my condition of escapee, hoping to survive like a hungry, stalked animal. I bit my lips so strongly that they bled. Slowly once again we approached the rails. We walked on, saddened, with our heads down, waiting for the opportunity to take our revenge. Isaac started the conversation: "I'm going to castrate them like oxen. Later I'll put a yoke on them and make them work until they burst." I was thinking of making the beasts dig the graves with their hands, to take out those beings they had executed, to take them aside one by one and give them life once again. I imagined everything and did not come to any logical conclusion. I had a fever, I was sick, my mind rebelled against reality.

We walked that way until the new day greeted us. We didn't give a damn about seeing the sun come up. We went without a course, without bothering about time. And all the while we walked, slowly, like turtles, with our feet swollen. Isaac bent down to pick up a piece of paper near a rail. I looked. It was a dirty paper, written in a small, trembling handwriting. Without lifting his head, Isaac said: "It must be from one of the people on that train. It's written in Yiddish. Let's see if I can read it. I don't know much, but whatever it says, I will never forget."

He stretched out the paper in front of his reddened eyes, which were swollen and shining with the strength of one who has something in his power that he will later be able to use against his torturers. Finally, after reading in silence, he read a few phrases out loud: "I don't know whether this letter will reach you. We are in a cattle car. They deprive us of the most basic needs for our cleanliness. For a trip of several days we have hardly a bit of bread and a few drops of water. We evacuate on the floor, men and women without any shame. There is a dead woman with us. When she was agonizing we called out for help. But the cars are sealed. Nobody came. And now we must endure the odor of death. They threaten us with their weapons. My sister and myself give each other hope and we keep waiting, in spite of everything. Will this be the end?" We were not wrong when we thought it was a death train going by as we watched from the forest.

Sleeping in the woods, stealing from the farms, walking at night, we kept on living, always on our toes, until the last days of summer went by. The soles of our shoes were torn, the cloth of our jackets was ragged, my pants were black from soil. We lived like moles, digging holes in the ground during the day, sleeping with an open eye, ready to gamble our lives for a pair of eggs, living on the edge, like criminals. Some farmers would give us a plate of cabbage soup, others would loose the dogs after us. But we kept on walking, a bit more confident after a stable hand indicated the way northward, toward that field they had talked about in the village.

The rainy days of autumn had begun when we finally found the way to Bershad. We arrived in the afternoon, wet, thin, and covered with mud. We went up to a huge door and walked in. We did it automatically, as we had done in the past, trusting in a higher power, ready once again to take a chance. We had known this from the outset. You gamble and you win or lose. We bet on a high card when we reached Bershad. The only thing we knew was that there was an orphanage for Jewish children. Nothing more. That was the card on the table. And we decided to play it.

It was a huge building, under the control of the Romanian authorities. And, as we found out later on,

✤

they were not as brutal as the SS and the Ukrainians.
However, the setting was not too appealing. Isaac and I
were registered and immediately sent to a dark pavilion
where there were more than two hundred children who
had lost their parents or were simply wandering about
the city like ourselves. In the eyes of all of them there was
a strange sadness, a frozen fear that reflected shyly in
their tired, dull, hungry eyes. We had reached our destination, and now what? We slept the first night without
paying too much attention to conditions in the orphanage. We were dead tired, with no desire for conversation.
We only wanted to rest, to be less of a fugitive. We fell on
the straw that served as beds, and let ourselves be taken
over by the torpor of hunger and sleep working together.
That night I did not dream. Surely my subconscious also
wanted to rest.

They woke us up at six. There was a cold, nasty wind.
Everybody got up when they heard the siren of the
orphanage. I began to recognize the place where I had
landed. Isaac, wiping his eyes, said: "I don't believe this
was our smartest move." I looked around and nodded.
Surely we were among our people, but at what price?
Thousands of steps marched in unison. The Romanians,
though less evil, were still in the status of slaves to the
beasts. We were still prisoners. I knew that Bershad was
open to everyone, but to leave was another story. Any
escape attempt would have dire consequences. The door
was open to come in, but closed to go out.

Well, you gambled and lost, kid! You didn't calculate
well. You should have thought before gambling, but you
came in without a second thought. You're locked in again
waiting, with no one to come to your defense if the slaves
decide to fill some graves. You must think. They've

⚜

trapped you, and now you must endure, survive. Those who went to the other side of the Bug must not remain unheard. It was your pact with the fallen ones. The next card might be your last one!

The noise of footsteps penetrated my ears like a hot nail. The others, who were already used to the routine, stepped out into the hallway and formed a line. Isaac and I did whatever we saw the others doing. In the daylight I could better see the components of the building, this complicated orphanage, which may or may not have been part of Bershad. The Germans were masters at psychological games. There were hundreds of children, bundles of eyes that looked everywhere. There were children of all sizes, of different backgrounds, good ones and street-smart ones. The only thing we had in common was the fact that we were Jewish and had no paternal protection. Orphans from seven to fourteen years of age. This morning, after eating a nondescript soup that tasted of nothing more than salt, we met the chiefs of our pavilion. They were three seasoned boys from Bershad. They had been the first to come in and were doing fine with the Romanians, something they bragged about constantly, perhaps in order to maintain their status of leadership. The oldest of them was called "Hard Tooth" because of his characteristic way of eating. He would eat an apple, core and all. On several occasions I saw him devour a raw potato in ten seconds flat. If the Romanians had seen him he wouldn't have lived to tell the story. Thieves were punished with death. The second one was a freckled boy with a round face who answered every question with a whistle. They called him "Canary." He was an expert in getting out of the orphanage and into the town in order to survive. He knew a lot of people outside and knew

⚜

whom to trust. Together with "Hard Tooth" and his other partner, they ran a counterfeit ring inside and outside in Bershad. They knew the buyers and the prices. The third one, a thin boy with dark hair called "Matchstick," was in charge of training those under "Canary" and "Hard Tooth." His experience was recognized by the chiefs of the other pavilions. They had even bribed some of the Romanian guards with a few bottles of liquor and occasional girls when they wanted to party.

Matchstick was feared not because of his strength, but because of his cleverness in dealing with situations. The only one who reigned by terror was Hard Tooth. His other two friends did not justify violence, but they needed some "protection" and so worked with their boss. At first we tried to ignore them, but we realized that it was very difficult to survive without belonging to the organization. We spent the first day walking around, exploring the possibilities of getting in and out. Isaac became listless and spent hours looking out into space, not saying a word. I was going crazy. I didn't want to walk around without him by my side. For the time being we were outsiders among the boys of Bershad. The rains started and the meals did not change, even though they left us alone. The Romanians carried out their assignment by keeping us locked in, with a minimum of food, until such time as the beasts would claim us. It was their duty. Survival was up to us, and it had a set price. The ones with the organization charged. The guards needed their hands greased.

On the third night, a bit recuperated from our journey along the railroad tracks, Isaac called me over to a corner. Hard Tooth scratched his ear, and right away more than a dozen boys fixed their eyes on us. The Canary

⚜

whistled, and Hard Tooth started to rub his hands. Isaac got up and looked each one in the eyes. Hard Tooth laughed with a dry, sick laugh. he said: "You, yes you," he said pointing at Isaac. "There are no secrets here. Whatever you are going to tell your friend, you can tell us. Isn't that so, boys?" The others laughed in unison, clapping their hands. Matchstick, encouraged by his friend's words, said: "Boys, here we all protect each other. It's the only way to endure, to survive. Don't you realize that the soup you eat won't give you enough strength to survive the winter? The snow last year ended up with more than a third of those who were in this region. In other places, the plague killed half. And all because they wouldn't listen to the organization. You would do well thinking about that and leave your secrets for when you find a girlfriend." There was more laughter. I few back, looking on like a mere spectator.

Isaac got up, rubbed his chin, and kicked the straw. He looked at Hard Tooth and spit at his feet. Canary let out a long whistle, and Hard Tooth moved over to where Canary was.

"Boy," I said to myself, "this is getting ugly. Be patient, don't jump, if you want to live, don't jump. Wait, measure the possibilities, consider that this is all done for survival. They are not bad. They've turned themselves into wise guys, always ready to take a chance. Calm down, don't come in until all the doors are open." Isaac spit again. The others kept quiet. He was the first one who had ever challenged the chief.

Hard Tooth raised his hand to hit Isaac, but the answer was swift. Before the boy's hand could touch him, Isaac kicked the aggressor's shin. Hard Tooth winced, letting out a whimper. Before anyone could do anything,

❖

Isaac had a knife in his hand. The blade glistened, ready to slice the first one to make a move. Matchstick and Canary remained stuck in their places and made signs with their hands to quiet down the active members of the organization. They hadn't counted on such a reaction from the newcomer. It was logical. The boys from Bershad only knew the ghetto and the road. Little did they know about the graves and the labor camps. They lacked survival experience. And now they watched Isaac fearfully. Where had he gotten that huge knife? Not even I knew.

Hard Tooth straightened up, grimacing. Isaac said: "I will decide about joining the organization. If I want to talk secretly, it's my business, and nobody better stick their nose in my affairs. No threats to me or to him"—he pointed at me. "And no squealing. If you do, before you come back, your belly will be open. All I ask is peace and quiet. Then, when I feel like it, I'll decide what is best for me." And with his index finger touching the edge of the blade, he made clear that any wrong move have been bad consequences. The others were amazed.

Hard Tooth outdone? Nothing like that had ever happened before! Matchstick, a smart fellow, called for silence, for everyone was talking loudly and the noise was unbearable. When they quieted down he said: "This is no time to stir up a fight among us about something that isn't even important. We have to stick together, otherwise we are lost. If our comrade wants peace and quiet," he said, referring to Isaac, "then give him what he wants? Is it worth fighting over peace and quiet? If he wants time to think, let him think. And don't get any foolish ideas about squealers. The organization doesn't pay any attention to them. Our comrade can have all the time he wants, and if he wants to talk to his friend, so be it. Are we always going to cry in hiding where nobody can see us? Sometimes a friend is our best confidante. Are we going to keep complaining in the latrines, while we evacuate in solitude? Our comrade must have his reasons."

The audience remained silent. Only every once in a while you might have heard a sound from Hard Tooth, who was still feeling hurt. Canary nodded. In just a moment or two Isaac had become a big man. His possession of a knife intimidated the members of the organization. They weren't used to dealing with someone who was ready and able to take action. Isaac went back to his corner, sat down, and put his knife inside his shirt. He didn't say another word all night. One morning he and Matchstick talked for a long time and finally Isaac came over to me. "Israel, tonight we have an outing. We're going for bread and butter. You already know what to do. Here it's a little easier. I don't mean that it won't be dangerous. It's the same game, but with more guarantees. The guards aren't as bad as the ones in Ladyzhin. Some of them will keep quiet if they get something out of our smuggling. Are you game? It'll just be you and me." I bit my nails. I was flattered by being able to become who I was, but I didn't trust the members of the organization. Their operation was somewhat primitive. They didn't bring in very much, considering the risks they took. If it really was easier to get out here in Bershad, then it should be possible to bring much more back. It hurt me to see the five- and six-year-olds wandering the streets in ragged clothes.

I couldn't look at their eyes, those huge eyes that begged for a piece of life, for a helping hand. The organization did nothing for them. It had not been shrewd

❧

enough to use them. Children of that age, properly trained, could be very helpful. As I thought about this, I began planning to form a brigade made up of these little ones, because they too had a right not to die of typhus or tuberculosis when winter came. The atmosphere in Bershad was better than in Ladyzhin, so a little kids brigade would only be a matter of proper training.

I had been thinking about this for quite a while, and that same evening, before we slipped out into Bershad, I shared my thoughts with Isaac. "You're becoming really serious about survival. We'll go over the idea when we get back. I don't see it as an impossibility, and it may help a lot of us to survive the winter." That was all he said, and then he showed me the exit and entry plan the organization had given him. We would go out near the latrines, then would climb the walls of the infirmary, and from there to the wire fences. Several hundred meters on we would make contact with a certain farmer. That was it. He would give us some bags, and then we would come back the same way. "I looked at Isaac. He smiled: "Israel, we'll do just the opposite. Just follow me and you'll see." That was it. Isaac was an authority on this coming and going business, and there was no reason to question what he said. I nodded and extended my hand to let him know that I was at his command. The rest of the time we spent watching the kids wandering about. Isaac seemed to be interested in them. In the darkness their skinny figures looked like tassels moved by the wind. He patted my back. It was time to get out.

Just as we had planned, we went out the opposite way from what Matchstick had marked on the map. Isaac had figured the route beforehand. It was fast and easy. We went out behind the chapel where the Romanians

✤

conducted religious services. We got so close to the wall that the palms of our hands were covered with scratches, but it was worth it. There was almost no surveillance in this area, and it was very dark. Once we were past the wire fence it began to rain quite hard. I felt a pain in my joints and thought about arthritis, a pretty common disease among the inmates of Bershad. Isaac crawled for a while and I followed him into some bushes that offered some sense of security. We waited there for a bit, looking at the watchtowers. Everything was normal. The guards were busy playing cards and talking about women. In that sense all guards seemed to be alike. They usually passed the time talking and playing rather than standing guard. I remember that in Ladyzhin, just before we were deported, one of the beasts was saying to another: "Heinz, how much do you want to bet that I can kill a Jew without even aiming?" The other replied: "As much as you want, as long as you can kill him with your eyes closed, like I do." And he moved his machine gun just in front of my nose. He started laughing when he saw me walking away as fast as I could, with my head stuck between my shoulders. That day I thought that they could smell us, that they knew even the most minute details about us. But later I realized that the beasts and their slaves would probably not be able to distinguish their own mothers in a group of four people.

We walked through the countryside. Isaac motioned for me to stop in front of some trees that were losing their leaves. There were no houses in the vicinity. I still did not understand Isaac's plan very well. From inside his shirt he took out a huge sausage and two half-pound loaves of bread. He smiled: "We'll bring this as a proof that we made it. You're probably wondering why we had to leave

❧

the orphanage since we could have hidden anywhere? Because they blew the whistle on us. Hard Tooth doesn't like me. He told the Romanians we were planning to sneak out tonight. The way I figure, there wouldn't have been any guards along the route he suggested, to make us more confident. The farmer who was waiting for us is probably soaked by now, poor guy!" He laughed again. I could hardly understand him. He liked to speak in metaphors, like the prophets. He uprooted some plants. "This is what we found, right, Israel?"

Well, if that's what we had to say, fine! Isaac turned to me again. "The sausage and the bread? I stole them from a guard. But don't worry, I saw him steal them from the kitchen with the consent of the cook. So he can't say anything about it." I was still in awe of his style, his way of knowing and functioning. He put away the stuff again and we went back, not without filling up our pockets with bits of the plants.

When we got through the wire fence again, he stopped at the walls of the church. "Isaac, the sausage and the bread are for the little ones. We have to start feeding our army." He gave me his knife. I shrugged and followed him into the pavilion. We came in. Hard Tooth and his two friends looked at us with wide-open eyes. "Beat it," Isaac said. Matchstick looked like he was ready to make trouble, but Isaac pulled out a huge knife, probably also stolen from the kitchen. Even I was frightened by its size. The three boys turned pale and started to tremble. At a sign from Isaac they got up and started to leave. "If you say anything, you're dead, you shitty squealers!" Matchstick swallowed hard. His Adam's apple moved up and down his skinny neck. Canary wasn't able to whis-

❧

tle. I felt really good. I jabbed Hard Tooth with the tip of my knife to make him move faster

We pushed the three of them up against a corner of the wall outside. "I don't like your organization a bit, it's a piece of shit. Squealers are a disease to be wiped out like rats, and you three are rats. From now on, Israel and I are through with you. We can walk on our own feet. We don't need you. Stop shaking. I'm not going to slit your throats like a hen or a goose. Relax, your time hasn't come yet. But if I did eliminate you now, nobody would claim you and no one would care about three corpses up against the wire fence." The trio breathed a bit easier. Isaac went on. "But remember this: you don't play dirty tricks with the resistance, and if you do, you'll pay for it! That's the law. Oh, and here's something for you," he said, throwing them the plants we had pulled up outside of Bershad.

We went back into the pavilion and didn't see the three of them the rest of the night. The following day, after the required lineup and marching, we began selecting the kids who would make up our organization. We picked out five hungry children with huge eyes. Isaac studied them intently. I too looked them over, more impressed than interested. They looked as if they had just climbed out of a sewer. Their thin little bodies were filthy and covered with a dark crust. They cried from joy when we shared the bread and sausage with them. They ate fast, perhaps not wanting to wake up from what seemed to be a dream. They were eating! Isaac arranged a meeting for that afternoon. They agreed. It was the first step. We had to build up their confidence, make them realize that we had a chance of surviving the freezing nights of winter. We were going to survive in that tunnel of misery, inside the sewer, against all odds.

We ran into the three organization chiefs that morning. They pretended they had not seen us. Isaac nudged me with his elbow and whispered in my ear: "They believed our story that we belong to the resistance." I looked questioningly at him. He explained that there was an organization in Bershad that applied "an eye for eye" quite literally. "The Romanians themselves are afraid of them, not to mention the Germans. The resistance is a reality, Israel!" He talked emotionally, with bright eyes. Fighting Jews? I didn't understand the whole thing. How could it be, if I had seen thousands of people crossing the Bug with bowed heads, not uttering a word of protest?

Maybe Isaac was beginning to come down with the madness he so often talked about. "Soon I'll be in touch with them. They're beginning to see what I can do. How else do you think I found out about the squealers? You have to have contacts everywhere, people who know you because they owe you favors." Until then, because everything had happened so quickly, I hadn't wondered how Isaac had found out about the squealers. I didn't ask now. He would probably answer with metaphors or in ways difficult to understand. Isaac survived on his connections and his light touch. The thought of the resistance began to take shape in my mind, and I decided to dig deeper, since I did not feel safe in the pavilion. I decided not to leave Isaac's side. I had to learn and I could not waste such a teacher. That afternoon he assembled the children once again. He talked long and to the point, without elaborating on anything philosophical. The question was to survive at all costs. And the life Isaac

⚜

promised was centered around food, around the bread and butter we would get outside. And quietly, because otherwise—They agreed. From that day on Isaac began training them, teaching them how to steal from the kitchen, hide in the chapel, know all the ways to get outside. And the five responded as we had never imagined. They even began to bring Isaac coins from time to time. He never asked where they were from. The effect of that "otherwise—" had been grasped in its entirety: they would die with that acrid taste of hunger in their mouths if they did not do something about it. And while Isaac took care of our group, I was assigned to listen, to find out everything I could and store it in my memory.

I engraved in my mind every detail about the town, the people, the guards, and the sporadic but punctual arrival of beasts. I came and went. I began to know the sky, to know the signs that it was going to rain hard. That was the best time to get out. I learned how to lie easily, to make believe I was stupid. I did not "see" what the Romanians didn't want me to see. Nothing was noticed. When someone asked about my people, I answered that I didn't know anything. I invented explanations, making believe that I was nothing but a refugee who hoped to stay in Bershad for a few weeks. That's how I found out about the network of squealers and about the organization that protected anyone who came in with something of value.

I found out about the underground sexual commerce in the town. Some of the prostitutes gave me food. I looked so down-and-out that they were moved to shared their meager bread and butter with me. There were also some boys who served for the exclusive use of the officers. I had a well-defined status with them. I was their gofer. They trusted me because of the impression I conveyed.

And thus I won the confidence of the boys and girls. They talked freely in front of me, not hiding anything. And then I, showing an idiot's face, would begin to drool. They thought I was stupid, but that was my job, as Isaac's deputy

The information that I obtained this way I passed on to Isaac, who began to make plans for the five little boys. He knew about the weaknesses of this or that officer, about the valuables the guards were hoarding, the weapons they kept in certain places. And the ones who talked the most were the boys, confident of the brilliant future promised them by the officers who used them in their homosexual practices. From these poor souls I found out about some grenades that had not yet been accounted for. I immediately alerted Isaac. He put his five pupils in motion, and we appropriated eighteen grenades together with an instruction manual.

Around this time we had moved out of the pavilion run by Hard Tooth and taken over the space left by two boys who had died of dysentery. And in this new hole, where nobody suspected me, thinking I was an idiot and Isaac was crazy, we established our largest warehouse. Food and explosives were hidden in the same hole, under the straw that served as our mattresses.

I kept working, looking for arms and explosives. With these items, we would make our debut in the resistance. One of the girls, after sleeping with the driver of one of the beasts, told me that there were some machine guns in the trunk of the car, and she described them, going to great lengths to help me understand. It was a comfort for her to talk to me, because she was sure I couldn't understand anything, and thus she saw in me, the idiot, a way to vent her anguish, to justify her life, to explain that in order to survive you had to reach out to extremes imposed by the master. She showed me a card the Bershad authorities had given her in order to obtain certain foods that were prohibited to the others in the orphanage. I almost took it away from her. I wanted to engrave it in my mind. I found an excuse to leave, always drooling, to the place where Isaac was. I told him about the machine guns in the trunk of the beast's car. His eyes became so wide I thought they were going to pop out. Machine guns! That meant getting into the resistance through the front door! He disappeared, leaving me immersed in my own thoughts.

He went out quickly, probably in search of his protégés. There was no time to waste, so he quickly set in motion the first plan that occurred to him. We weren't there to ponder. They went without me because we had decided not to go into the town together. That way we couldn't both be killed at the same time. I stayed on the roof of our warehouse, perhaps looking like even more of an idiot and thinking about the wealth of information I had gathered from our young informers. I was trying to find a light in that tunnel of misery, in this darkness that sometimes put me on the fringe of madness. "Isaac, have you ever looked into the eyes of those poor girls who give themselves over to the utmost excesses, trusting in the future, desperately hoping they will continue to be the favorites of the slaves? Their eyes are dull, dry, isn't it so? And have you ever looked into the eyes of the boys who play the role of women in order to satisfy the aberrations of the slaves and the visiting beasts? They too are like liv-

❖

ing dead." I bit my lips thinking about this terrible world, comparing it with another system of annihilation, slow but efficient, with a far more sophisticated technique. I was learning too much, and therefore had to put my thoughts in order and remember everything. Once I joined the resistance I would have more than one reason to fight. I would fight for those who had been forced to cross to the other side of the Bug and for those who were being buried alive, taken in short steps to the grave. Isaac was right about madness, I could see it right there in that tunnel of misery that was the orphanage of Bershad.

I rubbed my hands and thought about my parents, those faraway figures who had remained at the Stone Cross, there in Ladyzhin, close to the graves brimming with our people. I looked at my torn boots, my ragged pants. I touched my face and took a deep breath. I wanted to make sure that I was alive. But was taking action again being alive? To be alive meant wandering around Bershad, measuring each post, the number of wire fences, the watchtowers and the faces of the guards. Did being alive mean seeing the emaciated bodies of boys my own age who could hardly stand on their feet and those with huge eyes, a sure sign of hunger and malnutrition, looking out, asking for hope, for a piece of bread and butter? Did they have parents? Hadn't they been born like plants on the swampy edge of a lake? Why was it that some, in order to survive, terrorized the weaker ones? I couldn't explain to myself why every little corner was an empire dominated by the "powerful" who exacted a price for their "protection." And only "idiots" and "madmen" like Isaac and me could escape from this. We had to pay for the children, otherwise they would not be left alone for a moment.

⚜

I looked around at the faces of some boys who never moved, who always sat quietly, waiting, trusting that the soup would get to them at the right time. They never moved, hardly ever spoke, they lived in their own circle, among the shadows of the pavilion and the straw that served them as a mattress. Perhaps they were already dead, and their quietness was the period that elapses between death and decay. I looked at them more closely, but I did not exist for their dull, completely defeated eyes.

A strong smell of dampness came up to my nostrils. It was to be expected—the rain never stopped, and the water was rotting the wood. I pondered my status as an idiot. If I kept playing this role, maybe I would eventually end up as the real thing. Wasn't I already an idiot? I thought about the daily shooting I had heard in Ladyzhin. Those nights and days of terrible anguish had now become routine. They were the price I had to pay in order to survive. I wondered what had happened to Canary. I hadn't seen him anywhere around town for several days. Perhaps the plague had gotten him and he was now in the infirmary or in that white house which I had not yet been able to enter. It wouldn't have surprised me if it were a "treatment" area like the one at Stone Cross.

Everything began to spin in my head, I felt it big, heavy, like a rock. My eyes fixed on the cracks in the ceiling, and once again I felt trapped among the slats of that railroad car that for twelve days had rolled along with us inside immersed in madness, screaming, and death. Isaac came back after about two hours. He was pale and sweaty. "They told you too much. There were only three machine guns, and we almost didn't make it. Two went down and I don't know what will happen. They'll probably kill them, but before they do, they'll make them talk, they'll break every bone in their bodies." He talked fast,

❖

afraid that at any moment the beasts and the slaves would be upon us. I shuddered and put my hands together in an attempt to gather strength.

"Two went down," he told me, "and they'll make them sing. They know how to do it. The beasts know their techniques too well, and the prisoners are too young not to loosen their tongues. Everything is lost. This card is going to cost us everything we've gained up to now. " In the meantime Isaac took out the three guns from a huge sack and put them away in the hole underneath us. I saw him fondle one of the machine guns. "They're not going to take me alive, and they won't take you either. Better to make them kill us first. Do you understand?" His last words were almost a scream, a voice clamoring for hope, a future, a bit of this life that had once again became mired in the coldness of waiting and uncertainty. He put everything away, covering it well with straw. Including a box of ammunition that he had carried in his underwear. "We'll let them kill us," I replied with conviction. I didn't intend to be caught with my hands raised in surrender. The card was to be played to the end, with the loser sharing his luck with the grim reaper.

I almost fainted when I saw a couple of boys hanging from their thumbs from a post in the center of the Bershad market square. Their faces covered with bruises and there was blood coming out from the corners of their mouths. They were hanging like pieces of meat on a hook in a butcher shop. Their eyes, which had shined when they gulped down the piece of bread and butter, were so swollen they were almost closed. A loudspeaker began blasting orders. "Everyone line up in the square. Everyone is to line up in the square." Immediately the slaves lunged at us and hitting us with the butts of their guns took us to where the boys were hanging. When they had us lined up and looking at the tortured boys, a short officer with a comical look strutted in front of us, probably to show the beasts that he was a good slave, brandishing a small whip. He grimaced and swore after every word: "Pigs, is that how you repay the hospitality we have given you? Do you see that pair of bastards hanging there? They are murderers, worms of the worst kind. In cahoots with others, they have stolen the guns that were in the car of the marshal who is honoring us with his presence. They have stolen the war possessions of this honorable representative of the glorious Reich. And those murderers, that pair of bastards, will confess in front of you the names of the other members of their gang. We already know who they are, but we want their accomplices to give them away, to teach you a lesson." He calmed down a bit. I felt the earth open under my boots. Isaac looked on impassively, showing no sign of emotion on his face. The officer resumed: "Of course, if the accomplices decide to turn themselves in, their lives will be spared and those two hanging there will be tried for robbery—" He was interrupted by one of the boys hanging from the post: "There are no accomplices. We didn't steal anything."

The slaves went up to the boy and broke his legs with blows from the butts of their rifles. But he kept on screaming: "There are no accomplices. It isn't true!" They kicked him in the head and left him unconscious. Then the other boy spit at the SS men, yelling: "You murderer sons of bitches!" The beast who caught the spit on his face grabbed the boy's torso and pulled downwards. The boy bit his lips. We watched silently, not moving. The SS yanked the boy's body. The poor kid's thumbs turned

❖

blue and then separated from the rest of his body, stuck to the rope like a couple of knots. Crazed by the out-pouring of blood, the beast took his bayonet and slashed the boy's wrists while shouting: "Murderer!" And from the mouth of this little boy not a sound came out, he simply bit his lips until they tore due to his unbearable pain.

Acting on orders, the slaves kicked and beat the boy. He kept bleeding. The SS man used his bayonet again, this time chopping his feet, which had curled up in pain. We swallowed in silence, resisting an impulse to jump on these rats. Later he cut the knees and the elbows, and whatever remained of the members. In this orgy of blood, one of the slaves used the point of his knife to gouge out the eyes of this bloody mass that every once in a while still moved. The SS officer took his pistol and with one shot finished off the minimal life that remained on the wet ground on this autumn afternoon.

The boy, in his effort not to scream, had bitten off his own tongue, and a piece of it was hanging over his chin. When they turned to the other boy, thinking they'd be able to make him talk after what he had seen, they dis-covered that his throat had been slit from side to side. Probably someone from the resistance had done it. In order to spare him a horrible death, he had taken advan-tage of the boy's unconsciousness to cut his throat. A Romanian soldier could have been the culprit. There were some members of the resistance among the troops. The slaves were beginning to become aware of their mis-erable condition.

They gave orders to lock us up until they found the guns. Isaac and I sat in our corner waiting. The boys whose quietness I often watched did not move either. It seemed to me that they were no longer able to think and were unaware of the infanticide that had just been committed. They just kept waiting, their eyes fixed on a distant point, their hands on their skinny knees and a strange expression on their faces. When I least expected it, while pondering the situation, they got up and opened the door of the pavilion. I saw them disappear. Less than five minutes later I heard a terrible explosion. We all shuddered and an intense cold filled my body. Isaac wiped away the sweat that had started to run down his forehead. We waited, me with my idiot's face and drooling. Isaac talking to himself. We didn't want to be found asleep or shivering when the beasts and their slaves got to our quarters.

It was the moment to play a difficult role, gambling with the card that a pair of martyred children had spoiled for us. We could hear the steps of the troops outside. They screamed, swore, and gave orders. Someone, perhaps a frightened officer, yelled out: "They are terrorists!"

After two days of being locked up and a few more superficial searches, since the Romanians were not as methodical as the Germans, they let us go. We had to be more careful now. After putting all our things in order again, Isaac said: "Israel, go back to what you were doing, I need information. Four of the grenades have disappeared and I don't like that." I didn't like it either. It meant that someone knew about our hiding place. I saw myself hanging from my thumbs like our comrades. I went back, again as an "idiot," to the rooms of the boys and girls who satisfied the sexual appetites of the officers. They received me with some disdain, convinced that I had come for the piece of bread that every once in a while they would give me. A girl pointed to a broken comb and asked me to comb her hair. I started to do it, moving

❧

my hands clumsily in order to gain time and be able to eavesdrop on the conversation she was having with her friend. "Did you see? The accomplices of those two boys committed suicide. The sergeant who slept with me last night told me that the terrorists, knowing they were going to be caught and tortured, blew themselves up with Molotov cocktails and sticks of dynamite. At the same time they blew up the guns they had stolen from the German's car. I don't know what they looked like. They say that it was impossible to recognize them." I began to put things together. Those boys who never moved were the ones who stole the grenades. They had probably planned it a long while before and took advantage of this opportunity to throw the investigators off. They knew what Isaac and I were doing, but did not turn us in. I felt an intense desire to live for them too, for those boys who gave up their lives in order to allay any suspicions about those of us who were putting together an arsenal in order to join the resistance.

But—and this question drilled my brain—why suicide, that escape from life without taking action? The fight was to survive, not to die without gambling on the highest card. I felt that the walls of this tunnel of misery were sticking to my skin and trying to suffocate me. Deaths, suicides, massacres, prostitution in its vilest form, hungry children, rabid slaves, bloody beasts. Madness echoed in every corner of my brain.

What if I was already mad? Didn't you have to be crazy to survive in such a world? Me, a child myself, combing the hair of a girl internally destroyed who only wanted to live in the present time. A girl who lent herself to the vilest demands for a few sardines and a piece of white bread. My guts froze when I thought: "What if she's

❧

an escapee from one of the graves, a dead girl who has just risen in order to get a couple of days of life that are still owing to her?" My hands trembled and she demanded: "What is it, boy, is this the first time you ever touched a woman's head?" I restrained myself from screaming that she was not a woman, that she was still a girl like so many others I had seen holding rag dolls in their arms.

I kept quiet, but my mind was still turning. I left without asking for the piece of bread they usually gave me. That day I wandered around the town. I was drowning inside that sewer. I thought about death, about being tortured, about the piece of tongue hanging from the chin of the boy who did not want to talk. He had a right to trade his life for ours, but he hadn't done it.

He chose to swallow his words, to forget he knew us. I could still see his mutilated body and his deformed face. That little boy, just like his partner, knew that the resistance was the way ,and they knew that it was a way through which blood and terror, massacre and genocide ran every day. The price exacted for our survival was going up. They were charging us too much for feeling cold and fear, hunger and terror.

I felt old. I carried too many lives inside me. The obligation to live for them. Walking about in the orphanage I fed my desire for revenge, I filled my brain with an only thought: "They will have to pay for what they did!"

Isaac and his group never stopped. I kept passing on information. They left Bershad and came back with some food and dried fruit. Winter was harsher than ever.

It was snowing all the time, but we did not stop. We were committed to endure, to live in order to take our revenge for what they were doing to us. The wire fences were covered with snow, and the guards remained in the

❖

sentry boxes. I looked at them, swallowed bitterly, and went on toward the zone of the "special ones." Everything, even the stones, was engraved in my mind. The wire fence reflected in my retina and from there went to my brain. Nothing went unused, everything had a purpose. Our arsenal grew, and so did our group. Finally, because of the many operations we were carrying out, a fellow from the resistance got in touch with Isaac and me. We explained what we were doing, but kept some things to ourselves, of course. He marveled at our method for getting out and listened very carefully to everything we told him. He almost fell on his face when Isaac showed him one of the grenades we had hidden under the floor where we slept. The man examined it as if what he had in his hands was a huge diamond. He looked at Isaac questioningly. "I know where you can get these," Isaac told him teasingly.

The man, knowing he wouldn't get any more information from us unless he clarified our situation with the resistance, nodded: "All right. I'll tell them and we'll see what we can do. It's all right, boys." He looked at a couple of boys who were watching him attentively. "Listen, you'd better be careful. Those kids can sometimes be dangerous. What are you doing, you scoundrels!" he yelled. Isaac reprimanded him. "Don't offend them, they're my bodyguards." The man from the resistance opened up his eyes. How could those children be the ones who came in and out of Bershad, the ones who stole ammunition and passed on information to the partisans? Surprise showed in his long face. Finally he had no alternative but to smile and lower his head in respect. "Pardon me, comrades," he said to them. The children remained in place without blinking. The man, for he was

⚜

fourteen years old and for us that was already older, understood very well that our group functioned and didn't beat around the bush like many others.

He said he would contact Isaac within three days. "Imagine if we show him the machine guns, he may die of fright," said Isaac laughing. I scratched my face and asked: "Can we trust him?" Isaac looked at the tip of his boots and said: "He was the one who warned me the first time we went out. I know him. He's a nice guy. Sometimes he talks about Palestine and the obligation we Jews have to go there. He talks about a country for the Jews and says that there are many there planting seeds and that they're waiting for us to help them harvest. He's a good guy." I shrugged. I only accepted.

Our group kept on working, but the situation became more and more unbearable. The slaves were aware of our outings and demanded more than we were able to give them. We had to plan things differently. Isaac was trying to find a way out that the guards or "protectors" could not interfere with. Everybody had to be paid off, and the rope was getting tighter every time. in the zone of the "special ones" a layer of silence started to form. One suspected the other. Obviously the informers were already doing harm in this area. The girls were careful not to talk about delicate things, or to show the bills and coins they had taken from their lovers. The hand of terror had already reached this front, which up to now had remained outside. I had to increase my foolishness in order to maintain my role of idiot.

Some shouted at me, some boys even hit me, but I never said a word, with my ears wide open for any information I could gather. I realized that they were deporting people assigned to that section. They were taken to the

❖

east. Some boys and girls had been sent away in the train
that left Bershad every Monday for an unknown destination. I could imagine the destination. The slaves and the
beasts had to get rid of people who already knew too
much. I found out through Isaac about the advance of
the Red troops, and the beasts were accelerating the
process of extermination. They did not want to leave any
witnesses. Here in Bershad there was human material to
be annihilated. Their biggest victims were the boys and
girls forced to prostitute themselves in order to satisfy
the degenerate appetites of the officers. As the Russians
drew closer, and the partisans became ever more daring,
the slaves and the beasts started to plan the extermination of what later would be their accusers, those boys
they had violated and stripped of all dignity, of their ability to dream, of carving a future for themselves, without
being branded, traumatized, dead while alive, as they
were now. Thus the lack of trust, the fear of talking, the
fear of being deported. In their misery they began to
understand the necessity of surviving, of entering the
game of the concealed card. And me, without being able
to say anything, with the words dancing in my mouth.
How could I speak, if I was an idiot, and idiots don't do
anything but obey in order to get a bit of bread and butter? If I talked, if I let myself be known, I would never get
out of the area. I was a witness to all of them, knew a lot
of their stories. They would probably think I was an
informer. No, I couldn't say anything. I had to continue
with my job of listening without giving a clue, of seeing
without blinking, of not seeing what they were hiding. It
was hard to gather information in this state of affairs,
but there was always something to find out, even if it was
a certain document, the number of soldiers who would

❖

come in at a certain date, the passions of the officers, their ways of operating, things that would be of vital importance to the chiefs of the internal resistance in Bershad.

In this tunnel of misery I was collecting phrases, words, material for the trial that later, when the war was over, if it ever ended, the beasts and the slaves would have to face. I put away everything in my memory in a very precise way. In the evenings. I told Isaac what I had heard without omitting a single detail. Everything had a value, an incalculable price.

The fellow from the resistance came again. He looked us over, from head to toe. He made sure there was nobody else around, aside from Isaac's bodyguards. Then, a little more reassured he said: "Tomorrow you will talk to the chief. He is interested in your work. Eight o'clock at the latrines." He didn't say any more. He left the way he had come, from one moment to the next. He surely had to avoid some guards, informers, or beasts.

At that time, the harshest of the winter, everything was very complicated. Every day they caught someone who was trying to escape from Bershad in search of a bit of food. Accusations were the order of the day. Some talked under torture, others because of fear, the rest because they were squealers. The squealers, for every item of information, received a cup of hot soup and half a carrot. That was the price they had put on our heads. It was unsettling to know that the Monday train already had more cars. This indicated that east or west, it didn't matter. Once deported, they were going straight to the grave. Some of us had already died of typhus or cold.

Others did not come back. They were probably caught by wolves, or got lost in the snow, or maybe just went

✤

mad. We started to consume what we had stored away under the floor. The following day Isaac went to a meeting at the latrines. I, in the meantime, went to the infirmary. I knew the building from the outside and knew that there was a small opening in one of its walls. I had to go because one of the boys, one of the smartest and most resourceful of them, was running a fever, which was an indication of a coming death from typhus. I went outside and walked around a few times so they would think I was trying to warm up. Then, avoiding the surveillance, I went in through the small opening. I slid through the hallway and went to the pharmacy. There a woman with a huge belly and thick glasses was passing the time reading. However, she noticed me. I thought I was finished lost and waited for her to start screaming. She was surprised, perhaps thinking that I was one of the characters in the book. I smiled and put my hands in my pockets to take out a few wrinkled bills.

This surprised her even more. I took advantage of the situation and said: "A friend is running a fever. Here's the money for you to give me something that will help him." I threw the bills on a table and put out my hand out for her to give me the medicine. I put my hand in my pocket once again, but this time looking for my knife. If she screamed I would have to slit her throat. I was inside and was not going to let them get me. I waited. She took out a bottle and a few pills and gave them to me as she took the money and put it inside her bra.

I ran through the hallway, got out through the hole, and went back to the orphanage. I was trembling from fright and cold. I had just done a desperate thing, but it had turned out all right. The nurse should have

❖

screamed, but she didn't. I didn't know why. The money was probably a good reason. Everybody liked to get a few bills, especially if they didn't have to work for it. I got my money from the zone of the "special ones." They stole it during the night and I stole it in the daytime. They were not going to suspect the idiot. Those who were succumbing to the slaves outside needed it more. The "special ones" had heating in their rooms, we had typhus. Survival was based on speed, on mental agility, on not thinking twice before taking the first step.

I went to the sick boy and gave him a few sips of the bottle I had gotten at the infirmary. The boy, who was about seven, swallowed with some difficulty. He coughed constantly. I stayed by his side, constantly thinking, feeling the stings that assaulted my brain. "Be on your toes, Israel, any wrong move and you'll fall like the leaves in autumn. Keep quiet, move silently, watch and don't talk. Your memory has to be on the alert, it's your only document. Things don't look good. The tunnel is getting narrower. The defense brigade is powerless. They are forced to watch us in order not to die. They will survive in their own way. The only ones who are doing anything are the resistance, and Isaac is in touch with them. Work hard, endure, avoid the typhus, live for those who went to the other shore of the Bug. You have a commitment to live for those who remained at Stone Cross, to keep alive the memory of your mother's anguished look. Come on, Israel, you can't fail."

I went out again. I was nervous. Haunted by images of the deported, of the little prostitutes who sold themselves for one more day or life, of those boys who lived in their miserable world agreeing to the whims of the cor-

❖

rupt officials. I thought I saw them in the frost that covered every surface, in the lead gray of the sky, and among the wire fences.

Finally, Isaac emerged from the latrine. He looked serious, with his hands in the pockets of his miserable jacket. We looked at each other and signaled to meet at the orphanage to iron out the details. He went his way and I went mine. We could not establish contact in the open field. A conversation between an "idiot" and a "madman" had to arouse suspicion. And the guards, though as drunk as sailors, never took their eyes off us. They knew that in each one of us there was a witness, a member of the resistance. They were afraid, the promises of the beasts vanished in the face of the Soviet advance and the continuous partisan attacks. The situation was turning ugly for the slaves and the SS.

When we met, Isaac explained what we would be doing in the resistance. "We will start as soldiers. For now we have to watch what the guards do and when they change shifts. With your trained mind, you will not fail. I know it." He was excited, and talked gesticulating and happy. I was also excited, knowing that I was on my way out of that tunnel of misery. And I would come out alive, in memory of the dead, whether the ones in the graves or the walking dead in the zone of the "special ones." I was going to survive, to fight for something concrete, freedom!

The boy I had given the medicine to was also starting to smile, he was regaining the strength to begin his way to freedom. Outside, the snow never stopped for a minute. It fell, covering the ground and the roofs, filling every space with cold, but its frozen hand did not reach our burning feelings. The resistance! The resistance was the door that was opening to let us see the sun!

❖

8

Good-bye to a Friend

It's been a week since Isaac told me that we have joined the resistance. So far, however, we haven't done anything. Nothing has happened. Apparently some obstacles have come up and we have to be careful. One false move and we'll die with our tongues stuck to the roof of our mouths. This is what I think about as I sit in a corner of the room looking for a bit of warmth. The snow hasn't stopped and the boy is still coughing.

I tried to go back to the infirmary, but there are too many slaves around. The deportations are continuing in the zone of the "special ones." I have to be careful not to go there too often. No one is safe, not even an idiot. Things are complicated now. Getting in and out of Bershad isn't as easy as it used to be. The slaves, probably because of a Nazi order, keep detaining the kids who are trying to get to the outskirts.

Our group has started to fall apart. Some are afraid, others are sick and dispirited. It doesn't do any good to tell them that we have to survive any way we can. They don't understand. Day by day their eyes become huge, impenetrable lakes. The constant detentions and the rumors about the terrible tortures to which some of the transgressors are subjected are getting to everyone who is compromised in some kind of movement.

We can't stop them. We ourselves feel the same way. And so they withdraw into their corners, hands in their pockets, waiting for death the way someone else might wait for dawn.

We're getting weaker. Small groups can't survive very long. The leaders of the "organization" were right about that. And our guys walk away telling us that they can't do anything inside or outside of Bershad. Even outside things are more dangerous now. The farmers, in this harsh winter, don't think twice about stealing everything we have and then turning us in to the beasts. They know that for every Jewish child they turn in outside of Bershad they will get a few loaves of bread and a good-sized package of sugar. They hunt us the same way they hunt the rabbits that cross the fields. We have become valuable commodities for their subsistence. In our corners we rationalize the acts of those who give up. They probably want to die in peace, or maybe they have some private hope deep in their hearts. In the tunnel everyone grabs at even a shadow that shows an air of confidence. But we know that they won't talk. When they go, they leave all their memories with us. They immediately forget that they ever knew us. They know their silence will help our survival. They leave now that we need them so. The one who was coughing is burning with fever. I have put some compresses of snow on his forehead, but he's not getting better. He has been delirious for a while. He mentions his mother, talks about flowers and a small turtle walking on top of a mound of sand. He says his mother opened her head with a frying pan, that the blood flowed and he caught it in his hands and gave it to her to drink again. Sometimes he keeps quiet and sweat covers his face, which every moment turns redder.

⚜

Isaac has covered him with the straw from his mattress, but he keeps trembling. He coughs and wheezes. Some look at him without understanding, others look at him thinking that soon it will be their turn. This winter is filling us with cold inside, turning us into people who wait in misery. To survive is almost impossible. The slaves are killing us in their own way. They allow the cold to kill our hopes, and when that happens you die of typhus or tuberculosis. It's so easy. All you have to do is wait, and eventually your fingers turn black and break. Many have been eaten up by gangrene, and others have died of tetanus. I look at my coughing friend and can't accept the idea of dying just like that. I rub my hands forcefully and look for a way, for a breath of life, that will stop that fever from wreaking havoc in that skinny, trembling body. The fever goes up, sweat drenches his face and his neck. His eyes are glassy and he goes back to his delirium, his speech ever more garbled. A fetid smell comes from the place where we have laid him down. A voice from the back says: "Leave him alone, he's rotting away, and no one likes to be seen in his own rot." His body trembles and his fists are clenched. He tries to smile, but the smile turns into a grimace that shows a row of yellow teeth. His wheezing has turned into hoarse, quiet breathing. We watch as he struggles to swallow a bit of damp air.

The winter claims many victims in Bershad, and the orphanage pays a price. There are too many orphans, and the fewer mouths to feed the better. His eyes open, his face turns blue, he is very still. Isaac and I look at each other, the others stay put. He's dead. He died a few feet from the infirmary; a few feet from that fat lady who only takes care of sick people in summer or early fall.

❖

During the winter she does not fall for "pranks." "Many of them only want to come in to warm up, taking the place away from a someone who is really sick," I heard her say one day. I look at my friend. He seems asleep. He's not sweating any more and hardly expels a slight odor. I get up. It is obligatory to inform the authorities when someone dies in the barracks. I put my hands in my pockets and face the cold air that hits my face, hurting my nose and my ears. I walk fast, trying to warm up. My boots dig into the snow, and it feels as if I will never reach the office.

I glance at the same wire fences. The watchtowers are in the same place. Some slaves, wrapped in woolen greatcoats and armed with machine guns, look at me. I stick my head in between my shoulders and pretend that I'm wearing a scarf.

To defeat the cold you have to imagine warmth, pretend you're walking on a fire, and breathe convinced you're drinking hot soup. My fingers are numb. No, they've only gone to sleep. You see that stuff that looks like snow? It's the hot, dry sand of the desert. That's why it's so hard to walk. Everybody knows that it's not easy to walk on sand. If you're going to report a death, don't cry. They enjoy seeing people cry. You will say, "Sir, someone in our room is gone." But how to avoid the cold and the numbing of the fingers?

Ideas swirl around in my head and my feet hurt. I feel as if someone is pricking my ankles with a needle. The skin of my feet sticks to the leather of the shoes. I laugh, thinking about my socks. There's no room for one more hole.

I get to the office. One of the slaves looks me over. The other one points his gun at me. They don't trust anyone.

⚜

Anyone could bring in a bomb and throw it in the face of the man sitting behind the desk, that pig who does nothing but put checkmarks next to names. I go in. They stop me after a few steps. The man is drinking some hot tea. He looks me up and down. He sticks out his chin and asks: "Well?" My fingers are still numb. I would give part of my life for a sip of that tea, but they would kill you for a single drop. "Sir, someone in the barracks died of the plague." The man furrows his forehead: "The plague? You're crazy. Here people die from heart failure, from stroke, from pneumonia if it's summer. Up to now nobody has died of the plague, do you understand? Nobody! Remember that! " I bite my lower lip. "Well, he died of a cold heart." I'm furious. The pig writes something down in a yellow folder. He smiles: "No need to dramatize. If you had just said heart it would have been enough. How dare you talk about the cold! Do you know what cold is? When I was little I felt real cold." And he told me about a childhood that anyone in the orphanage would have wanted. Finally, but not before I had agreed with every word pronounced by his mouth with its three gold teeth, I was able to leave. He asked for more hot tea in order to deal with the "complications" of his job.

Once again in the snow—they searched me just in case I might have stolen anything. The watchtowers with their drunken guards, the swearing slaves, the roofs of the houses completely covered by snow. The frost and the hail together with the wind that keeps beating against the faces of those of us who are outside. But we have to survive, imagine, live within the possibilities of the tunnel.

We didn't know what the slaves did with the body. Nobody knew. They came for it, put it in a stretcher, and

⚜

that was the end! Everyone looking somewhere else,
away from where the body had been. We were living in
death and were afraid of contagion!

Isaac has turned more introverted than usual, and
when he talks it is in a peculiar way. "Before this is over
they're going to gobble us up. We're their favorite dish
and they're hungry."

We are afraid of them and of ourselves. I saw a bird
that was unable to land on the roof of the watchtower.
They shot him and the bird disappeared in the sky. Such
are the memories of those who live near Bershad. They
try to remember, but at the first noise they don't remember anything or know about anyone. "Isaac, do you know
why the kid who died was delirious? Because he didn't
want to know that he was here. He was looking back at
his turtle, his mother's blood, and the flowers and sand
in his garden. Here we all want to live outside, we are living somewhere else. Do you see the way they're starting?
Everyone is looking for something. A message, anything.
Others live because of a commitment. Mordechai has an
old letter from his brother. Tell him to read it to you." I
turned: "Hey Mor, show your brother's letter to Israel."
Mordechai, a thin boy with big hands dragged himself
over to us. He had been limping for several days—they
say because he had jumped over the chapel wall. Nobody
asked him, but we were sure that he had drunk a good
part of the wine they keep there for the religious ceremonies. When he heard steps he got scared and had to
jump. He looked at me. Isaac told him to read the letter.
Mordechai took it out and spit on his fingers. He had that
habit. Probably the only thing he had left.

To listen was a way to pass the time and think about
ways to leave the camp. He read slowly.

⚜

"Dear parents: Even if the sky were made of paper and all the seas were made of ink, I could not describe my suffering to you and everything I see around me. The camp is in a clearing. They take us out early every morning to work in the forest. My feet are bleeding because they have taken away our shoes—we work almost all day without food, and at night we sleep on the floor. (They have also taken away our covers.) Every night drunken soldiers hit us with wooden clubs, and my body is black and blue like a piece of burned wood. Sometimes they throw a raw carrot at us, or a beet, and it is a shame how we fight each other even for a bit of a leaf. A boy escaped the other day, and they made us stand in line and shot one out of five. I was the fifth one, but I know that I won't come out alive. I say goodbye to all of you. My dear mother, father, brothers and sisters, and I cry.—Hayim."

I thought about Ladyzhin, my parents, and the graves they filled up with those who had been forced to go to the other side of the Bug. Mordechai put away the letter and snorted like a tired horse. Isaac nodded. "I need to see you after the soup."

I thought a long time about Mordechai. About his letter and those eyes that never stopped darting about, even for a second, while he read what his brother had left him, that piece of paper committing him to live in his name and that of his family. His parents had died in an air raid, before the beasts started to deport us, scattering us around the land. I had never paid much attention to him. I lived in my world, and he lived in his. And now, through Isaac, I had come to know part of Mordechai's world, to know that he endured, he survived, because of a yellowing letter that he kept inside his jacket.

After eating a greasy soup that was too salty, I went

⚜

to meet Isaac. At first it seemed strange that he hadn't told me anything about his plans these last few days. But I waited. That was his style. We met by the latrines. He made sure there was nobody suspicious around and watched carefully while he cleaned off the grease that had collected around his mouth. The cold soup had turned my stomach, but I kept living, waiting for Isaac's words. Mordechai looked like a pole stuck on the floor. His could have been mistaken for a body that had died standing up. He looked without saying anything, and hardly breathed. Isaac said: "Let's get started. Tomorrow at dawn we're going to join up with Mordechai's people. We're going to blow up one of the watchtowers in Bershad. But first we must place the explosives and get out of here. After the explosion we come back the opposite of the way we left. The Romanians and the Germans won't suspect us, they'll never believe that the orphans of Bershad have taken to blowing up watchtowers in their spare time. They will think it was the Russian partisans. That will frighten them. And what does this have to do with us? It's very simple. A second bomb will explode seconds later in the infirmary. Then we'll rush in and take the medicines we need. The rest we'll blow up with grenades. The partisans have planned everything. Of course that doesn't mean they won't suspect us. For now, we three know each other and I know two more. We operate in threes, that way nobody will be able to give too much about the resistance, in case one of us has to talk. Our mission is to set up the explosives, get out of the orphanage, and come back the opposite way. We get to the pavilion and that's the end. The rest is up to other brigades. And you, Mordechai, be careful." He nodded. The shadow moved in the dark and smiled, saying:

⚜

"Relax, I know what I'm doing, and the dynamite is not wet." I opened my eyes in wonder. "Was Mordechai another Isaac? One was just like the other.

We agreed to meet at dawn. Isaac would let me know my role. Mordechai got lost in the shadows, always at the same pace, with his head down. In our corner, while I counted the bits of straw on my knee, Isaac started to talk. For once he didn't seem to care whether anyone was listening. "That Mordechai is a good guy. Looking at him it's hard to tell that he's an expert on explosives. No one knows how he learned, but he'd be able to pass the hardest test. Many times he has gotten out of Bershad and worked with the underground. They give him some food and then he comes back. They say he's waiting for a sister who is still alive and wandering somewhere. That's why he hasn't left. Oh, your assignment for tomorrow. You know all the ins and outs of the town and ways that even I don't know about. The information you keep in your head will be a point of reference for when they put the explosives at the base of the watchtower. Mordechai will place them and you have to memorize everything the guards do. A look down and we're lost. You'll be our antenna. Mordechai will act according to your intuition. My role has to do with getting out of and into the orphanage. Everything will be fine. " And he gave me a piece of dark bread with butter, which, even though it was hard and bitter, tasted wonderful. Where had he gotten it? Only the devil would know.

We had already gotten used to not asking about the daily happenings. What was important was effect, not cause. We survived and that had to be enough. I closed my eyes to face the ghosts that haunted me whenever I sat in the dark. But now everything seemed different. A

❧

bunch of circles tried to meet at a certain point that moved in a spiral projecting inside my ears, making me go into a distorted dimension. I seemed to be screaming, calling for my parents, and embracing a maternal figure, thrown at an immense speed against a wall that kept moving away from me. It was a vertiginous game that filled me with panic. It must be the sublimation of all my fears of the last few days, the product of the long wait to join the resistance. I thought that I was awake and the figures of the dead of the orphanage were calling for revenge. I couldn't be sure whether I was dreaming or a victim of the fever or simply crazy. I was used to living under the diverse aspects that the beasts and the slaves had forced me to. I could change my personality with the wink of an eye.

I needed to endure in order to survive. But tomorrow at dawn I was betting an important hand . To be part of the resistance was like therapy. I needed action so as not to let myself be taken over by anguish. I had seen many go mad, talking to a stone and then hitting their heads with it in an attempt to kill themselves.

In the resistance I would drown everything that now depressed my spirit. I was going to let out the interior world that turned in my insides, that hurt my stomach when I found myself incapable of acting, like when I saw that man in the office drinking a cup of hot tea. At my age I had no understanding of ideologies. I had no idea of what the Russians or the partisans stood for. All I knew was that they were advancing, making headway in a bloody war and trying to vanquish the beasts and the slaves. But what were their intentions toward us? I held men in uniform on a value scale. They were murderers. I had seen men in uniforms massacring people, taking children from the arms of their mothers to kill them in their presence. No, I didn't know anything about Russians or partisans. I was only aware of one thing: the ones who lived, who survived, were members of the resistance. Those of us who had a debt to collect joined the resistance. And I had plenty to collect. The dead in the graves on the other side of the river Bug reminded me that I had to act. And I did, I do, and I plan to keep on doing. I was thinking about my people, just like Mordechai was thinking about his, and God knows what Isaac was thinking about, although, I suppose, the same thing. In matters of survival he was the spirit that did not let us get down, the force that turned into deeds.

I woke up in the middle of the darkness. The cold went through my bones, and I had to move my legs to get the stiffness out. Isaac grunted and yawned. He showed me a grenade and told me how to activate it. It was easy. All you had to do was remove the pin, wait a few seconds, and throw it. It would explode almost immediately, belching rubble left and right. He whispered in my ear: "If you get caught, activate it and put it inside your jacket. You'll be blown up fast, before they can recognize the body. Mordechai already has his." My blood curdled.

The placement of the explosives got mixed up in my head. There were only two alternatives: either you lived or you died. No putting your hands up to say, "I'm turning myself in!" I had looked at all the possibilities except suicide. If they caught me, how could I answer the call of those who had been executed in Ladyzhin? I kept quiet. I needed to think with all the faculties that still remained in my brain. "To survive while you're placing a bomb under a watchtower is pretty complicated," I thought. "Israel, you're going to take a big step. You're going to

⚜

gamble more than what you have. And after all this, what's the resistance giving you? But is it fair that the beasts and the slaves keep doing what they want to us? Is it worth it to wait for death, seeing how others are being killed? Isn't it sometimes necessary to go to one extreme in order to know the other? You have been gambling from the beginning, so what difference does it make whether you die today or tomorrow when before, you too could have been selected to cross to the other side of the Bug. And when they took you away from your parents and forced you to get on the truck, weren't you already condemned to death? It's the same thing, Israel, in a little while you'll be in a similar situation. You were condemned to die from the outset. Since then you've done nothing but escape, and now you're going to do the same. Get ready. Hold the grenade without fear, look for your instinct not to fail you. If you come out all right, won't it be a battle that you win, one more step toward your victory over those who have haunted you, making you pretend to be a fearful, stammering idiot? This is your war too, and you're part of the army of the resistance. By fighting back you'll be shouting loud and clear that you're alive, that those in the graves, your parents, are still alive."

I shook my head. Hundreds of ideas went around. Everything revolved around survival, living to the fullest, expressing myself. First the deeds and later the questions. Didn't the beasts also act that way? I touched the grenade in the darkness. It was cold. Who would think that something so small could cause such damage, that it could blow up a whole structure? This gave me an idea. I could be like the grenade, small but deadly. I started to understand the value my deeds had for the leaders of the

❖

resistance. I felt more confident. All my faculties were honed to the point that I heard the snow fall. The breathing of those who slept came to me like a huge murmur that screamed out: "Act!" I stroked the grenade as if it were one of those sweet apples my grandfather used to give me on the farm. I felt it part of me.

And while I thought, I dreamed or came back to reality, I don't know which. Mordechai came over, slapped my thigh, and indicated that it was time to get moving. We got up slowly, without making noise, crawling to the door, very close to the cold walls of the barracks. Isaac opened the door a bit, looked around, and signaled for us to get out. The searchlights were moving around without any direction. The guards were probably drunk. With the image of the approaching Red Army in their heads, they did nothing but look for excuses to get away, and those who couldn't, escaped through alcohol. They looked, at all costs, to avoid the reality that was taking shape. The Russians had defeated the Germans at Stalingrad, and their advance resonated in every corner of Ukraine.

We went out. The first impact was like an electric current through the spine. A frozen wind was blowing. We moved slowly to the end of the exterior wall. I stroked the grenade, and that gave me renewed strength. Isaac ran into a small dark alley. We did the same. About forty meters away were the columns that supported the watchtower. I opened my eyes wide. The plan was starting now and every detail was vital. The position of the guard, the crossing of the searchlights. We had to be alert to every sound, with our ears ready to pick up the faraway voices of those they were probably executing somewhere in this Europe stamped on by the black boots of the beasts. At first my eyes burned, but I had to cry in silence. It was-

⚜

n't the time to rub your eyes. A missed second and I could miss some important detail that later might turn expensive. I looked up and saw the dark figure of the slave moving in his post, with the strap of his machine gun hanging from his shoulder. He was moving to get some warmth, walking from side to side.

When I saw the searchlights going to the other side, I ran out. I moved fast, always looking at the man in the watchtower and the direction of the searchlights. But we had to stop constantly, burrow into the snow and cover ourselves with it. It was the only way to avoid the white light that illuminated every inch of the orphanage. It took us half an hour to advance fifty meters.

Finally we got to the base of the watchtower. There, a bit more secure, since the lights did not reach that point, Mordechai took out the sticks of dynamite and with amazing speed, since our hands were still numb, he tied the charge to the posts and then connected the cable. In the meantime, Isaac cut a hole in the wire fence. It was still snowing, which was to our advantage. But at the same time the cold pierced us like a knife. Once Mordechai finished we didn't wait a second to get out through the hole Isaac had made. We ran as fast as we could, without the man at the watchtower even noticing us. He had fallen asleep at his post, trusting that his partner in the other tower would cover for him.

As we ran into the field, Mordechai ran out the cable he had tied to the sticks of dynamite. Isaac made us stop at a certain point. "Mor, is everything ready?" Mordechai nodded. He turned to me. "Israel, have you decided yet where we'll be going back in?" I too nodded. I had thought about it from the beginning. The most secure

❖

place was the one assigned to the "special ones." In the commotion nobody would take notice of three boys running through the hallways. They would be too involved with themselves.

Isaac took out a small box, connected it to the cable, and activated the switch. Without giving it too much thought, we went to the place we had chosen to get back into Bershad. We ran, rolled on the ground, got up again, and went on. When we were almost to the wire in front of the zone of the "special ones" we heard an infernal noise. The watchtower was flying through the air wrapped in a red flame. We didn't stop to look. We went in and stuck to the walls. The searchlights were turning fast, looking for the perpetrators. The slaves were coming out of headquarters while the sirens went off. We got in exactly as we had planned.

Everybody was running around. They were screaming, clutching their belongings, as if they were going to protect them from the ceaseless random shots. We ducked into a corner. Isaac shook me by the shoulders. "Look what you've done. How are we going to get back now? We're finished if they realize we're not there. How are we going to get out of this mousetrap?" It was the first time I saw Isaac so nervous. The boss, the idea man, was now seeing himself trapped, ready for the first idea I could come up with. Mordechai stayed put, with his hands in his pockets.

I took them to the first window that faced outside. Twenty meters away were the latrines and beyond them the orphanage. "When the infirmary explodes, we jump, we crawl along the latrine wall, and"—the idea did not really crystallize but I couldn't think of anything else—

"we wait for the second explosion and get out," I said. We didn't have to wait long. A second, even brighter glare illuminated Bershad. The lights went out immediately.

The resistance had thought things through. By hitting the power plant it would be easier for them to move around. We began running. In about a minute and a half we were at the door of our room. There were the others, looking fearfully at what was going on. Some said the Russians were coming, others that they were going to kill us all. Some slaves fired in the air. Mordechai shouted: "Inside, these people don't like it when we know what's going on outside. They don't want the partisans to know about us." We ran inside. Isaac breathed a little easier. Mordechai laughed: "You're not all there, kid," he said.

Isaac grumbled and took a bottle of vodka from under the boards. We all drank. "Just one swallow, so there'll be enough to go around," he said, and put it away. The noise did not stop. We heard the sound of sirens, of soldiers' fast steps and shots in the air to scare the "Russians." And, as Isaac had said, it was not long before the slaves came in to do a head count as they did every night.

"No one's missing here," said a fat soldier with an oily face. The commanding officer said: "Take a good look at the ones with wet clothes. The fact that they're all here doesn't mean that some couldn't have gotten out and come back." My stomach churned. We were soaked. "You lost, Israel, it wasn't your hand. You should have thought things through."

I swallowed slowly. The slaves told the boys sitting across from us to stand up. They touched them and made them show their feet. The fourth one was a sick boy who was about to leave this world. The slaves, still unused to the smell of typhus and TB, recoiled in horror.

⚜

Just like the beasts, they lived in fear of the plague. "What's wrong with that one?" asked the officer. Another boy with an egg-shaped head and a dull look in his eyes answered: "He's sick." The slave looked around and Mordechai, without even getting up, said: "And the boys on this side are dying. That's why we have separated. Those that are more or less all right to one side, and the really sick ones on this side." It was a sting.

The slaves, as if pulled by a magnet, retreated to the center of the room. They did not dare to continue their search. The mention of the plague had spooked them.

A third explosion, which we had not expected, came from the officers' quarters. Instinctively I put my hand to my belt and it turned cold. There was the grenade Isaac had given me, and the slaves were less than four meters away. If they get closer I'll pull the pin. We're all going together. But they left right away, turning away in fear of the "plague." We looked at each other for a long time. Nobody was able to say anything. That night nobody could sleep.

At dawn we were all forced to go out, even the sick ones. They lined us up and a squad of slaves stood in front of us, pointing their guns at our heads. There were also SS beasts, with their black uniforms and the hats with the skull and crossbones in front. They looked at us contemptuously. The one with the highest rank went to a microphone. Before he started talking, he blew his nose and affected an effeminate grimace. "I don't like what happened last night. We know for a fact that it was the Jews, since they started this war. If you only knew how many lives the Third Reich has lost because of you, you would be ashamed of being Jews. Thousands of brave men have died because of world Jewry. You will pay for those responsible for what happened last night. I'm very sorry, but my mission is to fight against the murderers." And he stepped down as he straightened out his gloves.

They were going to kill us, just like in Ladyzhin. It was obvious that the beasts saw nothing but Jews everywhere. If the Russians made them retreat in the steppes, it was not the Russians who did it, but the Jews. The winter was the fault of the Jews. Every defeat had us for a scapegoat, and they took out their failures on us.

Panic showed in our faces. The beasts, with their sticks, were pointing. And they chose the ones who seemed stronger. I realized that and I immediately put on a miserable face. Isaac and Mordechai did the same. They passed us by and chose the boy next to Isaac.

Fear made me delirious. The beasts called us murderers and considered themselves missionaries of a saintly labor of extinction that went beyond anything imaginable. They talked about a war against the Jews in order to justify their genocide. More than two hundred boys were pulled out of the line, their heads bowed, waiting for the sentence. We watched sadly, but what else could we do? The resistance had begun, and many would have to pay with their lives so a few could survive. Otherwise we would end up in the graves, like those who had crossed to the other shore of the Bug, and we were not ready to let ourselves be trapped like mice!

I had won again, but with sadness, looking at the sentenced ones with their eyes fixed on the ground. The beasts had chosen the strongest. The sick would die without the obligatory shot.

The branded ones were shivering. With their bodies they were going to initiate the graves of Bershad, the bridge between being and allowing themselves to be led.

⚜

I had already learned the details in Ladyzhin. Suddenly one of the condemned boys started to cry. An SS man turned to him. "If you know a guilty one—" We felt that the earth was going to open under our feet. The boy moved his head from side to side. The beast hit him in the head with his stick. He fell down,, losing consciousness, blood coming out of his right ear. The beast started kicking him and swearing: "Nobody knows anything. Everything happens miraculously. But you can't fool the Reich!" He ordered the selected ones to take off their shoes. The others were watching us, ready and willing to shoot. They needed to see blood run, smell the agony, relieve the fear that was engulfing them.

When the two hundred were shoeless, with their naked feet in the snow, the officer who was giving the orders barked: "On line, to the end, always to the right!" We saw them march off with their hands above their heads and without the slaves taking their eyes off them. They got lost when they turned the corner. They made the rest of us raise our hands. The slaves began to search us again. They were looking for something nobody had. But it did not last. The fear of contagion made them stop. They were in fear of touching the bodies of those they had in front of them with their hands up.

They made us go back into the orphanage. I fell on the straw like a sack of potatoes. I was numbed, incapable of distinguishing between fantasy and reality. Outside, on the ground, lay the body of the boy whose ear they had blown away with a stick.

He was probably already dead. After the kicks he had gotten, his guts must have ruptured. I looked out. They had already taken him away. The slaves were fast workers. I looked at Isaac. He had a long face. He looked as if

❧

he were made of wax, eyes closed and an ashy look on his face. He was breathing with difficulty. He kept his hands inside what remained of his jacket. Mordechai was trying to sleep by his side. He kept his eyes closed and sometimes let out a dry cough. "Isaac, what do you think?" I asked. I didn't give a damn about the answer. I just asked to see if there was still any life in my friend. He grumbled: "Remember the madness? Well, it's starting to take shape again and now it's serious. Don't you realize that I'm already mad? Look into my eyes. In time we all go crazy. It's a slow process but it never stops. It advances slowly, but it always advances. It has caught up with me and I have to accept it. I'm crazy, Israel!" He let out a peal of laughter that sounded like an anguished scream.

Mordechai opened his eyes. He accommodated himself in his corner and wet his lips. After a while, like a mole coming out of his hole he said: "Relax, kid, we're all crazy in here ,and those that aren't die, like the one next to you. It's the only alternative. Either you go crazy or you die. In the end it's all the same thing. Did you see how much blood was coming out of that boy's ear? That's the way my mother bled. That's how we're all going to bleed when we least expect it. It's very simple, you are selected, they put you in front of the SS, and you fall on the ground with a broken head.

"Afterwards they finish you up with kicks. Then, in order not to scream, you have to believe you're crazy, be crazy or else you die. Anyone who cries is dead; anyone who moves a bit is dead. Anyone who doesn't eat is dead, and in order to eat you have to be crazy. Isn't it crazy to risk your life for a piece of stale bread, for half a bottle of vodka? To wake up is madness and yet we don't stop waking up; to open our eyes is to stay stuck in the filth.

⚜

Half of the boys they selected were in the resistance. The one who cried was in the resistance. Isn't it enough to go crazy?" And he kept licking his thin lips.

I lowered my head. I needed to meditate. "Israel, aren't you crazy too? If you're alive, you must be crazy. Survival is madness, and without it you cannot survive. Don't you risk your life every moment for a few apple cores? Don't you sleep on top of a dozen grenades and two machine guns? If they find out, you will wish you had never been born. The third explosion, wasn't it a product of your imagination?" I finally convinced myself that I was mad. It couldn't be avoided. It was part of everyday life.

Now the question was to act without asking too many questions. To listen without moving my mouth. I closed my eyes and tried to empty my mind. But it was impossible. My neighbor's breathing prevented it. I felt him dying with every labored breath. Perhaps that was the only thing left to do. I looked at him. He was a redhead with pale skin covered by hundreds of tiny freckles. His light green eyes were not moving. They were fixed on the ceiling, looking for I don't know what. Many died looking at a piece of meat. Others were sure that they were at home. I had planned to die seeing the wooden toys my grandfather had given me.

That day there was no soup for anyone. Thank God the winter was fading and the cold winds were not as intense. We stayed in the room for a couple of days, enough time for eight to die. When they finally let us out the man who kept the death records exploded: "What, eight? Have you gone back to suicide in order not to talk?" He took me by the neck and kept yelling. "Russian, that's what you are, a Russian spy! Your mission is to kill those who are involved in the guerrilla warfare. Atheist, you'll go to hell for your sins!" His words didn't make any sense, and he didn't care—he was simply venting his fear on me. Afterwards, a bit calmer, he wrote down the number of deaths and kicked me in the behind as a farewell. The guards at the door tried to hit me with the butts of their guns, but I avoided them by dodging as I ran. I got back to the orphanage with a deep pain in my chest. Fear, hunger, madness? I don't know! I felt like I had a stone in my sternum. That's when I started to cough.

In our corner there was another guest. He was covered with straw and Mordechai was guarding him., only letting those who could be trusted come nearer. The "nurses" came for the dead bodies and took them away without even looking at us. They were like automatons. They came, took their load, and left. I later found out they were inmates in a nearby jail, all condemned for crimes against the Reich. At least they were alive, for most of the inmates had been killed. Mordechai told me this, for he knew a lot about what went on in Bershad. When I found out, I justified their comings and goings without looking at anyone, without being afraid of the plague that every dead body represented. They lived in their world, and their madness was probably similar to ours.

When I got to the corner I could see the face of the boy lying under the dirty straw. His eyes were purple and swollen. You could see that his front teeth had been pulled out savagely. The odor from his gums almost made me vomit.

When I saw that miserable face, without a place for another bruise, I forgot about the pain in my chest. Isaac motioned for me to follow him. "We need cotton and alcohol. Can you get them?" I shrugged. But later I remem-

❖

bered the zone of the "special ones." There might be something there. I went in that direction, walking slowly so as not to arouse any suspicion. The watchtower destroyed by the explosion was being repaired. I avoided the path to the infirmary. The building was surrounded by the beasts and I did not want to risk it. When I got to the zone of the "special ones," they gave me a dirty look when I came in. They thought I had come for the piece of bread that they would sometimes give me. I went in without paying attention to the eyes that shouted: "Get out!" and sat down on a box. One girl pointed at me and said: "The idiot doesn't die. Did you see? When I say something, it happens." She smiled sadly. It was a wan, cold, dead smile. I didn't say anything, even though the pain in my chest was bothering me again. I tried not to cough. I was desperately looking for a rag, a bottle of alcohol. The girl who had pointed at me went to her corner and took out a bottle of cheap perfume, applying a bit behind her ears before putting it away among her things. There Israel, that will do it. As long as it stings. You have to steal that bottle and the two towels hanging from that nail. I got up and started to walk around the room. I heard curses against my pestilence.

Suddenly, when I got close to the place where the girl had put away the bottle of perfume, I made believe I had fainted. I fell over her things and my left hand dug quickly until it found the bottle. I put it inside my jacket. Some of them came over to see what was wrong with me. The women were scared. They quickly pushed me into the center of the room. One screamed: "He has the plague." The "special ones" were afraid of contagion. I took advantage of this opportunity to get to the towels. They moved away from me in horror, afraid of any contact with a plague carrier. I held on to the two towels, shivering and

❖

slobbering, while I coughed. The screaming became deafening. They cried, kicked, and called the guards.

I took advantage of the confusion to flee with the rags. At the door I put them inside my jacket, and when I saw some slaves coming in I told them: "There is one with the plague in there." Some opened their eyes and tried to stop. They did not want to come in contact with the plague.

I got to the orphanage without any problems. I don't know what happened to the "special ones." It was the last time I went there. From then on I had no news except about the continuous deportations. I gave the bottle of perfume and the towels to Isaac. Mordechai whistled and shook my hand. "You're one crazy kid." They started to clean the wounds of the shivering boy. We gagged him with a dirty rag so that he couldn't scream. Isaac tore the towels in long strips and soaked each one with the contents of the bottle.

It must have stung badly, for the boy was writhing in pain and three others were holding him. His wrists and ankles were raw, as was a good part of his groin. He was black and blue all over. I swallowed my question. These were the new rules.

We acted, but did not know why. To live was the theme. Those who survived could ask all the questions later on. For now, we had do what was necessary to achieve our goal. I sat down with my head between my knees. That way my chest hurt less and I could control the cough.

I gritted my teeth in a vain attempt to lessen the pain. "Israel, the madness hurts, gets inside your bones, it makes you walk over and watch a fellow writhing in pain because his body has been partially destroyed.

"Did you see his gums? They're huge in comparison with the pain in your chest. Did you get a good look at them? They were oozing blood, broken, covered with red mucous. And the wrists and the ankles. What happened to him? Did they try to saw them off? Come on Israel, you have to survive, you have to get out of this hole. Your parents are alive, they're looking for you." I shook my head. Thinking about my parents always moved me terribly. It filled my stomach and made me feel terribly alone.

At that moment, what with looking at the injured boy and the deep pain in my chest, I felt awful. I relaxed and waited for the shot in the back of my neck that would make me fall into the grave. Wasn't it enough what I had lived through?

I was beside myself. I saw nothing but the anguished faces of starving, decaying people always on the lookout for a scrap of food. I coughed and decided to keep on, to live through the madness they were forcing on us. I got up again and left the room. I walked hunched behind the walls of the latrine and reached the wire fence. I got there fast, without looking back—pushed by something, and that something protected me. Before, I wouldn't have taken such a chance. I went out without any plans, just to escape the horrors of Bershad.

I walked for a while. Behind me, beyond a few tree trunks that remained upright, challenging the last snows of the winter, I could see a column of smoke going up to the sky. I thought about a house, about the people on the outside, about playing another hand. I went toward the house, calculating what I was going to say in my halting Russian. From less than a hundred meters away I could see the farm.

It was a small cabin. I knocked on the door. "Partisan," I said. The woman who opened the door let out a small cry and covered her mouth. "Guerrilla." I repeated, so that she could put her thoughts together.

⚜

Immediately someone grabbed me from behind and lifting me up carried me to the back of the cabin. Two men
with uniforms very different from those worn by the
slaves and the beasts gave me a look-over. The older one,
with a huge black beard parted here and there by a few
white threads, said to me after slapping his calves: "So
you're a guerrilla, huh? How do I know you're not from
Bershad?" I looked him in the eye and, stammering, said:
"Because I know you're a Russian soldier, just like your
friend. Or what do you think, that in the organization we
don't know deserters when we see them?" The two men
looked at each other. They were probably waiting for me
to identify myself. But my curt answer was a slap in the
face. When I saw his reaction I went on: "Don't you know
that the Red Army is almost here?"

I told them what I knew about the Soviet advance, the
same gossip that went around Bershad: the German
defeat at Stalingrad, the despair of the SS when they felt
the Soviets at their heels. I made things up, creating situations. I told them about the participation of the guerrillas in the explosions in Bershad. They listened and
nodded. Surely the slaves and beasts were looking for the
saboteurs and they had to hide in the hills, enduring the
bad weather before being able to go home again. The one
with the beard, never taking his eyes off me, said: "And
what do you want from us?" Wow, he had swallowed the
bait. Israel, now don't give them too much line or you'll
lose them. They bit and you have to hold them tight. You
must take advantage of their lack of information so that
they will start creating their own dreams.

I looked at them with an air of condescension. "We
need alcohol, cotton, and some fresh vegetables. Also a
bit of salt. Oh, and don't try anything, my comrades are

⚜

waiting outside and they get impatient when we don't come back on time. Gentlemen, if it isn't too much trouble."

The woman ran to her bedroom. The two men asked how they could join the guerrillas. I replied that next week I would have more information while we evaluated their patriotism and considered the possibility of their having collaborated with the enemy. The words came out spontaneously, strong, hard. The younger one turned red with fury. "We are Russians and this is our battle. How can you accuse us of being collaborators?" The older one, pacifying him a bit, said: "They're right. Don't you see how they work? They send the young ones, the big ones wait. They don't want to be recognized. They have every right to suspect us. Didn't we suspect the comrade?"

I stood up, holding back the cough and the pain that drilled my chest. The woman came back with a bottle of alcohol and a full bag of cotton. She also had a bag of bread, vegetables, and a small bottle of vodka. She gave it to me without a word. But she suspected that I was ill. "Kid, you're sick, very sick." Looking for strength where I had none I answered: "No, it's nothing. My chest hurts, but it's a passing thing." The two men, perhaps believing that my report would determine whether or not they would be accepted by the guerrillas, made me sit down, and the one with the beard told the woman: "Mumushka, bring a bit of cough syrup and a spoonful of oil." They made me swallow it almost by force. It tasted like hell, but it was medicine! I thanked them and told them that I would be back within a week. I went out with what I had gotten tucked inside my jacket.

When I got to the trees I looked back at the cabin. I saw a window open. They were watching. They wanted to

⚜

know if what I had told them was true. Israel, if they realize that you're from Bershad, they will come after you
and give you a good beating or maybe turn you in for a
sack of sugar. I reacted right away. I let out two whistles,
one short and one long one. Then I raised my arm three
times and whistled again. I saw the window close. Had
they swallowed the story ,or were they biding their time
to come get me? I started running as fast as my feet
would take me. I was scared, seeing a pair of huge hands
that were trying to grab me by the neck. I stopped to
catch my breath when I got to the hill where I could see
the wire fence at Bershad. Nobody was around. The
hands had been an illusion, the men in the cabin had
swallowed my story, even though I had to ask myself
whether they too were hiding something, since they had
been so forthcoming with my requests. They had probably done something that would now get them in trouble
with the Russians. They were not crazy, they did not
know about the tunnel, they hardly knew fear. We, on the
other hand, lived in madness, among the ghosts, knowing that death slept in every room, seeing it every day in
the faces of the slaves and the beasts, always on the lookout for the first opportunity. We had no time to think
about good and evil, we existed and the game was won by
whoever had the strength to hold out. I waited for night
before returning to the orphanage.

There were no problems. Luck was on my side. I came
in slowly. The pain in my chest had subsided a bit, but
the cough did not leave me alone. Mordechai approached
me. "Where were you? We thought you had been caught
in the roundup. Almost everyone who was outside the
orphanage was apprehended, and they're all in the basement of the officers' quarters. We still don't know what

happened, but something is wrong. Do you see that boy?"
he said, pointing at a body covered by straw. "They tortured him last night. He and four others escaped. Do you
see his hands and feet? They hammered nails into his
wrists and ankles. His groin and testicles, as well as his
butt and the tip of his penis were burned. They pulled
out his teeth and shoved nails under his nails. Do you
know what they were asking him about? How many
tanks, planes, and soldiers in the Russian army! I'm sure
the others are dying if they're not already dead. Who
knows that kind of thing? Not even the Russians!"

The beasts and the slaves were beginning to see the
collapse of their macabre empire. Their defeats were
mounting and they were taking it out on us. We had to
be careful. It wouldn't be strange if they would start
deporting us, sticking us in graves so that nobody would
talk. I forced away the idea and went up to Isaac and the
wounded boy. I took out the bottle of alcohol and the bag
of cotton. Mordechai looked on with his mouth open.
"You went out, kid, didn't you?" I shrugged and coughed.
Isaac was looking at the cotton as if it were gold. He
stroked the bottle of alcohol and looked at me in disbe-
lief. "Were you in the infirmary?" I said no with my head.
I smiled while I coughed and took out the bag that the
mother of the two Russian deserters had given me.
Mordechai's eyes popped out. Isaac opened his mouth so
wide that I thought for a moment that he was going to
scream. "Where did you get the money? Just a while ago
I counted ours and it's all there." I coughed again, but
this time took the bottle of vodka and took a swig. "It's
mine, for my cough, I mean. No, there was no need for
money. Let's say they gave these things to me in
exchange for putting in a good word for a couple of guys

❖

who want to join the guerrillas. I was Igor once again. Remember Isaac?" His pale face opened up in a grin of satisfaction. Without meaning to, I had developed my own style, my way of surviving. "They'll be waiting for me next week," I said, while Isaac pulled up the boards to put away the precious bag of provisions.

The wounded boy, screaming and writhing each time we cleansed his wounds with the cotton and alcohol, began to heal. Isaac went out of the orphanage and always brought something back. We had divided our operating zones. He went north, I went east, Mordechai had set points to go to and we did not change his itinerary.

I returned to the cabin and came back with another bag, this time a bit bigger. Of course I had to tell them that on my next visit I was going to bring concrete information from the chief. I could see their eyes shine. The two deserters were beginning to wash away their guilt and now, by if they joined the guerrillas as I had promised them, the Russian army would overlook their treason. That was their thinking. I sold them illusions, and the deserters paid me with food, with the elements to endure and survive.

One of the operations of the Jewish resistance coincided with an attack by the partisans made on the headquarters in Bershad. More than a third of the building was destroyed by the explosions, and the zone of the "special ones" was completely demolished. We, with our heads between our knees, heard the detonations and felt the whistling of the shells that flew over the orphanage. It was the first concentrated partisan attack. They attacked as if they were an army, bombarding precisely the most vulnerable parts of the town. Surely the

⚜

Russians must be close. During that attack the Jewish resistance killed eight of the SS officers who supervised Bershad.

The beasts were corralled. One SS man, maddened by his crumbling empire, tried to take it out on us. He kicked the door down and pulled out his gun in order to kill the boys standing in front of him. Immediately a pair of knives got stuck in his chest. I didn't know where they threw them from, but the beast doubled over without uttering a sound, his eyes wide open and his hands curled on the black fabric of his jacket. They took him out, after removing his gun and his boots. Somebody spilled gasoline on him and the body started to burn.

It was a terrible night. The Russian planes flew overhead, dropping a shower of bombs. We felt them explode near us, in front, behind, everywhere. The deafening noise of the bombs made us keep our eyes open and our ears ready to catch the smallest detail. Everything got complicated when the beasts decided to close the doors of the orphanage. In the darkness, without knowing what was going on, many started to scream in despair. They hit the walls in a vain attempt to bring them down. They were screaming for a bomb in order to die once and for all and not be burned, roasted like chickens. Isaac, Mordechai and the wounded boy, already much recovered, tried to calm them down, but to no avail.

At dawn, after that hell, we looked at each other. Some had died during the night due to the advanced state of their illnesses. Five others had given in to madness. Only a few were left, and we waited for retribution by the beasts. We didn't have long to wait.

The sirens called us out. They made us line up. The beasts, their faces long and pale due to the tension of the previous night, moved around nervously. The slaves followed them without questioning the SS order to finish off the sick ones. This way the healthy ones would be deported to labor camps in Germany. Many stuck out their chests, rubbed their cheeks, and stood firm during the review. However, more than three hundred children were ordered out of the lines. That afternoon they would be sent in a special train, to a sure death.

Among the chosen ones was the boy who had been tortured. They found him sick with pyorrhea due to his lack of teeth. He bade us goodbye, saying: "I know you won't falter." We saw him disappear, running, forced to walk fast by the butts of the guns.

We found out from a Romanian maid about the death, during the bombing, of a good number of high-ranking beasts. Bershad had become a war zone. The SS were leaving and their posts were being taken over by regular troops of the German army. The Romanians remained at their posts, drinking more than usual. A few lower-ranking beasts who would be in charge of the final solution for us remained in town.

A last-minute order, from the general headquarters of all the Germans in occupied Ukraine, required everyone in Bershad to start working. Our job consisted of going to the forest to cut wood and bring it back. Other groups were assigned to dig anti-tank trenches and other types of defenses. The presence of the Russian army was imminent. We went out at six in the morning and came back at five in the afternoon. The food remained the same, and the number of crazed ones multiplied. Two boys attacked a German soldier. They broke his head with a stone and ran away. They were shot while running. The nights in Bershad were times of despair. With winter over, we had

✤

to deal with a horde of rats every night who were even hungrier than we were.

Our outings were becoming more and more complicated, as the German soldiers were unwilling to let anyone out because the approach of the Russians meant that anyone who went out could be a contact between the Jewish resistance in the camp and the guerrillas. However, while in the woods, we managed to go in search for food and money. Some farmers paid us to sell cigarettes to people in the area. I sold tobacco until the end of spring. I had the morning shift and in the afternoon I took Mordechai's place at work.

The escape system was simple. We let the guard count us in the morning. Later, one by one, those of us who had the morning shift started to hide in preassigned places. There was a path that Mordechai, Isaac, and I knew that led to the farmer who fed us a light breakfast and gave us cigarettes to sell. They all loved to protect the "Russian" children who had started to face life. Isaac did his thing on his own.

The number of German troops in the area increased, and this went against us, since the farmers had to give part of their crops to the soldiers. It turned even more difficult to follow the initial path. The constant presence of the partisans forced the Germans to double up their guard in the surrounding area.

We had to make do with the miserable soup we received at the orphanage, each time worse. The total of those still alive was fifteen hundred, and they made us work like mules. When we finished cutting wood they made us dig trenches, put up barricades, and reinforce the walls of the headquarters. They electrified the fences, and every night one of the beasts, one of the SS men who

❖

had not fled for lack of an order that allowed them to leave Bershad, came to the orphanage and took it out on anyone he wanted. I got a beating that only the alcohol and the cotton we had hidden under the straw helped me get through.

Isaac was worse every time. His depression showed in many ways. He didn't care if they saw him crying or screaming. Sometimes he would let out a peal of laughter without any reason. He started to drown in the madness of the crazy people, in that state that I avoided at all cost. I had already seen them. I knew them. The really crazy ones went up to the wire fences and got electrocuted. Others threw a stone at a German and waited to be shot.

Isaac stopped talking for a few days. He worked in silence, his head down, without any enthusiasm for the ideas that either Mordechai or I proposed. Our friends in the resistance kept us busy. My memory had become an archive for them. I remembered every place, all the spaces, the steps you had to take from one place to another.

I even served as a contact between the Jewish resistance in Bershad and the partisans outside. I knew that certain parts of the fences were not electrified and sneaked out that way, after going through the latrines from the inside, getting full of filth. On the outside there were too many guards and it was too risky to crawl against the walls, especially now that the number of searchlights was tripled and the town was almost as light at night as during daytime.

My mission depended on the details and on my speed. I carried messages and took the opportunity to steal food whenever possible or to buy it from whoever wanted to sell.

⚜

In the summer things got worse. Rubles had no value, and the only thing that was worth anything was the scrip issued by the Germans. The crops were bad and there was a scarcity of food. Our ration of soup was cut in half. The squealers came back. The beasts paid well to another who provided information about the resistance. The orphanage was in misery. There was nothing left in our hiding place except the three grenades, my switchblade, and Isaac's knife. Hunger got stuck to our guts and pressed tight. Mordechai started to diminish like a candle. Our workload increased. Little food and eight to ten hours of work with our hands, since any tool could be a dangerous weapon in our hands, particularly the crazy ones.

There were suicides all the time, a group of deportees, somebody who was massacred. We were living like animals. I forgot how to think. I lived to survive and held on to this idea with ferocious tenacity. "Hang on, Israel!" That was my motto and I thought of nothing else.

One night Isaac asked me to go with him on a job he was going to do outside of Bershad. We got ready and had no difficulty getting out, since I knew a way that had not yet been discovered by the slaves and their dogs. We got to the main post that held up the watchtower to the east; we got across and started to run. We walked several hours until we got to a cornfield, took a few ears, and went back. It was a lovely night The whole field was illuminated by a round moon. I ate young corn and it tasted like heaven. Suddenly a German patrol appeared in front of us. "Halt!"

I went down to the ground and started to roll as fast as I could. I got to a recently opened breach and ran toward the wire fence outside the town. I had to throw away the ears of corn. I couldn't leave a trace. One ker-

❖

nel and you'd wish you had never been born. They were
punishing the least transgression with the worst tortures. The beasts said that the robbery was not against
the farmers, but against the Reich, and that was punishable by death.

The dogs were barking and sniffing all over the place.
I took a chance, got to the closest watchtower, and went
in that way. Once inside I went into a latrine and stayed
there, standing until dawn, waiting for the door to open.
I could already see one of he beasts egging on his dog to
destroy me. But daylight came and I was able to go eat
the soup without anybody noticing my outing. I saw
Mordechai in the line, but I didn't see Isaac. The beasts
made us line up in the main courtyard. Isaac, with his
hands crushed because of the beatings, came in escorted by some slaves. They were dragging him, since his feet
were broken and he couldn't walk. His face was so black
and blues that he was almost unrecognizable. The voice
of one of the beasts could be heard over the speaker system. "Anyone who steals from the Reich will be punished
by death!" They repeated it more than five times.

My stomach turned. They tied Isaac's feet to the back
of a car and started its motor. And thus vanished the life
of someone who had been my friend, my comrade in sadness and disgrace, the light in the middle of darkness.

His body, dragged by the car, bounced against the
ground, leaving behind a trail of blood. The beasts shot
him in the feet and the hands to increase his suffering. I
bit my mouth not to scream. Isaac shuddered when he
felt the impact of the bullets against his flesh, but didn't
scream, didn't move his lips. He had swallowed his
tongue. It was his way of saying goodbye.

❖

At last, feeling his life ebbing once and for all, he raised his battered head to scream: "Pigs, sons of bitches!"

The car increased its speed and at the end what it was dragging was no more than a bloody mass that scattered its bones through the yellowish soil. The car didn't stop until nothing that could be recognized as Isaac's body remained on the ground. Even then the beasts fired into the mess that no longer resembled what just the night before had been a human being. "Dirty Jew!" the beasts shouted, pulling the triggers of their machine guns. I couldn't help myself and began to cry silently, feeling the my tears run down my cheeks. Mordechai did the same thing.

Back at the orphanage, once again in our corner, Mordechai took out Isaac's knife and said: "Sticking it in the belly of one of those bastards will be the only way to say goodbye to a friend!"

⚜

9

Getting Out of the Sewer

After Isaac's death the Jewish resistance blew up three fuel tanks in his memory. Mordechai told me about it—he was the one who had planted the sticks of dynamite at the depot.

You could begin to feel the loss of control in Bershad. The slaves didn't trust each other. They knew that some of their own men were just waiting for an opportunity to join the Russian offensive against Germany. The fear of falling into the hands of the Russians could be seen on their faces. The bombings were more frequent. The beast commander, a man named Karl, was killed when he tried to flee and his car was struck by a bomb. They burned him in the middle of the road.

We in the orphanage were able to mingle with the townspeople. It was a different world. The people of Bershad were living in tragic conditions. There were half-dead Jews still alive with their families. I couldn't believe it. The orphanage where we were imprisoned was part of an internment camp, a prison closed off to the populace of the town, a huge number of inhabitants along with many orphans and displaced persons.

Nothing changed. Bershad was still a center where the beasts and the slaves could indulge in a daily feast of blood. The town, that clutter of half-crumbling houses, was an enormous field, a center surrounded by barbed-wire fences and hundreds of guards with machine guns ready to vomit their message of death. I was beginning to understand where the principal locus of the resistance was. Perhaps Isaac had found out but didn't have time to tell me. He didn't talk about the houses so that I would not investigate. He created the illusion of being in a field, and he was right. When Mordechai and I went out to the Bershad full of houses, to that village about which I hardly had a notion aside from its being mixed up with the headquarters of the German regiment, we had quite a surprise. Thousands of people were dying there without lifting a finger. They would squeeze up against a corner and the next day someone would poke them with a stick. Anyone who didn't move was dead. Every day before the sun came out, the air vibrated with the croaking sound of their dying breaths.

The men of Bershad were not men; they had no idea that outside there was a vast steppe that could be crossed. They preferred to die rather than face the beasts and their slaves. But in spite of this arid environment devoid of initiative, the Jewish resistance survived and grew. We in the orphanage, those skinny figures who sometimes entertained themselves by searching for holes in the wall, were pillars of the movement.

At night the image of Isaac would appear to me: "Fight, endure, don't let yourself be taken away. Some of us have to die, it's the law. But those who survive must continue the fight." And I dreamed that dream for more than a week until I told Mordechai about it. I could see that he was moved. His eyes were shining, almost dancing in their sockets. When I finished he said: "I'm going through the same thing, but had no words to express it!"

⚜

When we came back to the Bershad that I had not noticed until now, Mordechai couldn't stop cursing: "You see them? They die peacefully, convinced that war is a new way of life. They seem to love hunger and misery, but when they see a rat they chase it. They make a soup with it and wait until the next day to continue their hunt. The rats are feeding them. Do you know what I think? That they're going to end up eating each other." What Mordechai was saying was true to a point. The people in the village looked like ghosts. They dragged their feet with pain and tiredness. They didn't lift their heads and hardly talked. The scene looked like a cemetery where the dead had been left outdoors. Women with their hair over their faces and torn dresses carried emaciated children who could hardly breathe. The older men went outside to cut wood, bring stones, dig trenches. They went motivated by fear, holding back in silence, allowing their madness to grow, as Isaac would have said. We were all strangers.

Our presence, once the walls of the orphanage collapsed after a bombing, was a threat to the survival of these people living in the silent madness that engulfed the village. They surely believed that we were after the garbage they ate, out for a bit of rat.

Madness was the rule. An old man, while still digging, drank the sweat that rolled down his cheeks and said: "The sewer, where is the sewer? It's the only way to know if I'm still me." And while he dug he kept repeating this phrase. I watched him for a while until he threatened me with his shovel. "What's wrong, haven't you ever seen someone dying while working? It's easy, you dig out the last bit of soil and you fall inside. Someone else will come and throw a bit of soil over you so that the smell of your body won't spoil the taste of the dirty water he drinks, while he keeps digging his grave and that of his family."

I look at him. The old man gives out a dry peal of laughter, toothless, pointing his yellow hand at the hole he has been digging since I don't know how long. Mordechai pulls at my sleeve. We walk through an alley that stinks of excrement. There is something in this new Bershad that leads me to mingle with its people, stones, and half-destroyed walls. My torn boots are full of moss; my hands easily peel off pieces of lime. The cats watch in pain. Many of Bershad's people have already eaten cats and mice. Hunger, the inclement weather, the anguish, the madness, having a family you have to care for any way you can. I'm beginning to understand the bowed heads of the men who go back and forth, retracing their steps. In this Bershad of the outside, things are more complicated. There are many squealers. The mothers fight each other for a cabbage leaf. The beasts have built a pen and those who are able to endure are allowed to live there. But there are still deportations, and graves in the forest. Anyone in the street after six in the evening is detained and taken to the Gestapo office. If he isn't dead when they finish with him, they deport him on the weekly train. I feel like I'm in the ghetto again, but this time I am a part of a crazy camp-ghetto. I suffocate looking at the sad faces of the little ones. The madness has been with me for a few days, and sometimes I have nightmares in the daytime. I walk, I dream, I'm part of a world different from this one. I feel like getting up and then diving headfirst into the ground. I need these people to realize that if you want to, you can live, and life, even if you lose it, goes on in the resistance. It hurts me to see the pallid faces of the men with their heads bowed. I feel like I'm

❖

choking and have to keep looking without seeing. This is a dirty game where nobody wins. Everybody loses; nothing is risked in this artificial world of Bershad outside of the orphanage. Its alleys full of garbage only incite riots. I look at the bleached wood of the windows and the cracks in the doors.

Thus life in the outside world is, after all, very similar to life in the orphanage. I haven't been well since Isaac died. I feel sick with each step I take. I move painfully, digging my soles in the dust, angry, clenched fists in my pockets. The presence of the beasts and the slaves drives me crazy. It must be the constant waiting. Everybody talks about the Russians, but all we hear is the sound of their cannons. The Germans hide in their Panzers and wait. They're afraid to advance. The people of the resistance know this, from Mordechai, from me, and from everyone else. In the mornings I leave my cave and walk around the Jewish quarter, each time more decimated by the continuous attacks of the Gestapo and the SS.

The resistance has joined the guerrillas. Here we're all essential. I have to see, smell, put my nose inside this new world of Bershad that I had not known before. Every day at five in the afternoon I give my report: "Those who are still here are low-ranking officers. The big ones left a long time ago. Today they took the guy that lived on the corner, red as a beet, to the office of the beast commander. They pierced his tongue with a hot nail and burned his eyelids with cigarette butts. He didn't say anything. Today he's in jail and we have to wait until tomorrow. This information came from the fellow that works in the prison." I work among the garbage, I move through the narrow street. I know the Eight O'clock Way. It's a way through the rooftops that got its name because it's the

⚜

one we use to move around after curfew. Now, in the summer, it's easy to follow. We'll see how well we'll be able to go through it this fall and winter. If the Russians don't come before then, there will be plenty of broken legs among those who try it. I keep peeping through the cracks. Everything is worthwhile. To know that there is a fireplace in a certain house has its value. I crouch in the shadows and cover myself with garbage. Through Mordechai, I know that the squealers know about me. I am careful not to be caught. I could end up like the guy who turned beet red. He didn't talk, but they broke his arms and legs and now gangrene is eating him up. The beasts are all alike, regardless of rank.

In the last few days they've been worse than ever. Five women were hung by their hair. They tore off the beards of three poor old men who were not capable of digging a trench. I understand that the last Gestapo agents will be leaving tomorrow. They're getting nervous with the noise of the advancing Russians. The beasts and their commander, who is a lieutenant down on his luck, swear that they're going to finish off all the Jews in Bershad. Yesterday they showed what they meant by executing eight whole families in front of everyone. The accusation was the same: "Guilty of causing the war."

The resistance bombed the slaves' headquarters for more than half an hour. The time has come to go underground. Every Jew found in the street is executed without even a "Halt!" Each day it becomes more difficult to walk through the narrow streets. I haven't been able to go back to the orphanage, nor will I. They have started to deport the boys who are still there. Mordechai and I endure. It's a fight against nature, against the environment, but we don't give up. I have learned to jump from

❖

one rooftop to the next and eat a stolen apple while I run as fast as I can, to avoid the dull stare of the squealers. I'm a citizen of the great Bershad that I didn't know. It is difficult to contact the farmers. They too are searched and executed for the smallest suspicion. The partisans roam the region, waiting by the roadside, ambushing any German troops who go by. Every path is covered with blood. Refugees are starting to flood the roads. They go, others stay, the rest die in despair. You can smell death in the four corners. Sometimes it gets mixed up with the odor of gunpowder. You walk fast, stuck to the shadow of a wall that threatens to fall on you.

The personal solitude is terrible. One starts to lose feelings and the preservation instinct grows. I live like a mole. I go from hole to hole, with dirt in my hair, a dirty face, and a cough that sometimes leaves me completely exhausted. But I don't give up. The kingdom of the tormentors is falling. I see their pale faces when they hear the thunder of the cannons and the airplanes that go by announcing the Red Army.

Part of the orphanage has been blown away. What used to be our area no longer exists. The last beasts have fled. The resistance attacks them, leaving some wounded and others dead. The partisans finish off the wounded. They don't want to have anything to do with the SS. We know that some Gestapo members are hiding in the area. The resistance and the partisans are looking for them. We have debts to collect. This piece of history isn't going to remain blank. My job gets a bit complicated. They have asked me to identify the collaborators. I cover the Eight O'clock Way during the day. I look at the porches; search the faces, trying to interpret the grimaces of those below. Some hide their belongings. I store every face in my

⚜

memory and later inform the resistance. We hide in the basements, living off a meager ration that sometimes we have to win in a frantic fight. A few days ago we attacked the kitchen of the police headquarters; two of our people were killed, and we barely managed to get away with three bags of flour and two of potatoes. The German soldiers patrol all day. You can tell they're tired. Their brown uniforms are tattered and they are obviously ready to give up as soon as the Russians come in. I don't think they will offer much resistance.

This morning a whole contingent of beasts came in—about two hundred. The German soldiers look at them with distrust. I think the SS and the regular army do not get along very well. Around ten in the morning, the resistance attacked a food convoy. Nobody was left alive. It's logical. The Jewish guerrillas and the partisans have nowhere to hide their prisoners. The SS have started to search every corner. Some Jewish families have been caught. I saw it from the third zone on the Eight O'clock Way.

One of the SS men who just came in ordered some Romanians to shoot them, but the soldiers refused. The beasts took out their guns, but the partisans and the sharpshooters killed them all before they could fire. The Jewish families were saved miraculously. After the shooting, they hid in an alley. The Germans are disconcerted. The Romanians don't listen to them any more, and the SS are continually being shot at. They know they're trapped. The only way out would be by air. They start to look for us like hunted animals, but they always encounter the snipers who turn up where they are least expected. The Ukrainian slaves keep drinking vodka. They prefer to be killed while drunk. Mordechai places a charge of dynamite in the car of the beasts' highest-ranking officer. It blows up to heaven and nobody dares to leave the headquarters. The Nazi flag is tattered. The men in the black uniforms are now careful when they go out.

A few Romanian soldiers stopped me on one of my outings through the narrow streets. My stomach turned. If they had shot at me, they would not have missed. But they made believe they didn't see me and walked away. They were probably from the resistance. It's almost impossible to sleep. The explosions can be heard closer every time. The water supply is non-existent. It's dangerous to go for a bottle of water. The men with the bowed heads seem to have come back to life. Their lives have a value they had not expected. Many of them have enrolled in the resistance. Even the women participate in one way or another, despite the danger. Everyone suspected of a crime against the crumbling Reich is shot on the spot without a trial. The squealers try to wash away their treason by participating in some skirmishes. I don't know how the chiefs of the resistance will evaluate that.

We know that the beasts have annihilated the Warsaw Ghetto, but not before they had to kill its inhabitants block by block. One of the survivors is here. He tells us how he had to flee that hell through a sewer. He talks about gas chambers, about millions of deaths. Some don't believe him; others, like me, do. The man from Warsaw takes out a letter written by Mordechai Anielewicz, commander of the resistance in the ghetto:

"What we have been through is impossible to express in words. We realize that everything that has happened surpasses our wildest imagination. The Germans were forced to flee the ghetto on two occasions. One of our units was able to keep its position for forty-five minutes, another for six hours. A mine, placed by us in the middle

❧

of a brush factory, exploded. Some of our units attacked the Germans and made them run for cover. Our losses are minimal. This too is a victory. One of us died heroically while firing his machine gun. I am aware that we are doing something big that has great importance. From now on we adopt guerrilla tactics. Tonight three groups go into action. They have two missions: reconnaissance and the gathering of arms. Remember, pistols don't have any value for us, we rarely use them. We are in urgent need of hand grenades, guns, machine guns and explosives. . . . It's impossible to describe the conditions in which we live in the ghetto. Only a few of us will be able to endure all this. All the others, before or after, will die. Their fate is written. In almost all the bunkers where the Jews are hiding by the thousands, it's impossible to light a candle for lack of air. But in the face of all this I must confess that my life's dream has come true. The armed resistance of Jews is a reality. I'm a witness to the heroic resistance of the Jewish insurrection. I hope to see you again. —Your friend, Mordechai."

The man stopped reading and looked at us for a while. "He was killed, but not like the ones they sent to the gas chambers. They had to kill him fighting!" We kept quiet, thinking, wishing to fight a battle like the one in Warsaw. A man with gray hair and big purple shadows under his eyes said: "I come from Bialystok, and I swear that eight hundred Jews were burned alive inside the synagogue. Twelve hundred were killed in the middle of the street. These are facts that the Jewish defense committee already has in case anyone doesn't believe me." And he pushed back his hair with his hands.

Yes, the beasts could be fought, they fell, and the resistance knew it as well as the partisans, and many of us who had heard the contents of the letter had already

⚜

seen some of the SS die. Those who were still here were dying of fear. We felt better. That evening, after the meeting, they gave me five grenades stolen from the Romanians and I covered the eight o'clock route to the assigned point. There I squeezed the grenade, activated the pin, and a door was blown into pieces. I slid fast between the tiles and went to the second spot. Then I threw two grenades over the roof of the building in front. The fire came after the explosion. I saw the Nazis run out like rats leaving their hiding place. The sharpshooters who were everywhere immediately shot down those who reached the street. When I got to the next roof I found Mordechai and two other boys. He said: "Israel, now we have to get to the anti-aircraft gun. That one we blow up together." We walked a few meters, jumped a wall, and got to the place where the gun was. Two soldiers were guarding it. A searchlight was going around, illuminating every piece of land. We hid behind some bushes. Mordechai took out a machine gun—I had no idea where he got it—and shot the soldiers. They fell dead on the grass. The searchlight tried to find us, but other shots, from a different place, knocked it out. We immediately ran to the AA gun, pulled the pins from our grenades, and threw them inside. Crossfire was covering us. We ran back to our original post and there, with our faces against the ground, heard the deafening sound that crowned our mission. We climbed back up the walls and got away via the eight o'clock road.

The following day the Germans searched insanely for people to execute. Everything they did showed fear. They shot a couple of old men who were digging in the garbage for something to eat. They massacred them while shouting: "Murderers!" Part of the Romanian army had joined

⚜

the partisans and the confusion was growing every minute. The Soviet air force returned to Bershad with their small one-engine planes. They bombed without pity. The arrival of the Soviet army was imminent. The last attack of the resistance, in conjunction with the partisans and some Romanian defectors, took place against the headquarters of the SS and the high command of the regular troops occupying Bershad. This small town in Ukraine had suddenly become a hell from which the remaining beasts would not get out alive. There was not one person affiliated to the movement who didn't participate. Mordechai, three others, and I blew up the corner walls in order to block any motorized attempt to help the beasts. The walls fell down while the roof blew to pieces. The sharpshooters kept up a crossfire between the door and the windows of the upper floor. Everything had been planned. We had to make the beasts come out so that we could loot the warehouses without interference. The operation wasn't very easy. It took almost an hour and on several occasions we were almost lost. If not for the intervention of a Romanian regiment, which had executed its officers, the operation would probably have failed. These men reinforced us and surrounded the Germans, who were now in complete disarray. Afterwards, upon an agreed signal, we retreated fast, leaving no visible tracks.

That night we camped out in a basement. There was more booty than we could manage: machine guns, grenades, ammunition, bags of sugar, flour, salt, boxes of sausages. Nobody dared to touch anything until we were given the order to do so. We were well disciplined. If you wanted to survive, you had to avoid anarchy. We kept order in our misery. To survive we had to obey the rules we imposed on ourselves in order to reach our objective.

⚜

More than a third of the resistance members were killed in this fight, some because they were inexperienced, others because their time was up, others due to their own carelessness. The partisans also had a great many losses, but at least were able to obtain the equipment they needed: all the large-caliber weapons went to them. It had been agreed.

The following day only a few of us dared to go out. The Germans, after this attack, and after seeing their flag replaced by the red banner with the hammer and sickle, were very cautious and kept a careful lookout everywhere. Fear was embedded in their skin. A patrol went by under the Eight O'clock Way. We saw their shining helmets and their dusty boots. The patrol had not advanced more than two hundred meters when it was gunned down by partisan sharpshooters acting like urban guerrillas in Bershad.

The sirens went off immediately and the German regiment opened fire crazily, throwing grenades at the walls, unburdening their impotence while shooting in all directions. Two went out in the middle of the street with their dogs, shot the animals, and then shot themselves. A grenade, I don't know from where, blew up the German flagpole and whatever remained of the wall after the previous night's incursion. The noise of motors in the air told us that Russian planes were approaching.

We ducked into the basement—and just in time. The methodical bombing made the walls shake. Children cried in the arms of their mothers, while the men raised their arms to heaven. Some old men prayed incessantly. Mordechai happily stroked his machine gun. The noise overhead became louder. Suddenly somebody came down screaming: "The Russians are coming, the Russian army is here! I just saw them; they're taking over Bershad. The Germans can't get away; they're completely surrounded. Come on out and fight. The partisans and the Jewish resistance are attacking from the rooftops. Those pigs are going to find out who we are!" and he went out again. I looked at Mordechai. He gave me a few grenades and motioned for me to follow him. Other boys and a few women did the same. We went up to the surface.

The horizon was darkened by smoke. Shots were heard everywhere. Explosions and screams. The Germans fought hard. The men of the regular German army were not giving up and maintained a constant barrage. Four men hid in a doorway and started to burn some papers. A woman recognized them: "They're from the Gestapo! Some partisans shot them, wounding them in the legs and knees. They screamed and tried to defend themselves, but it was too late. Three boys from the resistance had them pinned down, with their guns against their heads. I asked myself why they didn't kill them on the spot, but later realized that they were probably more valuable alive than dead. If they wanted to burn the papers, there must have been a good reason.

The fighting in the town square was especially fierce. The Germans had positioned a machine gun on the top of a church and from there were shooting everyone who tried to cross the square.

The Russians were attacking outside the town, while the partisans and the Jewish resistance were lashing out on the inside. The building where the beasts had taken refuge was subjected to unrelenting fire. I saw the bricks come down, then the walls and part of the roof. A brigade was formed to get rid of the Germans in the tower with their huge machine-gun. They chose five boys between

❖

five and eight. The boys took some explosives and went
out with their machine-guns in their hands while their
comrades covered their backs. I covered the Eight O'clock
Way. I went back and forth looking for something to blow
up. Those on the other side of the River Bug were claiming their revenge. The Romanians retreated, leaving the
field open for the partisans. But not the Ukrainians; they
kept firing while drinking vodka. I directed my first
grenade at some of them. I calculated the distance,
pulled out the pin and threw it. I crouched. The explosion
followed. When I looked again the Ukrainians were
sprawled on the ground.

Charging like a madman, I threw a second grenade
against a half-open door. The door shattered and a pair
of beasts fell to the ground. One of them was still screaming as he held in his guts with his hands. Mordechai
pinned him down with his gun and shot. The animal
could hardly move again when he fell on his comrade.

The Russians kept firing, but the Germans resisted
the attack. Those of us who remained inside were getting
low on ammunition and our morale was ebbing. The capture of Bershad was not going to be a bed of roses. The
voice of a comrade from the resistance could be heard
over a loudspeaker:

"Comrades, our dead claim revenge from their graves.
Listen, in the territory that Poland occupied before the
war there are hardly two hundred thousand Jews left.
The deportations continue to the extermination camps of
Belzek, Sobibor, Oswiecim [Auschwitz], and Treblinka.
On January 18 the second evacuation of the Warsaw
Ghetto started, as well as its heroic defense. All of the
members of the National Jewish Committee have fallen
and suffered heroic deaths. In Warsaw and the sur-

❖

rounding area only sixteen thousand Jews remain. The entire area of Bialystok has no more Jews. Only a few remain in the cities. In Volhynia, Podolia, White Russia, Silesia, Pomerania, and Lodz, with the exception of a few small ghettoes in Vilna and Lodz, there isn't a single Jew. The ghetto of Krakow is finished. The total elimination of the Jews of Eastern Galicia is underway. Every Jew found in a hiding place or in a forest is killed on the spot. Electric current, gas, asphyxiation by means of boiling gas, machine-guns, crematoria, this is the way for the millions of Jews of Poland and the occupied countries. The fate of every deported person is death. It's still going on. Synagogues have been burned down, Jewish cemeteries desecrated. During these last months the entire area east of the German border is to be completely cleansed of Jews. After this, not a single Jew will be found between the Oder and the Dnieper. Every day brings thousands of new martyrs. A day that goes by means new fodder for the camps of torture and death. S.O.S.! And if you can't save the witnesses of the worst tragedy in human history, we exhort you, for the blood of our children that was spilled, for our martyred mothers, for our desecrated sacred places. Take revenge! Damn anyone who takes pity! Revenge! Those who are about to die salute you! —Mordechai Tamarof!"

The voice continued: "This letter was written over a year ago, comrades! Are we going to allow the German border to remain clean of Jews? If we lose this battle we will lose the last chance to live for the millions that have been massacred!"

I felt an electric shock run through my back. I believe that everyone in the resistance felt the same way, since they all opened fire more strongly than ever.

❖

The letter—and God knows how it got to us—was a scream that came up from the very graves. And all of us, for one reason or another, had some part of us buried, murdered, incinerated, dead of cold and hunger behind some barbed wire. I threw a third grenade, but all I accomplished was to open another hole in the building where the beasts were hiding. I set out on the Eight O'clock Way again and fixed my burning eyes on the bell tower that still sent down its message of death. The noise of the shooting, the whistling of the bullets overhead and the thundering explosions were the symphony that accompanied my steps along this path built on the run over a rooftop about to topple down. Without a second thought, with my eyes fixed on my target, I kept walking. After about three meters, I could see the place that just a few days before had served as our synagogue. My head started spinning and I had to hold on to a gutter so as not to fall. I remembered the SS officer. I couldn't forget that face with the narrow forehead and turned-up nose of the beast with beady eyes who had stopped a pregnant woman, looked at her, and, laughing, shot her several times in the stomach while shouting: "I can kill a Jew even before he's born!" I knew he had to be someplace, hiding in fear. Because of him we killed three beasts, but we couldn't find him. I lay down on the Eight O'clock Way. I was tired, unable to move. The shots hit the roof tiles, whistled over my head, hit the walls. And there I was, lying down, with my mind alert, looking at every scene of the last few days as if it were part of a movie.

I saw the five detained boys. They made them kneel and shot them in the mouth, their blood running down the yellow dust of the road. Then they hung three children because they were supposedly part of the resis-

❖

tance. The Nazis didn't investigate. They took out their anger and fear on the most vulnerable.

Mordechai shook me by the shoulders, thinking that I was dead. I opened my eyes and stood up with great effort. It seemed that my whole body was full of stones. I felt heavy, tied to the tiles of the Eight O'clock Way. He gave me some water. I swallowed with difficulty and rubbed my burning eyes. The constant explosions, the shots, the crumbling walls, everything took on the appearance of a decisive battle, the one that would stop the SS from making soap with those who still remained from their huge genocide. I looked at Mordechai, and he took one of my grenades and threw it at a car going by the road below. Several bodies in black uniforms jumped up in the air. The wounded were nailed down by the fire of the partisans and the guerrillas. They fell like flies. I rallied and went to the end of the Eight O'clock Way. From there we could see the battle between those down in the street and the machine gun in the bell tower. Memories hounded me again. The farce of Balta, a camp for orphans that was supposed to have more "comforts" than we did. Most of the orphans who went there never came back. We found out later that they had been shot. The beasts played with us in their own way, and we responded in ours. To think that I almost fell into the trap of Balta. I had believed the whole story and left Bershad for a few days, but we came to our senses and twenty of us escaped.

We came back and joined the resistance and now, here at the end of the Eight O'clock Way, we look for something at which to aim our guns. You can tell that the Germans are beginning to give in. Those who went up to the tower in order to "clean it" have lost contact with the

❖

larger group. Mordechai says that the Germans are ready
to start blowing up the whole town of Bershad. They'd
rather have it in ashes with us inside than in the hands
of the Russians. The Jewish resistance and the partisans
are doing whatever they can in order to prevent this. The
battle in the alleys is like a game of chess. Every move
has a value. It is a game of intelligence that, if badly
played, can lead to checkmate. We have to be aware of
the collaborators, of those who want to escape, that
already see themselves trapped. Some Nazis are trying to
find a way out. They know that in the hands of the Soviet
army they will have to confess their crimes and there are
too many witnesses. Many people could not be exterminated because the Nazis ran out of time, and we're all
going to talk, to tell how they turned us into animals to
the point that they made us eat mice and cats in a dirty
stew. They should pay for this. We can't let them go. It
would mean losing the value of having endured, of having lived in the filth and misery. Those of us who are still
alive have to keep them alive so that the beasts will
answer for their crimes. This is the meaning of the skirmishes in the alleys.

Suddenly a tremendous explosion shakes every wall
while a red flame flies up to the sky. The resistance fighters cry out in unison: "The bell tower!" I open my eyes
wide. Yes, the tower has been blown up and the machine-
gun nest has been silenced. Its warped metal covers a big
part of the square. A group of partisans move up to headquarters. They kick open the door and go in. We hear a
few shots and then a white flag comes up, a piece of
sheet. The Germans of Bershad have surrendered!

They come out of their hiding places with their hands
up, looking distrustfully at their victims. They surely

❖

expect us to do with them what they did to us. But the resistance has been clear about that. They will be judged. After all, the soldiers were troops who had to carry out orders.

But the ones in the black uniforms, could they be judged? Did they judge us at the graveside? After the soldiers in brown uniforms come out, the beasts, the slaves, and lot of Ukrainians follow. From the rooftops, gunfire hits their legs and knees. It isn't time for them to die, but it is time to start paying for what they did. They double up and nobody helps them. Let them get up if they can, and if they don't, that's insubordination and it is punishable by death! They crawl like worms, weeping and asking for mercy. The Russians have already taken the town and are allowing the partisans and the resistance to assemble the Germans in the square. From the basements, the rooftops, the sewers, an accusing human mass starts to come out. The victims of Nazism float in the air like ghosts. In each of us is the memory of the lives of many.

Mordechai cries, holding his brother's letter. I think of Ladyzhin, of the Stone Cross, of my parents, of those that crossed to the other side of the river Bug to bow their heads before a shot to the back of the neck. Those in the graves are also present in the square. I feel them floating in the air, I can see their pale faces and their bones decaying one on top of the other. I close my eyes and see the road that for three days I traversed with a small boy of the resistance whose father had hidden in one of those graves. Before the Russians started their final push, the man was forced by the beasts to work on building a bridge in Nikolayev. With him were a few other men who could still stand heavy work. But very few came back,

❖

and he escaped. He ran away, but the only hiding place
he could find was a mass grave. I was going with his son
to bring a carrot and some water to his hiding place
among the decomposing bodies. Three days were enough
for me to believe what others had said. The pit was filled
with the human material massacred by the beasts. I was
a witness who would have to speak in the name of the
multitudes of people who would never rise up again.

In my madness the memories loomed stronger. The
memory became one huge platter on which everything
was engraved. I ran to the square, followed by Isaac,
Moshe, his legless father, the rabbi from the train, the
raped woman who was later assassinated in the ghetto,
the children, and the old men. The dead world of the
graves came alive, got in between my feet and pushed me
toward the square. There I would recognize the beasts, I
would point out the hangmen, and would identify the
slaves and the collaborators. I ran forward, paying no
attention to where I planted my feet. What was the difference? Wherever I stepped I would leave my mark,
denouncing the beasts whose treatment I had endured.
My madness was turning rather lucid.

I looked at Mordechai, who was running at my side.
We were going to point out those who had branded us.
The trumpet of justice sounded in the sky, resounded
from the soot-covered walls. It reverberated in the ground
we were walking on. Hoarse voices shouted out from the
stones, stuck to our ears, drilling. We were going to exact
our price for having lived and what they owed us for the
souls they had deported night and day in those railroad
cars, for those who had been mixed with soil and lime-
stone. We were going to collect a price they would never
be able to pay because it was a stain that went beyond

❖

every conceivable limit and that in a thousand years would not cover even a quarter of the bodies that could be sensed through the stink of their decayed flesh.

The Russians lined up the Germans and the Ukrainians in the center of the square, the regular soldiers to the right of the beasts and to the left of the Ukrainians. The Romanian and Ukrainian soldiers were loaded on trucks. Their long pale faces bore no resemblance to the faces of the soldiers who had started the war. Now they were the defeated and were being taken to a special camp. The beasts remained at the mercy of the partisans and the resistance. The Ukrainians were for the Russians. After all, they were traitors to the Red Army. The solution for them was fast and final. They were shot without a trial. They were deserters and traitors, besides the charges levied on them as collaborators and murderers of the Russian people. There was no discrimination between officers and common soldiers. The men of the Vlasov Army paid the price of treason to the Russian flag.

No one cared. The annihilation of the Ukrainians must have been planned by the Russian high command. With every shot they shouted something about Babi Yar or Kiev or Stalingrad. The Russian troops were highly motivated, for they were collecting the blood of their massacred brothers, of the widows, of the raped and martyred women. In Bershad, not one Ukrainian was left alive. In about an hour they were all dead.

Later the Russian partisans and the resistance lined up a group of beasts and collaborators they would have to judge and later report on to the new occupying authorities. That's where the big wigs of the resistance came in. Our participation was hardly centered on anything we

❖

could communicate by the written or spoken word, as long as they could prove we were of sound mind. A boy, recognizing one of the beasts, started to cry: "That's the one who killed me. Yes, I saw him open my belly and take out my guts to chew them up. And he gouged my eyes out and put them in a bottle." He was already insane.

The boy was talking as if he were one of the dead of the massacres he had witnessed. There were many like him. The partisans listened but didn't pay much attention. They simply said: "It's enough."

When my turn came, they didn't want to believe the story of the train, of the Stone Cross, of my escape. I saw them looking patiently at me, sure that it was all a product of my imagination. When I realized this I said: "I know you don't believe me. As the Russians advance you will discover that what I told you is true," and I walked away without saying another word. Mordechai didn't want to talk.

We spent that night and the following day walking through the destroyed alleys, through the dust and garbage. My personal pride was deeply bruised. To have survived, to have played my last card over and over again only to have the grownups believe that it was all a pack of lies was very hard on me.

I looked around and kept seeing the sad, hungry faces of the children, the paleness in the faces of the mothers, men staring into space as if to say: "Well, now what?" I was wondering about the same question. I couldn't stay in Bershad, this town next to the orphanage that I barely got to know during the last few days, when the Russians were already breaking in with their cannon and bombing. It hurt me to know that there had been something right there that I had been unable to take advan-

❧

tage of for lack of knowledge. Stuck in a corner, digging my nails into the walls of the barracks, always playing to exist. I swallowed hard. Isaac knew about Bershad. Why hadn't he told me? A boy extended his dirty little hand, waiting for me to give him some food. I took a piece of cracker and gave it to him. He waited for another piece, thinking the beasts were still there and he would need another piece in case he woke up in the basement. I shrugged. The boy looked at me with his big black eyes and grunted. I understood why Isaac hadn't told me anything. There was more misery outside than in the orphanage. Inside, at least, we were organized and were able to pin our hopes on the farmers. Had I known the town of Bershad, some of our illusions and hopes would have been diluted by the misery and the vulnerability of its people. Isaac knew but didn't say anything. He knew that many of us wouldn't survive. It was not a favorable environment for the gangs from the orphanage.

At first I accepted these ideas, other times I rejected them. I came and went, walked everywhere, sometimes I would look into the place where they kept the beasts and the slaves, most of them with wounds in their hands and legs. I looked on them as rats waiting to be executed. Shivering, with teary eyes, they begged for mercy. Those in black pleaded that they had been following orders, the others blamed the Germans. They were long, ugly scared faces. Not even the people who were tortured had such faces. The beasts and the slaves made me sick. I ran into Mordechai again in the street. He and I would stay together for some time and then each would go his own way. In reality we didn't know which way to go. We talked about our homes without any concrete knowledge or information. Mordechai told me to sign up at the Office

❖

of Displaced Persons, giving the name and place I came from. They said you could get information there about relatives and friends. We went there. There were many people in the line. We stood in line. The Red troops were going from side to side. They arrested the collaborators and those who were under suspicion because of the work they did. If anything could be proved, they would be shot on the spot. The Russians didn't want to jail the murderers. Their conclusion was fast, devastating, ready to annihilate the German enemy. They went to Berlin. There they would resolve their problems in a different manner.

But the Red Army advanced now, avenging their dead, their people who had been crushed by the Nazi boot. For this reason, public courts of justice were instituted and the charges were read. If the accused was found guilty, he was shot on the spot. To spare the lives of those who for four years had conducted a reign of terror and death would mean to keep alive a seed of evil that later on might germinate again as the dark fruit of Fascism.

I waited in line, trying to focus my attention on something that would not be the anguish of not knowing which way to go. A woman was telling her friend: "The Russians have liberated some camps and villages. I hope I'll be able to join my husband. He was in Ladyzhin, and I understand the camp was liberated more than a month ago."

My stomach churned. My parents were there. Could they be alive? Would they be looking for me? All the darkness dissipated. Thinking about my family and the possibility that they were still alive sent me back into my madness. But now I was dreaming, looking for their faces. The line kept moving, getting nearer to the small

❖

office that the Soviets had improvised to carry on the task of reintegration. We displaced persons advanced slowly, but advanced nonetheless with a shred of hope. I waited, dreaming about my mother's face, my father's strong arm. I was coming out of the sewer, albeit a bit dirty and weighing half my original weight. But thin as I was, I had just been given the strength to endure, this time definitely. I looked at the woman who had spoken about Ladyzhin and wanted to kiss her, to thank her for the news she had just given me. But I held back. My name would probably already be in the records. I put my hands in my pockets and waited. I played with the minutes, passing the time by getting into an unreal world. Fields covered with flowers, my parents running toward me and me running toward them. Ladyzhin liberated, no more Stone Cross! The word "liberation" had a beautiful ring in my ears.

When I got to the improvised office, a uniformed officer asked me to sit down. He asked for my name and place of birth. Later he asked about my doings and finally nodded. "Kid, stay here in Bershad. Your last name is known and you're one of the ones they've been claiming for several days. Come back tomorrow and I'll be able to give you more information." And he pointed to the door.

I was walking on air. My parents were claiming me. They were alive and on their way to Bershad! And what if it was all only a product of my imagination? Lately I had found it difficult to distinguish truth from fantasy.

I waited for the next day in a huge bomb crater. Curled up into a ball, I indulged in mental machinations of all sorts. I went along a dark road that had no end. The Russians flattening the beasts and me behind looking at the human misery. I walked alone. The story about my

❖

parents was a lie to help me endure. Mordechai talked about becoming an avenger. He wanted to kill. When the resistance asked us about the treatment we had received from the beasts. Mordechai hit one of the SS in the head with a stone. "I'm gonna kill him. We have to kill them. My sister, if she's still alive, must be thinking the same thing." I grunted. He stopped talking, understanding my mood. He took out a piece of dark bread and gave me half. A boy with black hair and a huge scar that covered his head from side to side began to speak:

"The Russians are here. The Germans couldn't run away and now they are standing trial. Everybody is moving around. They talk about camps where people came in through the door and left through the chimney. We Jews were exterminated and there are hardly two or three on the road picking up the bones of what once were whole villages. Liberated, so what? Others can celebrate, we're in the same spot and they don't need to put us in a ghetto because we are all destroyed. What a fiction this liberation is! I don't remember whether I had parents, whether my brothers were real or a figment of my imagination. I don't know who I am or where to go. I've been dead for a long time. They came to the house, they pushed us outside and ripped out my grandfather's beard. Then the darkness. The train, the boxcar, some boards—some of us jumped. We walked long and hard, dying of hunger and thirst. Some just lay there with their mouths open, looking for a heaven that didn't answer. The other dead ones dragged our feet to where we are today. We lived with the mice, the filth, and the sickness. How many managed to survive? I found two of my gang, they had smashed faces and didn't laugh like before. The Russians killed them with their damn invasion!"

⚜

Mordechai stood up and responded: "Some die, others are already dead like you. Death has been coming at us from all four corners, you can't blame the Russians if one of their grenades exploded in someone's faces. They were attacking the Germans, not the partisans or the guerrillas. And how many of us died? Many, but many more are left. What do you want? To have a chest full of medals that you can't eat?"

A strange voice came from a pile of straw on top of a wooden crate, broken down by the dampness and the battle. "Don't talk so much! The guys on the Jewish Committee talk about going to Palestine. That's our country, and that's where we should go. That's what liberation is all about!" The one with the black hair laughed. "So why are you still here?"

"I'm waiting for weapons. There's going to be trouble, and a lot of us in the resistance are going to Palestine—" I hardly paid any attention to these conversations. Some talked about politics, others about women. I looked at them as if they were ghosts. I was again living in my own world. My corner, myself, the ceiling, some tiles about to fall down, the ever-reddening evening sky. A warm breeze hit my face bringing in the smell of garbage. We were still in the filth, liberated with the smell of excrement. The words went in one ear and out the other. Optimistic phrases clashed with angry speeches. I looked at some bits of straw. Thin, a bit coarse, yellow, very similar to the ones in the dream I had told Isaac about. I opened my eyes and saw myself surrounded by a bunch of boys. Some were talking, others were looking at the sky or had their eyes fixed on the floor. I didn't panic. Probably all the streets of Bershad were full of displaced persons heading home in the wake

❖

of the Red Army. I asked for one wish. I asked for my parents to be alive and to find me.

I smiled when I made this wish and began to examine myself. Eleven years old, wearing torn shirt, pants, and boots. I touched my neck. I could have planted potatoes in the dirt I found there. I was covered with filth and had nothing to arouse anyone's envy. I looked at Mordechai, who thought I was hungry and took out another piece of black bread. I broke it into small pieces and threw a piece to whoever looked at me. Some thanked me, others returned angrily. Mordechai asked: "Israel, are you staying?" "I'm going to wait for my parents," I said, nodding. And there was no shaking or fear in my words. He looked at me. "All right, I'll stay with you for a couple of days. If my sister doesn't come, I'll have to go look for her." And he stroked his pistol again. "And if I don't find her, if she's nowhere, the Germans will pay for it! Do you understand?" I nodded, even though I didn't understand much. What could Mordechai do with an eleven-shot pistol? I looked at sunset, which brought with it the possibility of a warm, stench-filled night, more so now that the Russians were opening the mass graves to investigate the truth of the accusations.

The odor of decay filled every space. I thought about the sewer that the dark-haired boy talked about. Yes, this was like a sewer, the exit from a well of filth to one of garbage. The heat increased considerably. The alley seemed to come on top of us. Its torn walls, its destroyed windows, the faces that came up through the unhinged doors, it was all an explosive whole that could blow up any moment. And this suffocating environment, together with the anguish of the wait for the dawn of a new day, so that they would tell you whether your name is known

❖

or not. I began to have difficulty breathing. I was getting
dizzy. Because of the heat and the smell—

Displaced persons crowd into the alleys, each one
thinking that he'll be recognized, that someone is looking
for him. Others enclosed in their silence, feeding their
hatred and their need for revenge, a way to regain what
has taken from them.

I sleep and the nightmares return. I am with a group
of people going to be executed at the edge of a mass
grave. The dead wait with open arms. The beast is about
to press the trigger at the back of my neck. Far away, in
the front rank of the vanguard of the Red Army, my parents cry out that he shouldn't shoot me. The beast begins
to move his finger, my parents are farther and farther
away, and the Russians disappear. I fall into the grave
and there, to one side, between two thin bodies
Mordechai is loading his gun. He smiles: "Aren't you getting out of here?" His a voice sinks deep into my brain.
Somebody touches me on the shoulder and I wake up,
certain that there's a hole in the back of my neck.
Mordechai repeats: "Aren't you going to get out of here?"
I rub my eyes. Could I be still dreaming? Mordechai's
hand grabs my shoulder more firmly. I open my eyes,
and a blinding sun hurts them.

It's another day, but I'm still sure to be in my nightmare. The sun is strong and the odors are getting
stronger. The latrines are full, and there are long lines of
hungry people waiting in the hot sun for the bowl of soup
the Russians will give them. A couple of women are fighting over a rag they found in the street. One hears curses
from the houses, because of the lack of fresh air, of water,
of a place to breathe. Others are cursing God. The liberation is beginning to take shape in my mind. We have

fought for freedom, but is this the freedom we risked our lives for? I look cynically at the rooftops that made up the Eight O'clock Way. That's where I ran, risking my life, spying on the beasts, sticking my nose in the homes of the collaborators. And now the people who live in those houses are killing each other for a piece of wool or half a dozen potatoes.

Mordechai takes out another piece of dark bread. I eat it avidly. I'm hungry and hot, wishing to disappear into the horizon. Refugees keep pouring coming into Bershad. The parade of misery never stops. They come looking for a friend, for any piece of news. Others simply pass through. The village is only a point of reference in their wanderings through a destroyed Europe. Perhaps they think there's something left of their homes, that someone might have survived. In spite of their ragged clothes and their curses, there is hope in their eyes. You can see the strength they are gathering to start the reconstruction of what the war has ravaged. They walk slowly, their eyes fixed on the dusty road, and drawing narrow lines with the staffs they carry in their hands. But we Jews, where can we go? Is there anything that is still ours? Many of our assets have been auctioned by the Germans or confiscated and given to people who didn't know how to manage them. Our eyes carry a terrible question that even today the world cannot answer: "Why us?"

By ten o'clock I was standing on line outside the office of missing persons. Mordechai was in front of me. The heat increased every moment. The last days of summer were coming on strong. I felt more than ever that I was in a sewer. The line moved very slowly. Inside the Displaced Persons Office, they were probably giving more details. In the war you always hope the dead will not be your own.

⚜

Finally, after almost three hours of waiting, my turn came. The same officer as the previous day, albeit a little more tired and disheveled, looked me over. He smiled. He obviously hadn't forgotten me. He finally found a sheet of paper: "Your parents are among the survivors at Ladyzhin. With a bit of time you should be able to reunite with them." I couldn't help it. I lunged at the man to kiss him. It seemed impossible that all this would be happening. They were alive and were coming to join me. Some soldiers pulled me away but when they saw that I was crying, they put me down and patted me on the shoulder. The officer ordered me: "Comrade, salute!"

I stood at attention, I'm sure ridiculously, and extended my hand. The man took it in his and shook it. I left the office running, wanting to cry to the four winds that my parents were alive, that they were looking for me, that they were not on the list of missing or executed persons. It was a miracle that they had survived the Final Solution to the Jewish problem."

When I saw Mordechai I wanted to share my good news, but I stopped when I saw his long face and reddened eyes. We looked at each other like a pair of strangers. After a while he started talking. "She was killed in Maidanek. The minute she got there she was gassed or flattened out, what's the difference? They killed her, those sons of bitches, and they're going to pay for it! Mordechai is going to die, but first a lot of them are going to go, you'll see!" He began to sob with his head against the trunk of a tree blackened by fire. He cried openly, raising his hands to the skies as if asking permission to execute his revenge. I stayed with him for the rest of the day, afraid that he might do something crazy. He had lost hope, and from a hopeless man you can expect anything.

⚜

A new contingent of the Red Army was now camped on the outskirts of Bershad. They were probably resting while preparing to continue the offensive. In the afternoon Mordechai sat on a rooftop. He insisted he wasn't going to come down until he had killed a beast in the name of his sister. Night came and Mordechai was still up there, waiting for his prey. We explained in every possible way that it wasn't permitted, the Germans who had been caught were prisoners of war, but he stayed on the roof with his gun in his hand. I waited downstairs and couldn't help falling asleep. I was tired, hot, and hungry. Up on the roof, with his eyes wide open like an owl, Mordechai awaited his prey.

Around midnight we heard some shots. When we looked around in the alley we saw two ex-SS agents with their mouths open and holes between their eyes. Mordechai was nowhere to be seen. How had the SS men gotten out of the detention camp after the partisans and the resistance had filled in the necessary forms? The Russian soldiers shrugged, and some nurses came in and took the bodies away. Maybe the Russians had cooperated in this, in order to frighten any beasts who still refused to talk or to sign documents implicating them in crimes against the Russian people and the rest of the displaced persons. For now, nobody talked about the executed Jews, who had been massacred, gassed, squashed like insects. They talked about the Russian people, who now were going back to their countries of origin.

We Jews were still parading like ghosts. Sometimes they gave us something to eat. Other times they looked at us with pity; some people avoided us because we brought "bad luck."

In the morning, unable to sleep a wink, I found myself standing in front of Mordechai. He looked at me as if he

⚜

were going to give me a piece of bread from his pocket, as always, without anyone knowing where the devil he had gotten it. He smiled bitterly. "I still have nine bullets and new clip." My blood froze in my veins. He was the one who had shot the two beasts, and he wasn't afraid to show his gun and talk about the bullets he still had left to keep avenging his sister's death. He put away the gun and took out his piece of bread, but this time it was white. He rubbed his nose and said: "You have to have friends everywhere. Last night two SS officers talked too much after they found out about their friends." He offered me a sip of vodka. "They did me a favor, and I did one in return. Do you know that they consider the SS the same as Vlasov's Ukrainians, that is, they are to be shot without too much ceremony." For a few minutes he looked quietly at the blue sky that covered the whole countryside. I told him that my parents were coming for me and he could stay with us. He didn't say anything in response except for a long sigh. He got up. "We'll talk," he said, and began strolling among the throngs of refugees filling the streets of Bershad. I chewed on the piece of bread he had given me and pondered what I would do if I were Mordechai. He was alone, he had nothing to lose. He was alone in the world with his gun, nine bullets and a spare clip. His only hope was lost in an extermination camp. He was probably reading his brother's letter again to give himself some hope and not fall into the despair that precedes suicide.

I started to walk around Bershad. People saw me go by. Some looked at me inquisitively, crying out with their eyes, asking why I had been saved instead of one of their relatives. A woman laughed and held on to a piece of wood that kept rocking. Some children were making fun of her. Some old men, who could hardly walk, were chew-

❖

ing their ration of black bread and had to stop for a rest
every few minute. Madmen were everywhere. There were
crowds of them among the refugees. They laughed, cried,
hit each other, they kept looking through a small hole
they had dug in the floor and I moved among this miserable web looking for a bit of air, a bit less of the bad odor.

When I walked in front of the headquarters I heard
my name called out by some people passing in a truck.
My parents were in Bershad! Without asking her pardon,
I stepped over a woman who was lying on the ground and
ran toward the place were I was being called. How would
they be? Would they cry or jump in joy when they saw
me? Would they be surprised to see me so thin and with
eyes so big? As I tried to approach the newcomers the
soldiers stopped me, but I managed to slip through their
legs. Perhaps they thought I was a thief. I crossed the
street, running as fast as I could. Breathless, almost at
the point of collapse, I reached the people getting off the
truck. I looked up, and there they were. I ran to them,
and they ran to me.

⚜

10

On the Path of the Dead

Time began to pass less slowly in Bershad. Now that I was reunited with my parents, things had changed drastically for me. Everything seemed different. I still felt the intense joy of my first encounter with my mother's trembling hands. With my parents by my side, I knew that the beasts had really been conquered. I was myself, my hands were my hands, and I became aware once again of values that had vanished during my ordeal, holding on to my madness to endure. We had overcome, had defeated the genocidal urge of the executioners. We had had not fallen into the pit. In my happiness, I lost sight of the terrible tragedy that surrounded us.

I was a child who had recovered his parents, finding what I had thought had been irreparably lost. It was somewhat akin to having your hands cut off and suddenly finding them reattached to your wrists. I was so elated that I ceased to be aware of the immense human mass sliding along the roads looking for whatever remained of their homes.

The day of the reunion, my piece of dark bread tasted like heaven and the sound of shooting from the front gave us some security in order to set out for Belz, our native city. I looked at my mother and touched her face. I wanted to know that I wasn't in a dream from which I would have to wake up. I held on to my father's thin, callused hand, digging my fingers into his palm, not taking my eyes from each gesture he made. I was entering a new world, knowing myself to be a passenger in an unsealed wagon. I wanted to turn around and scream to the half-torn walls and the stones that we were as free as birds that flew across the sky without fearing the shells of an anti-aircraft battery. I even touched myself to be sure that I was still Israel, the boy who waited, the one who had walked through the ghetto, who had survived in Ladyzhin, and who had later escaped to become a member of the Jewish resistance.

Feeling my mother's hands on my head, and mine in my father's, I knew I was privileged, that I was receiving more than enough for having endured. My mother smiled, perhaps holding back the emotional outflow that stirred inside her. The same with my father. We each lived in our own dimension and tried to find an outlet for our emotions, our hopes and illusions. We hugged and cried for a long time, letting the tears roll down our cheeks. We savored the prize of having endured when there was no other hope but the grave. Our cry was existence transformed into life, in new strength to start once again.

But this didn't last more than a few hours. Suddenly the wasted figure of a child made me come back to reality. It was true that we were together, but we would still have to endure and survive. The war wasn't over. The bombing resounded nearby and the walls of Bershad still trembled with each explosion. The displaced persons kept to the side of the roads, waiting, with big eyes and

⚜

long faces. We all looked at each other as if asking. "Now what?" The anguish manifested itself in the children's cries, the curses of the adults, the constant grumping of old people who could hardly move. It was a terrible, bitter picture, an enormous filthy multitude following in the tracks of the Red Army.

We were a small point in the huge crowd walking along the road, holding onto the hope of getting to our homes and finding our belongings. Dull eyes that harbored no illusions, that almost denied hope. A human tide filled the roads, leaving behind the residue of misery, an acrid smell between the threatening sound of gunshots and explosions. Women looking at every passing face in the hope of recognizing someone.

Reality had a bad taste. The taste of a broken road, laid on a foundation of blood and corpses. We were going to leave Bershad, joining the human tide that followed the path opened by the Russians. My father made the decision to leave, and I didn't have time to say goodbye to Mordechai, or even to see him again. It wouldn't surprise me if he had already left and lay dead somewhere, killed while trying once again to avenge his sister's death. I searched for his face among the thousands around us, but apparently he had disappeared within his world. It hurt not to be able to tell him at least, "See you soon!"

We left Bershad at dawn after a night sleeping in one of its alleys. I yawned deeply and said my goodbyes, kicking the first stone that I found in my way. Thus I began my life as a displaced person, the life of a refugee feeding on the dream of a decent existence. Bershad stayed behind. My torn boots became filled with dust and pebbles that hurt my toes and the soles of my feet. But I con-

tinued, I couldn't stop the start of a new beginning. I had
to keep on, one of the many people who found refuge in
the wake of the Russian Army.

We walked without stopping for a good part of the
day, among the craters in a road that had been methodically bombed. Water was scarce, as was food. Little or
nothing could be gotten from the farmers. They wanted
to be paid, and all we had was our empty hands. We had
no money. The sum of our belongings was a sack of dirty
old clothes. Nothing of value. I looked at my mother's tormented face as she protectively murmured a few sooth-
ing words. I saw my father's hardened face, his sad eyes
looking for a solution to our problem. Everybody tried to
make do in the misery. My fingers moved inside the
pockets of my pants. I went back to being the escapee
who went to the farmers to get at least a loaf of bread and
half a pound of butter.

There was a blind man walking beside us, his hand
shakily grasping a cane. The road was in such bad condition that he wasn't sure whether he was on the road or
in the fields. He kept asking where we were. His cane did-
n't afford him the security he needed, and he looked for
assurances in the words of his neighbors. I walked by his
side for a while, listening to the hoarse voice that came
out of his sick lungs. A woman who was serving as his
guide answered each of his questions, but he refused to
believe what she said. In his blindness he was incapable
of understanding the darkness of the war and the black
world of the displaced persons. But he never stopped
walking. He clung to the hope of reaching the main road,
even though he was already on it.

A little before dusk we stopped to rest. Some of the
wounded clenched their teeth in order not to cry. The

⚜

blind man sat down and began muttering to himself, perhaps remembering a time when he had been able to see,
searching in his memory for the shapes the sounds
around him might have. I was surprised to see him smile,
moving his head while he said: "We're all going someplace. To each his own. I can't see anything. I haven't
been able to see for ten years. But you who can see will
also see nothing. You'll be as blind as I am. I feel the
night, and for too many, dawn will never come. After the
war, there will be many who will remain in the dark, like
me." An old woman let out a scream and the man was
silenced. The woman cried and tugged at her white hair.
She was demanding a sum of money that the Germans
had taken away from her, she talked about some pictures
and kept saying that her children couldn't have died. She
ended up on the rocky ground, exhausted after so much
crying.

My mother gave me a piece of bread, and I drank from
my father's huge canteen. Our blind neighbor smiled
again, but this time he didn't say anything. He was living
in his own silent world. He ate without appetite whatever the woman gave him.

Some children began to cry, while others played with
odds and ends they had found along the way. One of
them made believe he was shooting an enemy with a
dried-out branch serving as a machine gun. Another was
shaking a whip. His friends cheered him on with hoorays
and applause. A thin man without teeth kept watching
them. His hands under his chin, he followed each step of
the children's games. Tears rolled down his sunken eyes,
but his expression did not change.

A fairly young woman studied the piece of bread in
her hands, unable to decide whether to put it in her

⚜

mouth, perhaps for fear of not seeing food again. Her older neighbor was drawing figures in the sand with a twig. She drew a house with a horse next to it, erased it, and drew it again. My father began to talk with a man with a shaved head and his left arm marked with a black number. My mother looked at the stars that had begun to appear in the sky. When I asked what she saw, she responded: "The greatness of God." I didn't understand what she meant and tried to see if I could see it too. But in the shimmer of the stars I only saw the blasts of the machine guns of the beasts and the slaves.

The explosions at the front illuminated the sky with a red splendor and for a few moments the stars disappeared. I looked at my mother, and she, understanding my concern, stroked my hair and said:

"Do you know what is God's greatness? Look closely at that star, the one nearest to you. Do you see it well? After everything we're going through, there is something that still gives us life. A light that won't allow us to die altogether. When you're older you'll understand. But that light exists, and those who have died live there. They have joined in that star so that we will not forget them. That's why it shines so brightly, giving us strength to go on, so that each of us will tell the others that up there are the ones we are looking for. That is the greatness of God. He allows those of us who have survived to see those who have gone away, but He shows them to us in a beautiful way, dressed as a star. That's why, when you look at the sky and see the stars shining, remember the others, the ones who are still in their graves, and then you will have the courage to go on, in their name and in God's name. "

I scratched my head. In a way she was right. We had to go on in the name of the dead. The rest I didn't understand very well. The reality for me was in the darkness of

❧

the sky and the glow of the explosions. That was what I felt, smelled, and touched, and in my ears I could feel the rumble of the artillery while the smell of gunpowder filled my nostrils.

As the laments and curses increased, so too did the fighting at the front. The explosions were heard one after the other. Sometimes a shell would fall close to a group of refugees, creating panic. The darkness of the night would explode into a thousand lights, and we would fall on the ground and cover our heads to protect ourselves against the debris of the explosions. Suddenly a rumor spread that the Russians were retreating. Confusion reigned. The girl who, minutes before, had been contemplating a piece of bread, put it in her mouth and swallowed it and started to scream. The blind man swung his cane and asked again where the road was. "We're going to die in this forest. If we get to the road we'll be saved!" the poor man shouted, trying to get up, getting in the way of his own cane. The woman guided him among the people who were moving from one side to the other without knowing which way to go.

The frightened faces of the refugees turned a macabre color when illuminated by the light of the explosions. Some showed bulging, panicked eyes, contracted mouths, trembling hands stuck to the dirty parcels they carried, as if these pathetic packages were going to serve as shelter. Mothers grabbed their children and ran in different directions. My mother held on to me and covered me with her scarf. My father took us by the hand and we started to walk, shoving our way into the crowd, looking desperately for a way out. The explosions seemed to be closer every time. Red and blue lights illuminated the grimaces of our faces, and the burned-out trees by the side of the road seemed to poke fun at our escape.

❖

The blind man continued to walk at our side, guided by the woman. He was no longer using his cane. He was almost running. For a moment I thought he had recovered his sight. His steps were firm and fearless. We all ran as fast as our tired muscles allowed. The screams kept increasing, now mingled with the cries of the little ones and the hysterical screams of the women who yelled: "They're going to kill us! They're going to kill us!" Some fainted, and the men who still had some strength carried them off like sacks of potatoes.

We were like this for at least a couple of hours. Two terrible hours that seemed like centuries, during which some died because of the nonstop German artillery fire. Throughout this bitter time we were caught up in anguish and hysteria. People screamed and fainted, cursed and prayed in a panic. I felt like a prisoner inside four walls that threatened to crush me. My father's hands held on to my mother's and mine. While I ran I started to think: "Israel, this is the end. The beasts are going to win. You couldn't escape from their paws. Don't you see how they are making the Russian Army retreat? This is the last hour. Everything has gone back. What the devil is liberation?" At times I felt that the ground was giving in under my feet; that my feet were stuck to the ground and couldn't move. Other times I recovered my strength and began scheming how to get into the fields and join the Jewish guerrilla fighters and the partisans. Just as I began to feel that I could no longer go on , we saw a new contingent of Russian troops moving toward the front to reinforce those who were holding back the German attack. We stopped, full of hope, and while we waited our dreams came true. The Soviets made the Germans retreat once more.

❧

After a while we decided to retrace our steps, but someone said that we would be safer where we were, that the next day we could continue our miserable pilgrimage along the path of the dead. The blind man agreed and spat. It landed on the back of a hunchback who kept calling the name of a woman: "Masha, my Masha." My father, my mother, and I climbed up on the trunk of a half-destroyed tree and from there we could see the glare of the German artillery. I fell asleep in the midst of the battle noise and forgot everything. The tiredness and the anguish took me to a quiet place somewhere within me.

I woke up when I felt my mother's hand following the contours of my face, perhaps searching for scratches or wounds. The first rays of sun hit my eyes and I had to rub them to take away the burn. I didn't dream that night, even though nightmares usually plagued my sleep. When I got up I could see that many of the refugees from our group were already moving. My mother made me drink from the canteen and I ate a piece of bread. On our way we saw nothing but decayed flesh and dead men in the most convoluted positions. There were bodies with their mouths open. They probably died while attempting one last cry. Others with their eyes popping out and holding their guts. Legs and hands were everywhere on the sides of the road. Trunks without heads, unclothed, feet without boots. Many of the refugees took everything the dead soldiers had on them. If they didn't do it, others would. That's why, by the time we passed, we saw nothing but half-naked corpses, with their bodies burned-out and a terrible odor emanating from them.

My mother tried in vain to cover my eyes. I engraved all of these scenes on my mind. Men seemed to be born to do away with each other. Wherever we looked there

⚜

was nothing but corpses and twisted metal. It wasn't
unusual to see a burned-out hand gripping the sides of
a trench in an effort to hold on to one more second of life.
A thousand odors arose from each step we took. At one
turn on this path of death we encountered the blind man
again. He was walking with his head down, his hand
trembling on his cane and singing a mysterious melody.
The woman with him was holding a crucifix that hung
from her neck. A man who trembled constantly was being
led by his wife and son. On the sleeve of the boy was still
embroidered the yellow Star of David that marked us as
Jews. Some were wearing shirts from the dead soldiers,
brown German shirts and huge boots that made it even
more difficult to walk.

The advance was difficult. Sometimes the Germans
unleashed a terrible counter-attack that made us believe
we were lost, but the Russian Army drove them back
each time. Among the refugees confusion was our constant companion. Sometimes we had to retreat three
times in one day, which kept us in a paroxysm of terror.
About a third of our group of refugees were killed. Some
died on the road, others as a result of the bombing. There
was talk of death caused by cardiac arrest or exhaustion.
Someone even took his own life while retreating. He was
a little man, always chewing on a twig dangling from his
mouth. At dawn, seeing the Germans almost in front of
our noses, he took a knife that he kept on his belt and
cut his own throat. Nobody could prevent the hemor-
rhage that in less than a minute stained his shirt and
pants.

Anguish kept claiming victims among us. Fear of
falling into the hands of the Germans again led many
people to suicide. Our march on the death path exacted

❧

a toll in human lives. We all knew that we still weren't safe. We were hungry and thirsty. Tiredness and fear eroded our strength. My father's beard grew, and the circles under my mother's eyes became more purple each day.

Our faces showed the seconds that went by, the breath we still had. Our faces were a calendar full of painful dates; of waiting and illusions that moved farther away with every step we took. Hope disappeared whenever a tree fell down or a piece of shrapnel flew over our heads. My eyes were stinging and sometimes I tried to mask the cough that remained from my time in the Bershad orphanage.

We became once again inhabitants of the world of madness, of days that often were difficult to tell from night because of the thick columns of smoke that went up in the air, covering the sky with a dense black coat. The soil trembled under the torn soles of our shoes, hunger sliced through our guts, and thirst burned our throats. But we kept on walking behind the Russian Army. All of us longed to arrive at our destination, to know what had happened to our loved ones and our belongings. But despair went on among the swelling ranks of refugees. We found nothing but destroyed villages and decomposing bodies in our path.

Women cried, holding on to pieces of walls, covering with their tears what had once been their homes. Hundreds of fatherless children walked aimlessly in the misery, looking for something to eat in the garbage and the remains of the soldiers. We crossed through villages blown to pieces by the retreating Germans. Death walked along with us, pointing to a dark path and taking away the tiny bit of hope still harbored by those who had not

⚜

arrived in their hometowns. My father's beard kept growing, as did the circles under my mother's eyes.

We continued on behind the Russian troops. The blind man had stopped complaining in order to give way to every curse he knew. The woman who walked with him bit her lips and tried to calm him, telling him they would soon be home. And they arrived.

All I could see was a bunch of stones one on top of the other. People very similar to the ghosts that haunted me in my nightmares walked among the stones, which were starting to get wet with the onset of autumn. The blind man poked around with his cane and asked the woman to take him to his house. She opened her eyes wide and didn't know how to answer. The destruction was so total that it wasn't possible to invent even a small lie. The houses were unrecognizable, and it was difficult to determine where the main street used to be.

The angry ghosts watched us, screaming at us to go on. They didn't wish to share their misery. The blind man fell on the ground. He didn't ask any questions. In his darkness he began to understand the immensity of the war, the misery of the return, the pain of having walked so far to arrive at a place as dark as his blindness. Unable to contain her sobs, the woman sat down on a rock and began to cry. She didn't even move to help the poor blind man get up. He was doing it on his own, like someone lifting himself from a pit to arrive at a similar place. Some women were consoling their children, telling them that they could always start anew, that whatever was lost could be regained. The children shook their heads and looked at the desolate landscape. They had hoped to find the warmth they had dreamed of, but found only cold and the first drops of rain, which had begun to fall from the leaden sky.

⚜

We stayed in that village for a few hours, observing the despair of the refugees who had once inhabited this place that was once a town. They searched here and there, looking for a clue as to the location of their former homes, of their street, but in vain. Sullen-faced men emerged from the basements to look at the newcomers. Some recognized a friend and went over looking for a bit of hope. And between the two, the anguished refugee and the specter who had survived, a new hope was reborn. Between the two they were going to set out on the road to reconstruction. I looked at the blind man again and swallowed bitterly when I saw him crying and shaking his cane in defeat. His closed mouth held in the scream that wanted to break out of his throat. He couldn't see, but he felt the distorted images of a vase torn into a million pieces.

A pregnant woman looked down and touched her belly. The boy grasping her skirt kept asking: "Is daddy coming?" The old men looked like hooks that curved even more with every step they took. This was the most desolate village I had seen. The sign with its name was so full of bullet holes that I couldn't read it.

We pulled ourselves together and set out again. The noise from the front had become a symphony heralding the column of refugees advancing slowly along the path of the dead. Burned trees, ruined houses, men with their guts hanging out. Our march was slow, accompanied by foul odors, obstacles, and hunger. The collective insanity, the continued confrontation with death, the image of total destruction framed the sad picture of the refugees trudging slowly amid the residue of the explosions.

It started to rain and the road turned muddy, covering much of the destruction. I looked up at the sky, but didn't see the stars my mother had seen. Darkness filled

⚜

the heavens, which had also turned blind. I touched my forehead and the image of the blind man came to me, when he sat down to corroborate that what he saw with his cane was nothing more than the darkness of his own universe. Maybe we too were blind. Darkness filled every space, the ruins stuck to our soles. Death marked each step, and the noise of the cannons covered the horizon in black. We really couldn't see anything. Perhaps the images of the bodies were a figment of our imagination. It wouldn't have surprised me if madness had eventually been transformed to blindness. After everything I had lived through, nothing seemed strange. Everything became as logical as cracking a nut.

The blind man stayed behind, in the ruins of his village, weeping in the darkness about the blackness of a crumbling world. Madness and blindness became embodied in my mind.

It was a sign to keep enduring. I couldn't abandon those who had fallen into their graves, the victims who had been forced to cross the river Bug.

My father's beard, steadily getting long and longer, inspired me to continue, to keep slogging on behind the Russian troops. Water came in through the holes in our shoes, wetting our torn socks and chilling our bones. My mother's hair fell over her forehead, and dirty drops of water ran down my father's beard onto his ragged shirt. The rain made our progress more difficult. Every step was painful, our feet continually sticking in the bloody, filthy mud. Food was so scarce that I had to go back to my old trick of stealing, looking for anything to eat.

I always came back from the fields with something. A couple of carrots, half a cabbage, a bag full of apple cores. One person's garbage became another person's food, and we were the other person. I became an excellent garbage thief, and sometimes I still managed to find a loaf of black bread that a farmer had stuck away somewhere. I wasn't the only one. Many got into a fight over a piece of rotten potato or a cabbage leaf that later had to be cleaned of worms. In the path of the dead everything had a value to fill a pressing need, in order to endure and reach our only hope—our home . . . if it still existed!

It started to rain harder and the roads became so difficult that many of the Red Army vehicles got stuck in the ditches. The Germans took advantage of the situation to attack with artillery. We had to turn back, and then we were able to move forward again. It was a way back and forth between death and despair, savoring the bitter taste of anguish, our constant companion on our pilgrimage through the fields of death. We stopped for three days in a forest of trees that were losing their leaves. We ate the dried leaves that fell from them. Between the constant explosions of the grenades, we bit the roots and chewed on what little chicory remained The horizon turned darker and we kept waiting, adapting to the blindness that covered the front, sometimes resplendent in the red that followed an explosion and the last cries of a soldier who had fallen in the mud, fingers clenching in an attempt to hold on to the last breath of air.

More than once I had to go up to the front to procure the contents of a dead soldier's kettle. Walking in mud up to my knees, cowering whenever I heard an explosion, sticking my face in the mold and the garbage, I mingled with the bodies of the dead soldiers and searched their backpacks for a piece of hard bread. Many were killed in

❖

such attempts to find food right at the front. Our survival instinct made us risk our necks, calculating the time needed in order not to be caught by a bullet.

On some of the bodies we found dirty rubles, the precious paper the farmers exacted for their produce. During my incursions I thought about the boy who had talked about liberation. The refugees following behind the Russian Army were living the liberation in our flesh. We had witnessed the ghosts of the ruined towns that had been liberated. Probably none of us knew the meaning of the word, which was reserved for people in the big cities. We who marched on the path of the dead still felt the hoarse voice of the war, its explosive phrases, the lament of the dying, the last goodbye of the soldier digging his fingers in the mud, never to get up again. We still felt the need to endure against all odds. Along the path of filth, nothing was impossible; even death became something that many did not find disagreeable. At every moment life seemed to escape though our fingers, and then we were happy just to exist, marching on, stepping on the rubbish, digging our feet into the rotting bodies of the dead. In this exodus of life and death, existential values turned around from one moment to the next. Somebody who one moment was dispensing advice on how to endure, suddenly turned mad, talking about having ghosts in his mouth and of vampires that visited him at night to suck his blood. Others, who always seemed quiet, suddenly took their own lives. They remained hanging from the trees by their belts, with their faces blue and their tongues out. But this did not stop the rest of us. We had to go on.

The ghosts on the road became our friends. The constant rain hardly bothered us. We were a mass that

❖

moved along the path that the Red Army kept opening for us. The most bizarre scenes took place. A boy with long black hair confessed his love to a young girl who shrugged without understanding a word her admirer was saying. Others made love in the bushes, determined to live out the last moments of their lives. Many new insane people joined us. Women who claimed to be countesses and duchesses with large land holdings. A girl insisted that she was the Queen of England and we were her subjects. Some boys walked on all fours and barked. A woman pointed to her neck, insisting that was where they had shot her. She said we were all dead and this was the eternal pilgrimage of our souls. Some listened to her, others kept biting the small pieces of wood they had torn away from the trees.

The man with the marked arm who had spoken to my father was reciting a verse from a poem by Bialik. "The stars betrayed me. I had a dream and it disappeared." The sane ones nodded. My mother kept crying silently. As we got closer to the town where my grandparents—her parents—lived, her thin face developed a yellowish pallor.

It was drizzling when we reached the town. Some of it was in ruins, but a few buildings were still intact. The people here didn't seem so ghostlike. We even found some food to put in our dirty sacks. My mother didn't have to inquire about her parents. Before she even had a chance to ask, we heard that the first thing the beasts had done was to shoot all Jews. It was over very soon. The villagers said it as if they were telling a story. I understood that people forget quickly, that little matters to them if others die. The memory of those who had not suffered the devil's whip was too malleable and insipid, it seemed to me. Sometimes they didn't believe what we

❧

told them. They thought we were crazy. They truly celebrated the liberation, waving red flags and catering to the
soldiers who crossed through the town in a mad dash to
accomplish the final dismembering of the German Army,
which already showed the symptoms of a total defeat.

The Russians advanced swiftly, deploying all their
forces through the muddy soil of Ukraine. My mother
didn't cry. She had long felt that she would not find her
parents alive. What we had seen in Ladyzhin, in the faces
of those who crossed to the other side of the Bug, was a
sign that there was no hope for the survival of my grandparents. However, my mother's somber gaze revealed the
anguish and pain she was feeling. My father embraced
her, and she repeated the same verse the man had recited: "The stars have betrayed me. I had a dream and it
disappeared." I looked at the sky, and I saw gray, por-
tending more rain. I thought about the times when I slid
through these fields with my grandfather in a sleigh in
the winter. I dug my fingers into my torn pockets. We did-
n't even know if they had been buried or where. Could
they be in the shining star my mother had pointed out?
I walked for a while. I had to keep walking, living. My
grandparents also urged me to go on. I bit my lips in
anger and I cried, without fear of showing my tears. My
father stroked my hair and my mother tried to console
me, but ended up crying too.

I imagined my grandparents in front of the wall, with
their hands on their heads, looking in surprise at the
black mouths of the machine guns, perhaps hoping that
it was all a trick of the beasts to frighten them. The blast,
and then, doubling up, they dropped their hands and
their bodies fell against the wall in a last effort to conserve the warmth of life that was fast disappearing

❖

through the bullet holes. Later, they must have lain very still, their eyes open and their hair in disarray. I shook my head to let the idea go, but it wasn't possible. The evidence was beyond my imagination.

We left the village and continued our pilgrimage, with aching feet and backs twisted from looking so much at the ground. To look at the sky gave us a bitter feeling. Once again, we marched with the human wave that spread across the plain like a huge drop of oil. We moved slowly, marked by the war, with our ears full of explosions, living our madness and each time more conscious of the blindness that was invading our senses. We couldn't see. We simply advanced, like the blind man, feeling the road, sometimes asking ourselves whether we were walking in the fields or on a road. I didn't give a damn about anything. I invented possibilities, arriving at absurd conclusions, looking for a way to endure in the middle of this smelly, damp advance. In my mind the trees kept waving their branches in a continuous goodbye. I built a world of my own, full of memories of dulled eyes, of bodies intertwined in common graves.

The color of the explosions at the front resembled the blood of the victims executed by the beasts. On occasion, when we had to turn back because of a German counterattack, I let the others run and my parents had to almost drag me along. Death had ceased to exist in the world I had created. It was a world of the dead, a dimension inhabited by my grandparents, Isaac, Moshe's father, Moshe himself with his face full of sores, and his insane mother, Red, Mordechai with his sister's letter, the rabbi on the train with his cough, the blood running down the side of his mouth, Meitek who mutilated his fingers with his own teeth, the look in the eyes of the young girls in

❖

the zone of the "special ones," the bodies of the two boys who were tortured so savagely by the beasts and didn't utter a word about our organization—all the images mingled in a mass that filled my senses and made me dig my hands deeper inside my pockets. My father's beard was already bushy, the circles under my mother's eyes looked like lakes of purple water, eyes that no longer looked for the stars. Sometimes I wondered if she was thinking about anything at all.

Water ran down my face, I dug my boots into the mud, and chewed what little bread we could find. That was my life. Inside I was quiet, like a spectator. I saw all of the elements that had formed my previous life, when I had to risk everything at every turn. I looked at the stones and tried to start a conversation with them. They seemed like people with their coarse surface, their unlimited shapes, their sadness covered with mud and with the footprints of those who had preceded us. My back hurt, all my muscles were sore, my feet wanted to explode inside the wet leather of my boots. With each step my body lunged forward as if someone were pushing me. My condition of displaced person, of refugee who had not reached his goal, made me a friend to the footprints on the ground. I played with the mud, and told it about the star my mother pointed at. All my senses played inside me, and I hardly noticed the people around me during our long, slow trek.

Our miserable condition continued, only now it was raining harder. It was easier to get along, because my father had made some friends, who supplied us with bread and water. I didn't notice that happening, for I had begun to live in my own world. What meaning did the days have if the sun came up timidly on the horizon for-

✤

ever covered by the black smoke of the explosions? Where were all our difficult steps really taking us? Hopelessness took a hold of me, but just then the hoarse voice of a boy who was singing gave me a thread of hope once again. It was a good, loud voice that didn't allow a single note to escape in the midst of the symphony of shots that surrounded it. It seemed to me that I was waking up from deep in one of the trenches that I had seen along the way.

I went on, like the voice of the boy, feeding the half-destroyed illusions of those who heard his songs. I looked at him. He was a tall, thin boy, with a huge jacket hanging from his shoulders and a canvas bag fastened to his waist. His big, bony hands moved with a certain rhythm in the cold air that was starting to blow in the valley. His small, bulging eyes shined with every note that came out of his mouth. For a few moments I emerged from my private universe and, upon seeing the singer, made believe that he was seeing for the blind man. We all represented somebody else's role in one way or another. It was the double life of whoever sees himself hunted and stuck in a sewer from which there is no exit. Those who wanted to live had to submit to the rules of duplicity. Survival was a science you had to study in detail. The most insignificant error could cost you your life. Everything was useful in this constant deployment. Even the voice of the singer, who invented or remembered the songs of other refugees.

The Soviets maintained their line of fire and advanced, leaving the field covered by hundreds of dead. We who were advancing behind the troops took care to strip the dead soldiers of their boots and their kettles. Others stripped them almost completely. It was the law

⚜

of survival. The belongings of the dead were necessary for the survival of the wandering masses. Everything had its value. Half a loaf of bread was exchanged for a leather belt, a whole loaf was worth a kettle and a shirt. A business was created in trading what was left from the dead soldiers for the farmers' produce. For that reason many approached almost to the line of fire in order to take some of the possessions of soldiers who were still alive. Some even took a shirt off the back of a wounded soldier. I looked on without interfering. I was ready to exchange my life for anything. With every moment that went by I attached less importance to what was going on around me. I was fed up by so much misery, by walking on a path full of human waste.

From one moment to the next I gave up. Hope was vanishing in the face of what my eyes saw. My soul felt heavy inside of me. The rain didn't stop and my feet kept digging into the mud, as they had been doing from the shores of the Bug to the muddy edge of the Dniester. My footprints were imprinted in all the roads of Ukraine, getting ready for the road that led to Belz, our city, the town where our house was, the house we had abandoned to go to Czernowitz. Hope shined in my mother's eyes. My father stroked his beard with an air of satisfaction when he realized that we would be walking on our old street. I too began to dream. I would go back to my room, press my face against the windowpane, find some warmth in front of the fireplace. I would rub my hands and take shelter in the covers against the cold of the approaching winter. No more snow freezing my feet, numbing my muscles. I smiled and fixed my eyes on the road that led to Belz. I began to recognize places. The wire fences were familiar, even though I noticed that the path we were

⚜

walking on was just like the one we had been walking on before. There were blackened stones everywhere; the bark on the lower parts of the trees had been shredded and ripped apart by gunfire. The fighting in Belz had been quite fierce.

I feared for the house, and I noticed the same expression in my parents' face. With every step we took, everything seemed darker. The image of the blind man came back to me and I saw him grimacing behind us. I concentrated and his figure vanished in a light cloud that went up to the gray sky. I thought he had died and was now saying goodbye to those of us who had walked with him part of the way. I scratched my head and said to myself: "Stupid." I was paying too much attention to my imagination. I even doubted the voice of the singer whose notes floated out above our heads. I rubbed my hands and thought for a while. I could see the nearby forests, the hills, and the pebbles not yet covered with mud. At the end was the winding road that would finally take us to Belz. I felt a twinge in my heart.

Hope vanished quickly when we looked at the rubble before us. There were not two stones left together. Belz was a quarry. The few remaining inhabitants were unable to explain the destruction of all these structures that just four years before had stood proudly against the northern winds. Now, in mid-fall, we stood in a square where the only thing left was a pile of stones lying around every which way. We had a hard time finding the street where our house used to be. Finally we found it. The gate was gone and nothing was left of the walls except for a piece a few centimeters tall. The rest was a damp hole filling up with greenish mud. My mother sat down to cry, hiding her face in her hands. My father kept stroking his

⚜

beard. The dreams he had spun during the last part of our trek had vanished like soap bubbles. It hurt me to be alive, to know that upon arriving at the end of the road we were as much in the dark as the blind man. The images bounced against my eyes. Small stones got into the soles of my feet and I had to move my feet in order to dislodge them. I closed my eyes and saw a huge stone on which the word "liberation" was engraved. It was laughing. I opened my eyes again, scared. The image of my mother's crying burned in my mind.

My thoughts became a force that led me to keep marching on the path of the dead. Belz cried out to be avenged, for someone to explain what had happened. I swallowed hard and fixed my eyes on the faces of the people wandering about. I saw them parade in a ghostly walk that led nowhere. They moved slowly among the ruins, looking for anything, at least a marker that would indicate the fate of those who had remained. We didn't find anyone we knew. They had all left or simply vanished. Some people who had been living in the dark basements came out with their pale faces to tell what had happened. One man, bent and with a dull eye, said: "It was hell. The Germans and the Russians fought for close to three days, and while they fought, the special German brigades started to dynamite every street, blowing up the houses and the walls. They didn't want to leave anything to the victors in their retreat. Many died trying to hide, others in an attempt to run to the forests, the rest of us survived in the basements and the sewers."

He talked fast, without answering the questions that many were asking. Some of the survivors seemed crazed. An old woman talked about the Germans having horns and tails. Others said that during the battle the souls of dead German soldiers still fought against the Russians for a while, which held back the Russian troops and facilitated the blowing up of everything that was still intact. A girl pointed to the spot where her father had been shot. Two hungry children begged for a piece of bread and showed us their ulcerated legs. The rain kept on. My mother didn't move from the place where she was sitting despite my father's constant urging. She had nurtured too many illusions. She was crying, her hands trembling, her eyes fixed on the horizon. She had never imagined finding her house in ruins. My father was relatively calm, but he answered every question with a grunt.

The neighbor was cursing and hitting himself against the stones. He was claiming his house and pulling his hair out. I looked to my right and saw what was left of Moshe's house. The only thing still trying to stay up was a remnant of chimney. Some pieces of rotten wood were at my feet. I stepped on them for the simple pleasure of hearing them crunch. However I was still full of strength, I wanted to get out at once, go back to the crowd following the Russian army. Our goal was already destroyed, so it made no difference where we went as long as we got to a place that still had a few buildings. I talked to my father, and he mentioned Bucharest, the Romanian capital. Capital cities, he said, usually weren't destroyed like villages, and there would be places for refugees. But my mother didn't want to leave. She wanted to feel the pain in her stones. She was as if stuck to what had once been the floor she swept so carefully, especially for the holidays. I wandered a bit around what had once been Belz.

Stones, pieces of wall, blackened trees, people who moved like ghosts. We looked at each other, shrugged, and went on. Words seemed superfluous in this destruc-

⚜

tion. We understood each other in a language based on the expressive communication of a look that dims upon contact with the surrounding images, with those skeletons that survived in time. A disturbed child played with the stones and chewed on a piece of chalk. He laughed when his eyes met anyone who looked at him. But it was a dry, hoarse, faint laugh, and he was lost in his game, oblivious to the rain wetting his bag. He kept saying that with what he was gathering he was going to build himself a big palace. He opened his mouth with hardly two teeth in it and laughed for no apparent reason. He walked past me without looking, almost trampling me. A man was demanding a book he had lent to someone. Another was rolling a cigarette and didn't dare to light it, claiming that it was his last one. In his indecision he counted pebbles, balancing them in his hands and then throwing them on the ground. He looked attentively at the pattern of the stones and tousled his hair, looking for the correct interpretation of the message left by the pebbles on the wet ground.

Those who traded in the black market were busy. They sold black bread, canteens full of vodka, dried-out vegetables, ragged jackets with which to withstand the cold winter, and twisted boots that had belonged to some dead soldier. Even German shirts were for sale. Many came to this improvised flea market to negotiate for what they needed. But everyone was there to buy. Pickpockets abounded. I saw a boy steal the bread an old man had just bought, leaving the old man sprawled on the floor. None of the bystanders interfered. It was a common occurrence. Those who had nothing came to steal from the ones who bought whatever they needed at exorbitant prices. Nobody was safe from being knifed for half a loaf of bread, three carrots or a quarter of a half-rotten potato.

Hunger and despair afflicted the refugees. Everybody survived as best they could, and the Russian soldiers looked the other way. They were too busy looking for girls to satisfy their need for sex. And I, observing everything, came to the conclusion that I could be neither a judge nor a prosecutor. Circumstances were such that displaced persons of every faith and race looked for a bit of food, a blanket, and the security of another day.

I went back to the place where my mother was. When she saw me she got up and hugged me. She was on edge. A bomb had exploded a few minutes before and three boys had been burned to a crisp. My parents, not seeing me anywhere, thought I had been one of them. My mother hugged me, while my father reprimanded me severely. I didn't stir. Doubt, despair, the mounting anguish of believing that tragedy followed us had become the daily diet of those who ambled through this sea of stones. After a while, a bit calmed down, my father talked again about the possibility of going to Bucharest. There we could start again, think about a new beginning and try to get in touch with my mother's cousins in South America. We were again involved in a game of probability. We were back to weaving dreams, but now in another world.

An old man talked about letters he had gotten from America before the war. According to him, things were not that easy. Others contradicted him. Everybody had an opinion. We lunched on a piece of bread and some water mixed with vodka. The day went on, slow and rainy, wetting the stones that bore testimony to the existence of a village named Belz. We could still hear the noise of the cannons. Trucks full of soldiers waving red

⚜

flags and drinking Russian vodka passed by. They yelled, waved their flags, and fired their guns in the air. They were trying to lift their spirits before going to the front. We watched them, knowing that they were the ones who were going to pave the way for us.

My mother dried her tears, cupped her chin in her hands, and looked into space. She couldn't do anything. Water rolled down her face and her tattered shawl was becoming a heavy rag that stuck to her head. My father rubbed his hands while thinking about a way out. With my eyes, I followed the convoy of trucks heading for the place where the noise and flashes came from. A freckled-faced soldier threw a piece of bread and a bottle of vodka at me. I almost couldn't catch it because it took me by surprise. I saw him smile and then disappear without understanding the gesture, and a moment later I couldn't even remember his face. Many of them must have done the same. They must have seen in us as part of their own displaced families. I shrugged and hid the gift inside my jacket.

When my mother stopped crying we decided to leave again, this time for Bucharest. But we had to follow the road laid out by the Russian Army. This implied that we had to go by way of the city of Iasi, one of the last German strongholds.

We left after almost ten hours in the ruins of Belz. Once again we joined the ranks of the refugees looking for a future in a chaotic run from the disaster of their towns and their own lives.

On the path of the dead we started walking to Iasi, the threshold of our possible arrival in Bucharest. My father's beard kept growing and getting wetter, the circles under my mother's eyes grew deeper. She wasn't crying

❧

any more. All her tears had remained in the stones of what had been our house. I looked up at the sky. I didn't see stars and I remembered the verse recited by the man with the marked arm: "The stars betrayed me. I had a dream, it disappeared."

⚜

11

Fall Back, Comrade!

Watching the rain became a boring routine. We were following the Russian Army along a muddy, slippery road, constantly tormented by artillery shells and our other two enemies—the weather and the Germans.

Nature took care to make each step difficult, shells cut through bodies. A freckled girl never stopped cursing. She was looking for something, kept saying that things were not going to stay this way. She looked in anguish at the belly of her pregnant sister, raped by a soldier. Her sister, on the other hand, walked with her head high, not paying much attention to anything. She seemed to be flying through infinite space.

For a moment I centered my attention on the two sisters. The older one, with her freckled face, was always angry. Almost as if she were the one who had been raped. She rubs her hands constantly, closes her eyes, and talks to a rag doll that she carries. "Did you see? All men are the same. My father caused my mother's suicide. The bastard made her shoot herself. And you should know, you were my mother's last present. Come on, answer me." I looked at her with compassion. She was obviously disturbed. Her pilgrimage had affected her deeply, and now she was channeling her neurosis through the image represented by the doll she was carrying. Her sister was nonplused. She held her belly and fixed her gaze on the horizon. She smiled at every explosion, finding pleasure in seeing the trees fall, and crouching to avoid the shells overhead. Some of the others watched her fearfully. An old woman, her head covered by dark scabs, tried to converse with the girl but eventually gave up. The pregnant girl refused to come out of the protective shell she had erected around her in her march through the steppes.

Thus, among anguish, madness, and the bodies of those who had died from exhaustion and hunger, we traversed Bessarabia and Bukovina. We were getting close to the city of Iasi, which was still a German strongpoint. My parents pretended to be calm, especially my mother, who had not yet gotten over the destruction of Belz. She said little as we walked on, limiting herself to the most necessary communication. Whenever we stopped to rest, she would call me and start digging into my hair looking for lice. The pregnant girl looked at me, while her sister kept up her cursing. I warmed up to the one with the big belly. Her almost childish demeanor did not bother me. She was happy with whatever she got and was not frightened when we had to retreat looking for shelter against the continuous German bombardment.

The road was covered with blood. Soldiers writhed in the mud and then were still, begging for some water or murmuring the name of their mother or girl friend. I saw one, drenched in blood, rummaging in his bag for a picture of a girl. He found it, looked at it intently, and then died with a grimace for a smile. She must have been his wife. I never saw the picture again, since before I had a chance to get to his kettle, a grenade blew up, covering

❖

him with a reddish-black smelly substance. Even his boots burned out in the explosion. The pregnant girl, rubbing her belly, snorted and allowed her sister to put on her head a torn woolen cap that would protect her against the winter cold. Her white skin took an ashen tone against the burned red of the cap, forecasting a gloomy future for her unborn child. Her sister's freckles became more visible, and I couldn't understand the curses she kept spitting out.

We clearly heard the sounds of the battle the Russians were waging against the Germans for the city of Iasi. I had never seen so many flashes in a sky covered with blues, greens, and reds. All manner of activity and inactivity surrounded us. Stray bullets whistled past until they found something to bounce against: people crouching on the muddy ground; the pregnant girl sitting on the root of a tree, and her sister trying to protect her; my mother, clutching me against her breast; men sprawled on the ground with their arms covering their heads; water running along the road making ever bigger puddles and the trees losing their leaves. A boy about my age was dragging himself painfully through a ditch. He was munching on a piece of bread and had a swelling that covered almost half of his face. He did not utter a word. I could hardly look at him and couldn't understand why he was dragging himself. I was getting used to not understanding a lot of the things that were happening around me. Everyone had his way of surviving, so that explanations were meaningless. Many responded to the explosions by laughing nervously. We all ended up part of the unending battle. Fear, anguish, and panic became a fundamental part of each of us trying to survive against all odds. In my fear I ended up digging my hands in the

❖

mud that smelled of gunpowder. My mother was trembling, terror in her eyes. She swallowed hard and held me against her body. We were all part of a multitude that screamed out into the cannons' throat.

Fires surrounded us, the tree trunks were burning, and no less than three kilometers away was Iasi, being methodically bombed and defended furiously, ready to succumb to the Red Army, which did not give an inch. The noise of the battle came near with its devastating rhythm of destruction. A tree fell close to me, breaking the leg of a poor old man. The pregnant girl giggled. I could hear her sister's curses. I bit on a piece of bread and hid my head in my mother's bosom.

The explosions made me shiver. Their brightness hurt my eyes, and the smell of gunpowder made me want to vomit. With each blast my stomach turned and nausea invaded me. Even though I was in my mother's arms, I felt alone. When I closed my eyes I felt I was drowning, the ghosts came back to point at me with their vanishing fingers and an invisible chain gripped my body in an attempt to make me explode, torn to pieces like the grenades that fell nearby and that had already driven half of the refugees crazy. In order to escape I had to open my eyes and feel them burn against the rarefied air. The refulgence from Iasi bounced against my eyes, hurting my lashes and blinding me little by little. I chewed on a second piece of hard bread and looked around a bit with a strange calm, stuck in my own, shallow world. A red-headed girl, kneeling in the mud, kept her hands on her bosom and waited, as if the bullets that flew over us were not intended for her. An enormous sadness hung from her lids, forming muddy circles under her eyes. She looked a lot like my ghosts. Perhaps because of that I

wanted to know who she really was. There, still in the
mud, with bitten fingernails on her dirty, ragged skirt,
she was waiting for whatever might happen.

When I finished my miserable ration I shoved my
hands in my pockets and fixed my eyes on the wounded
and now complaining old man. A fat man with a double
chin tried to help him, rubbing his wounded leg, but the
old man went on screaming. Then, at last, he stopped. He
and the fat man were silenced by a grenade. We shook in
terror. Only the redhead remained impassive. I looked at
her with interest. "Israel, don't lose her, she's one of your
ghosts. Perhaps she can help you. Mordechai once told
you about the good ghosts who are always there to prevent tragedies. Remember Isaac nodding? Yes, she's one
of your ghosts that have come out. Don't lose her.
Perhaps only you can see her. Go and pull her back into
our nightmare."

I slowly moved away from my mother. The sister of the
pregnant girl looked at me angrily, like she looked at
everyone who got too near her. I moved half a meter away
and immediately felt my father's hand on my shoulder.
"Where are you going, crazy kid?" I couldn't come up with
an answer so I smiled like an idiot. My father smiled too,
but his hand remained on my shoulder and I had to satisfy myself with looking at my ghost from a distance. I
stuck my head between my knees and fixed my eyes on
the redhead, with her bony hands and her freckles, her
hair parted in the middle and falling on her drooping
shoulders. In my mind I was sketching a figure of the girl.
I almost captured the light that framed her profile, her
thin nose and somewhat receding chin. My ghost was not
ugly. She did not incite fear like ghosts do. I wanted to
leave my parents' side and run to her, touch her, feel the

❧

shape of my ghost, which remained impassive after each explosion. She didn't bat an eye when a huge tree broke in two and fell burning to the ground. She was quiet, nailed to the ground, not moving a single muscle in her face. If my ghost endured, so could I. The idea resounded in my mind. My father's beard covered much of his face; the circles under my mother's eyes already surrounded her eyes. It kept on raining.

From one moment to the next the noise at the front died out. The flashing of the artillery stopped. We looked at each other and couldn't see anything else but the sobbing shadows of a displaced group that got up to keep on walking. Word got around that Iasi had been liberated by the Reds, so it was time to get to the city and head for those smoking ruins we could still not see very well. My ghost got up, threw her hair to one side, and began walking toward Iasi. Just as Mordechai had said, she kept by my side, though at a prudent distance. But my eyes did not leave the figure advancing along the wet road at the slow pace of our tired, sick caravan. Iasi had finally been liberated from the Nazi beasts. The Red troops celebrated their victory over the desperately retreating enemies. They were holding a party over the still warm bodies of fallen soldiers who hadn't gotten away and had fought and died while dreaming of their girls back home or perhaps of drinking in a tavern.

We arrived in Iasi soon after the Soviets. The noise was overwhelming. Soldiers waving Red flags and running through the streets. Suddenly some Germans opened fire again. Walls blew up, houses fell down, buildings burned. The initial tumult turned to panic. Everyone ran for shelter from the German ambush. Soldiers and refugees mingled in a mass that tried desperately to

❖

escape the shower of German bullets. The bullets hit the doors, broke the wood, pierced bellies, and smashed foreheads. My father, my mother, and I flattened ourselves on the ground. My ghost stood under a portal, reclining against the stones and still waiting quietly. I wanted to run to her and bring her to my side, get her inside one of my nightmares, trying not to lose that image that had been comforting me ever since I first saw her.

From the top of the buildings the Germans released their shower of death. The infuriated Russians were fighting against an enemy they could barely see. The battle went on, street by street, house by house, door by door. Bullets whistled everywhere. They came and went, announcing their tragic message. A refugee went out into the street; he ran with his arms open asking for death. He had not gone half a hundred meters before he fell with his body covered by bullets. He doubled up, screamed, and fell, clutching his chest, destroyed by the bullets in the crossfire. With great difficulty we dragged ourselves toward some stones that had been part of a house now completely destroyed. There we huddled together. Splinters flew by and smashed against the nearby walls. The initial calm that had made us think Iasi was free of Germans became a shower of lights. The explosions went deep into our ears.

The cries of the wounded mingled with the avenging clamor of the Russian guns. Terror and a thirst for blood joined in a lone song of vengeance. The pain of the ambush became an enormous thirst for blood that needed to be satiated by the soldiers who just minutes before had been celebrating their victory in the streets of a Iasi full of hidden Germans ready to gamble their last card.

The Russians got over their surprise and began to recover their discipline. In an organized manner they

❖

moved forward street by street. They went into the buildings and killed the Germans. They took no prisoners. The
ambush had hurt them and many had fallen victim to
bullets fired from windows and rooftops when they least
expected it. The battle inside the city lasted until well into
the morning. All night we waited with our eyes open and
our bodies numbed from keeping the same position. It
was a hard fight in which many lives were lost, soldiers
as well as refugees. The streets were full of ruts and
craters, and the walls lost many of their bricks, weaken-
ing their foundation and creating a hazard for anyone
who walked past. You could expect anything to come
crumbling down at any moment. Bloody bodies of men
and women covered the streets. The dead lay in the most
grotesque positions, their eyes bulging, their hands
crossed, their bellies open. Others bit their tongues or
had them completely out. I saw a soldier with a mouth
full of mud and missing an arm. The hole in his shoulder
was still oozing blood. The wounded dragged themselves
painfully toward the army aid stations. One of them,
completely blind because of an explosion, was stumbling,
holding on to a wall and cursing. He stopped to cry.
Suddenly he took out a gun and shot himself in the head.
But he didn't kill himself. The nurses who picked him up
said that he would surely remain dumb and disabled.
Some old men walked in disarray, on crutches, on pieces
of wood, to a soup kitchen. All Iasi was covered in black.
Our faces were covered with soot. We looked like miners
coming out of a coal mine after being rescued from a
cave-in.

Like a crazy person I searched for my ghost. I heaved
a sigh of relief when I saw her heading for a place where
a big soldier was filling mugs with soup. Her face was full
of soot, but I could still see her freckles and the red hair

⚜

falling on her shoulders. German soldiers were coming out of the buildings. They had not been able to escape from the Russians. They were coming out with their hands on their heads. They had beards and pale faces. They looked at us fearfully, perhaps thinking that the Russians were going to turn them over to the populace, to be lynched in the middle of the street. However, the Russian commanders had them loaded in trucks and taken to a POW camp nearby.

The city had finally been taken, albeit at a very high price. We displaced persons began looking for a place to rest before continuing our march, although some wanted to stay. I once again encountered the pregnant girl and her sister. The first still did not say a word, and her eyes were still fixed on a faraway point. Her sister kept cursing, saying that she would take care of the unborn child so that her sister could search for the soldier who had raped her. Some of the onlookers smiled, probably aware that the girl calling them cowards and secret Nazis was insane.

We all found different ways to express our frustration and fear. A woman repeated over and over that the Germans had killed God, an assertion that many people seconded. My ghost, her red hair full of mud and soot, stood in line, ignoring everyone, a dented tin in her hands.

After a few minutes the tumult started again. The soldiers went by carrying bottles of vodka and other liquor. Some of the displaced persons, searching the basements, had also found liquor that the Germans had left behind. People drank to their heart's content.

The commanders of the Red Army unit had given their soldiers carte blanche, and they, taking advantage

❖

of this freedom, got drunk and danced with the few girls they found in the city. They went by, arm in arm, shouting *Hurrah!* and singing the *Internationale*. Some of the wounded drank in order to still their pain.

By nightfall Iasi had become a huge brothel of orgies and drunken fights. Two-thirds of the Russian soldiers were dead drunk and swearing to avenge their dead comrades. The sister of the pregnant girl, having downed half a bottle of vodka, began to recite poetry. "They raped you, sister, the same ones who now liberate you. They raped you, and the fruit of your belly will be born as a remembrance that once men were killing each other. Will he be a boy? Will you give birth to a girl? Who can tell from a raped woman? Maybe nothing, perhaps much. Fall back, Comrade!"

She leaned close to the swollen belly and started to kiss it with a frenetic intensity I had never seen before. It was as if she wanted to suck out what her sister was carrying in her belly. They were long, strong kisses, with a smell of vodka and the pregnant girl kept silent, like my ghost, who now was seated on the steps of a ladder half-destroyed by the bombs. I wanted to talk to her, tell her that she was part of my collection of ghosts. Yes, I was going to tell her each and every one of my nightmares. Then she would remember that she had once called me from the end of a tunnel and then disappeared so that I would feel the pressure in my throat, that terrible feeling of suffocation that almost made my eyes pop out. The image of the redhead settled in my subconscious and translated into the consciousness in an irrational need to touch her face and feel the cold liquid that ghosts have inside of them instead of blood. I tried to think of a way to escape for a moment from my parents in order to get

to her. I almost made it, but then saw a half-drunk soldier take her by the hand. She did not resist. She allowed
the Russian to pick her up and accepted his vodka-stink-
ing kisses. I woke up from my delirium and became conscious again of my madness. Perhaps it was a product of
my frustration at not getting to her before the Russian.

In order to rid myself of those feelings I returned to
my own world, into that place that many times I had
shared with Isaac and Mordechai. To survive, to endure,
to live in the name of those who had been forced by the
beasts to cross to the other side of the Bug. Everything
comes back to me like an avalanche. I wake up. I am
inside a damp basement. Some faces are watching me.
Others sleep. My father allows my mother's head to rest
on his shoulder. Darkness engulfs the room. A cold
stream of air hits my face. There are fifty or more people
in this basement. I don't care. But I feel the discomfort
and breathe a bunch of nauseating odors. The crying of
the little ones filters in through a hole that lets in the cold
air that has already frozen my cheeks. I want to scream,
go outside to get wet, rid my nose of the foul odor that
knots around my throat. I still cannot come to terms with
the rape of my ghost. Without her presence I lose part of
my vitality. Now I feel completely like a displaced person,
a refugee in search of a not-yet-defined goal. Bucharest,
the name sounds good, but there too we may be
ambushed. How many of those who are now dead were
also waiting to get there? And now what? They lay there
quietly, destroyed by the artillery. Their pilgrimage ended
in the streets of a city that never gave them anything. Not
even part of the hope they were feeding. I lean against a
wall. It is damp, but strong. The battle did not destroy it.
Perhaps because of that, people prefer basements.

⚜

Explosions take place up there, in the streets, against the walls of the houses.

I rub my neck. I try to rest. From outside come the singing and loud voices of the soldiers. They're getting drunker and drunker. Even many of the refugees are as drunk as sailors. Lying on the floor, they stink from the liquor they have downed. They drink desperately, perhaps thinking the liquor will drown the sorrow in their hearts and the mud on their bodies. We all drank, even the little ones, and now many were sleeping off their binge. Conquered Iasi welcomed us with its barrels of vodka. For lack of food, everyone opted for liquor. Iasi was a brothel that smelled of vodka, a huge bottle from which everyone drank: men, women, and children. We felt the burning liquor going through our veins. From my corner in the basement, I heard the soldiers and their mates for the night pass by. I saw the pregnant girl and her sister. They were sleeping off their drunkenness. More than half of the people in the basement were asleep.

A terrible explosion made us open our eyes. The noise came from the southern part of the city. Terror engulfed us once again. Someone said: "It must be the Russians. They blow up the buildings that are in the worst condition. For the safety of those living nearby." I half understood him. However a second, closer explosion made us stand up. There was no doubt that we were being bombed. The noise of airplanes was concrete evidence.

My mother kept me with her while my father went outside to see what was happening. His face was pale when he returned. "It's the Germans coming back. Now they are opening the way with planes and bombs, later the artillery will come. The Russians are all drunk, just waking up." I ran away from my mother to peer out a

⚜

small opening through which you could see what was happening in the street.

Some drunken soldiers were firing in the air in a vain attempt to bring down the planes that were strafing them. The Reds fell down, wallowed for a while, and then lay still in a puddle of blood. They were easy prey for the pilots, who from high overhead must have seen them as a bunch of marionettes trying to play at war. I saw the shots fly over the damp street, ripping the flesh of the wounded, finishing off those that were already half-dead.

In the light rain of dawn the bullets rained down. Soldiers and their girlfriends as well as refugees fell without a word, shivering when hearing the shots that ripped into their foreheads, legs, and bellies. They almost did not scream, probably thinking their death was part of their drunkenness. My father took me from my observation point to the rear of the basement. The children's cries increased. They cried with all the might that their weak lungs allowed them. The women woke up to start another round of hysterics. Some old people, between drunkenness and sleepiness, prayed. The world of the basement began to resemble a railroad car like the one that took us to Ladyzhin.

A look that seemed to cry out, "We're trapped, buried alive in this grave," was reflected in everyone's face. Sometimes, an explosion made the walls of the basement shake, and the women would scream, squeezing their children against their bosoms. The sister of the pregnant girl couldn't stop crying, while the pregnant one opened her eyes and bit her lower lip, holding her belly while she looked with dull eyes at what was happening around her. I felt an emptiness in my gut. Where was my ghost? The question turned mossy, like the walls of the basement.

⚜

Some children were starting to run from one side to the other, coming and going in all directions. They didn't know how to express their fear that they were trapped in a common grave. Now we could hear more clearly the cries of those who had fallen in the streets. A bullet came in through a hole and hit the neck of a poor old woman who did not even have time to sob. A rosary with huge beads rolled down the floor. Her neighbors crouched against the cold floor. We all became aware of the presence of death. The bloody body of the old woman, her half-open mouth and her bulging eyes, made us understand that we had to run for our lives. The strong voice of a soldier from outside came to us. He was shouting at a frenzied comrade who was trying to escape that inferno: "Fall back, Comrade!"

The Germans were back to retrieve what only hours before they had lost. Iasi was an important position and they were not about to give it up. The artillery kept showering us with shells. It was a constant crossfire. The Soviet troops were retreating, leaving behind everything they had acquired with so much blood. A shell exploded near the door of the basement, obstructing the entrance. Panic spread. We already saw ourselves in front of the Nazi beasts, bowing our heads in front of the ditches. The men were trying to open the door to no avail. The glare coming through the opening hurt our tired eyes. Inside the basement everything was screams, sobs, and the crazy laughter of the insane. Women and children, and old as well, clung to the walls. The rest looked for protection on the ground, with their hands over their heads. We heard the noise of the soldiers passing by our basement in boozy retreat. The liquor of Iasi became part of the ambush prepared by the Germans. This time their

❖

plan bore real fruit. Dozens of Soviet soldiers lay in the streets with their bodies totally destroyed. We in the basement looked at each other in a vain attempt to find a solution to our problem. Someone suggested that the smallest and thinnest of us could go out through the hole and remove the stones blocking the exit. There was no need to discuss the idea. Six of us immediately slid outside and started to pull away the rocks and pieces of stone that blocked the door.

Shells fell almost in front of our noses. The top of a building broke in two and collapsed with an infernal noise. We shook our heads and went on with our job. Our mission was centered on clearing the opening. A human mass of soldiers, refugees, and dogs filed in front of us, leaving Iasi. Shell fragments flew overhead as we tried to pull out the scorched wood and stones that blocked the entrance. Our fingers bled, our nails broke and our hands got swollen trying to open a hole in the middle of a wall of steel.

One of us, seeing a drunken soldier, took a grenade from his hand and, after indicating to us to get out of the way, threw it at the door. A big explosion shook the stones and the pieces of wood that obstructed the entrance. The door started to burn. We then began to smash at the door with a piece of wood we had found in the street. After a few minutes we had made a big opening that allowed us to see the anguished faces of those inside,

A few hundred meters away the bombing became steadier. The human tide was desperately looking for a way out of this pandemonium. Some of the wounded were carried away on improvised stretchers, the wounded not in much worse condition than those who carried

⚜

them. "Fall back, Comrade " was the watchword used to find the way out. We finally managed to open the door of the basement. Everybody came out at once, in a mad dash to escape what they already believed to be their grave. Old men, women, and children went up the stairs and into the street, which was ever more dangerous because of the explosions. The Germans attacked systematically. Their artillery hit the most vulnerable areas, destroying buildings and barracks from which they could be attacked. The liberators ran like rats, waking up from their drunken stupor, their eyes wide open in surprise, and we the refugees did the same. We kept close to the walls, sliding our bodies against the stones, bumping against them with mud sticking to our boots and up to our ankles.

It was raining. The multitude advanced in a terrible chaos. Curses and prayers mingled in a chorus. Bullets started hitting those who retreated. There were cries of pain when a bullet smashed through bones and flesh, and gestures of despair took on the color of the explosions. Next to me a man doubled over and started to vomit blood. His neck had been broken by a piece of shrapnel. The boy he had been carrying in his arms stood up, seemingly ignoring what had happened. He stepped into the middle of the street and began walking toward the area bombarded by the Germans. A distant cry let me know that he had been reunited with his father.

The pregnant girl walked with some difficulty, helped by her cursing sister. Some insane people embraced and began to sing and lament at the same time. Challenging death, they mocked those who were killed in the German bombardment. The drunken Soviet soldiers offered virtu-

❖

ally no resistance. They fired at random, without ascertaining the place or the target of their shots. In the middle of this crazy multitude I could see my ghost again. But she no longer had that inner calm. Now she walked fast, clutching her bag against her bosom, with anguish and panic in her face. I saw her scream and pull her red hair as if it were on fire. My ghost, like many of those who were running by, also had her madness. I felt betrayed. If my ghosts were frightened, if they were becoming part of the crazed crowd, who in hell, then, was I? What was I doing in this tide of people running toward a hypothetical exit without any assurance that there would be an exit?

I closed my eyes in search of my own ghosts, the ones that were still inside of me. I trusted those shapeless forms because I knew them. But it was difficult to get back into my private world.

I swallowed and turned toward the redhead. Without knowing why, my senses began to sharpen, so that every detail became engraved on my mind. I noticed the place where once a bakery had been. I ran inside to grab some loaves of bread. I crammed several into my coat and clutched six more loaves of black bread in my arms. But others were already doing the same thing. It was the law of survival, the need to take something in order to cover the need we were going to face in our retreat. The Russian troops were shooting at the locks on the doors in search of more liquor.

Some of them went inside a store never to return. A shell fell on the roof and the whole structure collapsed on top of them. We heard the screams, but nobody stopped. To stop meant sure death, and we who were fleeing were looking to survive, seeking a shred of hope that would

⚜

allow us to spin our illusions amidst the mud and the ceaseless rain. We found more corpses at each step. Blood and mud formed a compact mass with a characteristic odor. Death in Iasi smelled like vodka.

In a few moments we found ourselves outside the city. We were fleeing as fast as our legs would take us. The Germans recaptured Iasi, and we were again in a field, in the open, looking for shelter under trees scorched by gunfire. It was a sad, desolate scene. My boots smelled of dampness. The circles under my mother's eyes looked like stains. My father hardly allowed a grimace to show through his muddy beard. Some people were still a bit drunk and did not really understand what was going on. We had retreated about two miles from the city when we ran into a new, fresh contingent of the Red Army. For a few moments they were disconcerted by what the retreating troops told them. A muddy field full of corpses surrounded them. Many soldiers, still drunk, lay down to sleep it off.

The refugees stepped to one side. I watched the soldiers, who shrugged and held on to their arms. They had expected to be entering a city already under Russian control, and found instead their comrades drunk and carrying the weight of defeat on their muddy boots. My mother gave me a piece of black bread. I yawned and began eating, realizing what we had to go through once again. The hoarse sound of the cannons could be heard clearly. Now they began to answer on this side. The Russians, still proud of their victory in Stalingrad, deployed in a circle and renewed their advance on the lost city. Other contingents joined them. The deafening sound of the motors of the Soviet bombers reached my ears and I saw them cover the slate-gray sky. They were ready to fight for

⚜

every inch. We saw them advance, but the German artillery kept ravaging the Red troops. Soldiers were blown to pieces, their blood mingling with the rain and the swamp, which had become tired of so much bombing. The number of wounded escalated, and many of the refugees took up the weapons of the fallen soldiers in order to reinforce the troops. The planes fought in the air with everything they had. You could see them turn around and explode, falling in a spiral to announce their crash in a multicolor explosion. The pilots were black dots who opened their parachutes only to be killed by the Germans on their way down. I saw them twist among the chords in a vain attempt to cling to the life that was escaping from bullet holes.

The rain that fell from the sky was stained with blood. I kept chewing my bread, feeling cold and with my eyes wide open. I had to remember everything I saw. To forget would have been like forgetting I had been born.

I finished my bread and passed the time counting the dead I could see on the way to Iasi. I thought about them and about their families, who by now probably imagined them marching into Berlin shouting: "We won, Comrade!" Was it for this that they had been born? If to be born was to grow up in order to be felled by a bullet, then it wasn't worth leaving your mother's womb. The sister of the pregnant girl cried and kept clutched her rag doll. "Did you see them? They wanted to finish us off. They didn't look very friendly, did they?" Then, turning to her sister, "Did you see her cry? Of course not. We don't cry for anything. Did you hear me?" and she looked straight at the doll's shapeless face. The pregnant girl watched her without a word, with her hands on top of her swollen belly. It seemed as if she were laughing at the internal drama her

❖

sister was living. The angry one stroked her sister's face and fixed her eyes on her belly. She drew and put her ear to her belly. "It's alive, I can hear it cursing this situation. Isn't it beautiful, it already knows its mother is in the middle of this garbage. You'll see how, instead of crying, it will learn how to curse better than my father and my uncle put together. He's going to be born cursing, as we all should." Some of the other women looked at her dumbfounded and started to blush. One woman said: "Who gave you the power to utter such words? God knows what He's doing, and if we are born, it is to recover the time of those who die young. But you, damn you, dare to challenge the Creator and to say that the child will be born cursing. You should have been killed."

The freckled girl answered: "I can imagine how you must feel. You probably can't stand your own smell, and now you're telling me about virtue and pretty things. Don't you know that you smell like shit?" She began to laugh. The other woman lunged at her, and the two started pulling each other's hair and wriggling in the mud while shouting every curse they knew.

At first no one did anything, but finally a very thin man with a scar next to his mouth tried to pull them apart. The two women turned on him. They pulled his hair and pushed his head into the mud, ripping off pieces of his shirt and shoving them in his mouth. The man asked for help. Some boys who had been laughing at the spectacle pulled the women apart with amazing ease, and then kept them apart to prevent another confrontation.

With my hands in my pockets, I looked at the man who had tried to separate the women. He was trying to explain. The others were making fun of him. "Come on,

Motke, you never had an easy time with women. Do you remember the blonde that made you jump from a second story? Don't try to tell us again that she knew you were Jewish and was going to denounce you. Every time you tell the story you make a new mistake. Motke, you were born to be a good man. When all this is over, we are going to find you a good little woman, and you will treat her well so that she won't divorce you." The laughter made us forget for a few moments that we were against the wall.

The body of the redhead was reflected in my pupils, and I once again began to believe in the ghost that came out of me when I least expected it. I saw her go by with her head covered by an old shawl. But she was not the same as before. Her face was drawn and pale, with prominent cheekbones and an anguished look. She sat down a few meters away, put her head on her knees, and shuddered after each explosion. Since we were all in a group I saw no problem in getting closer to my ghost. My mother did not object and I managed to get away without feeling my father's heavy hand on my shoulder. Something unexplainable seemed to draw me to the girl, who could not stop trembling. I stood before her for a few moments, looking at the straggling strands of red hair that fell out of the faded shawl. Shyly, I touched her shoulders. She looked up at me as if I were an apparition or someone she had been expecting for a long time. I did not say anything. She touched my face, touching each one of my features. I suddenly realized that she couldn't see anything out of those beautiful eyes. My ghost walked so slowly because she could not see. That's why she would walk away with anyone who took her hand. She removed her hand from my face and began to cry sound-lessly. "You're a child, like my little brothers. You are a

❖

child, aren't you?" It was as if someone had hit me. Her words dug deep into me. She asked for a child to remember her dead siblings. I said yes.

"What color are your eyes?" I did not know what to answer. It hurt me to see her in the dark, asking for a color. "Blue? Yes, I know that color. I had a blue skirt my mother made for me when I turned twelve. It's nice to know that there is still someone with the color of my skirt in his eyes. Come on, tell me what you see. Fall must be beautiful"

I made a fist. I really didn't know what the hell to answer. "Well, this afternoon is not—" She cut me off in mid-sentence and forced me to sit in front of her. "You are going to talk to me about flowers. Flowers are beautiful, and you are going to tell me how big this garden is." I thought she was making fun of me. She had to know, even in her darkness, about the misery that surrounded her. But I saw something in her face that made me start to talk about gardens, to lie to her about flowers I did not even remember. "The garden is very big. The flowers are a bit pale. I believe it's because of bad weather. There are flowers with many petals, the leaves are swaying in the wind—" A nearby explosion made me shut up for a while. I saw her tremble, but she tried to keep smiling while the bullets hit the stones, the trunks of the trees, and the flesh of those who were exposed. My blind ghost asked me to talk to her about beautiful things, about yellow flowers covering the huge prairie, and a boy riding past with a bag of cherries in his hand. It was difficult for me to make it up. How could I talk about something like that when all I saw around me was a field full of mud, cries and dead people? But I kept up the lie. It was a way that I too could escape, for a while, from what surrounded us.

⚜

"I see a man on a horse in the distance. It must be the boy with the cherries. He's riding along the road that leads to the castle. Do you know there is a dwarf in the castle who makes beautiful shoes? Yes, he's a grumpy dwarf, but he's an excellent shoemaker. One day I will introduce him to you. Well, the yellow flowers have opened up and are going to start singing. They move their petals to greet the horseman. Some are bigger than others, but they are all sisters and they love each other; they look at the sun and begin to sing. It's a pity we cannot hear their songs."

My ghost, the blind girl, smiled through her tears. She knew I was lying, but my lies were helping her to escape our wet surroundings. She asked: "Can you see the horseman's face? He must have black curly hair because, you know, he is the prince who is going to take me to his castle." And she said this with tremendous certainty. "Yes," I told her, "he is a boy with black curly hair. He has a bag of cherries in his hand and is riding through the masses of yellow flowers that smile and greet him as he goes by."

The girl made a grimace, she doubled up and ground her teeth. I helped her to get up. I was about to ask what was wrong when she said: "Thank you, you don't know how good it feels to know that they are coming for me. You don't know how long I've been waiting for my prince. I used to write to him when I was little, but I never got an answer. Later I would go to the woods and ask my prince to come for me. And see, he's coming on the road I always thought he would. To be in love is the most beautiful thing on earth. You see the sweetest colors and hear the songs of the fairies. And my prince loves me and is coming for me. Make sure it is his face, otherwise I'm not going. Can you see him well?"

I swallowed hard. It was difficult for me to deny a blind girl what she wanted to see, but all I could see was a miserable scene that turned darker every moment due to the explosions. I looked at my ghost and saw her grit her teeth again, holding back a cry she did not want to let out. She asked me again if it was the prince with the black curly hair coming for her. I looked at her eyes without light. They shined with a strange light that I had not noticed before. I told her that yes, it was her prince. She smiled and took my hands in hers, resting her head on her chest. A thin thread of blood ran from the corners of her mouth and down her neck, dirty with soot and mud. I started to scream. My ghost was dying.

My mother was the first to come. Later a group of curious people joined us. A man with an almost white beard bent down and pulled up her face, and I could see a yellow pallor claim each of the features of my ghost. Blood kept flowing abundantly. Somebody took her pulse. "She's dead," he said matter-of-factly as he dragged on a cigarette butt. An old man noticed that part of her skirt was also soaked in blood. A woman fainted. When my ghost asked me to talk to her about flowers, her gut had already been shattered by a shell fragment. She had been taken away by her prince, and I was left alone in the middle of the mud and the people that kept retreating. I started to cry.

We went back and forth for several days. Autumn could be felt with all the weight of the rain falling on the road full of decomposing bodies. After my ghost's death I no longer trusted myself. I doubted every thought, thinking that everything was part of an endless dream from which I was afraid to wake up. I did not care to survive. If a bullet struck me, so be it. I walked next to my parents, going along wherever they went, without any objections. It kept on raining.

After a week of sustained attacks, the Red Army broke through the German lines. This time the conquest of Iasi was unquestionable. We went back to the city with a Russian artillery unit. We needed to retrace our steps in order to reach Bucharest, and, along with the Russian soldiers, we were able to get a few pieces of bread and a few mugs of lukewarm soup. They were good people, advancing toward Berlin waving their red flags. "Step forward, Comrade!" was the battle cry. And that comrade who had ran away drunk from Iasi was returning now with renewed strength and discipline, determined not to let his prey escape a second time. No more Fall back, Comrade!" The goal was straight ahead, at the end of the road.

The recapture of Iasi was difficult and costly. The road back was a virtual cemetery. Soldiers and refugees were joined in one mass, with their fists tight and their mouths full of mud. The odor was terrible. Birds of prey settled on the bodies for a feast. Our march was accompanied by nausea and the desire to run away as fast as we could. The return marked a new stage in the world of death. A little girl, her eye sockets empty, was holding on to a tree, her burned flesh mingling with the scorched bark. Her burned face was frozen in a ghoulish smile. Half of a body lay next to her. The head of a soldier appeared far away from his bootless body.

We advanced steadily toward Iasi. The Russian artillery was held up by the resistance of the Germans,

❖

who were entrenched in the suburbs. The battle would have to be fought house by house, street by street, like the first time. We were used to death and destruction. It had become part of our daily lives. The front had become our home. Some soldiers, who did not realize this, looked in awe at people who could find their way without weapons.

Just as we had imagined, the entry into Iasi was hell. A third of the refugees died in the attempt due to the bombings and the last shots of the Germans, fighting while retreating. The streets had been mined, and many trucks full of displaced persons and soldiers were blown away. Walls came crumbling down with the smallest noise. Drinking water was scarce, and we were all afraid of falling prey to an epidemic. The engineers of the Russian Army were trying the impossible in order to solve the problem of daily services, but their task was rendered even more difficult by the mines the Germans had planted everywhere. People wandering through the streets died without medical help. The occupying army prohibited anything that had to do with liquor because of what had happened the first time around. The doctors had their hands full with the number of wounded. The troops had priority over the refugees, many of whom rotted away waiting for an appointment they never got.

In the basement where we had settled in, stories went around about the massacres conducted by the Nazis. There were tales about camps that were virtual death factories. I tried to sleep, but when I closed my eyes, the face of my redheaded ghost with her blind eyes came to me. She wanted me to tell her about the rivers that swelled during the spring, the flowers that bloomed again to fill in the space that had been covered by snow. I felt

✤

my mother's hand stroking me, indicating that I must hold on, that our goal was near.

People in the basement talked about the future, about putting their lives together once again. A woman was talking about getting married. Two old men held on to the hope of two hens they had left on their farms. Now, with Iasi clear of Germans, we began to weave our hopes faster. Perhaps this was what liberation meant. To be able to dream freely, to see life in the stones and in the wet and cracked walls.

Hopes swelled as we heard more news. Reports announced the continuous advance of the Red Army. The Germans ran like rats to their former borders. Poland and Ukraine were already free of the Nazi boot. Romania had begun to form a new government. Bucharest, the capital, was free. This last news encouraged my father. At least we did not have to go on in the wake of an army, risking our necks at every step, stuck in a continuous nightmare, swallowing whatever we could get our hands on. Our road was clear and possibly without the huge amount of dead and misery we had found up to now. I heard the noise of planes flying westward.

I fell asleep, stuck in my tunnel, searching for an answer in my subconscious to the light that was always within the blind redhead, in my ghost who died with her guts hanging out without uttering a sound. The only thing she asked for was for me to tell her about what neither of us could see.

In a short time, with the city completely controlled by the Red Army, we were ready to start our journey to Bucharest. Winter was approaching. The rain never stopped. I saw a wall with dark shell holes. A thought crossed my mind. I recalled the soldier I had seen during

⚜

the retreat from Iasi, who had screamed: "Back up, fall back, Comrade!" I smiled. No, our steps now would go straight ahead.

I said out loud: "Straight ahead, Comrade!" Some soldiers, who heard me laughed and clapped. My father shrugged, and my mother watched me with eyes that seemed to swim in their huge circles.

⚜

12

The Exit

The noise of the planes slowly became more faint. The horizon no longer showed the red tinge of the constant death vomit.

It kept raining, and the drops rolled ceaselessly down my face as I looked at the line of the unchanging horizon before me. Destruction was everywhere. The trees leaned downward, as if defeated, at the side of the road. As we marched onward, we too looked down, like the trees. Our goal was Bucharest.

We were picked up by a Soviet truck on its way to the Romanian capital. We climbed in the back, and the first thing I saw was the cool stares of the other passengers. We sat to one side. The truck started. Somebody was complaining ceaselessly in the back. His dull eyes revealed that he was mad. He moved his hands in a vain attempt to reach something in the air. Others were scratching their skin and squeezing the bugs that ran through their tattered clothes. A girl with a red birthmark on her face held on to her father's hand and asked him now and then if they would find her brothers and her mother. The man looked at her, stroked her hair, and shrugged.

We kept bouncing on the boards we had positioned as seats. There were so many holes and slippery stones on the road that it was sometimes difficult for the truck to get by. I stuck my hands in my pockets. It was a habit I had adopted when nervous and wanted to relieve my frustration. That's how I stopped the bitter flow of thoughts that left my brain to start to dance in my throat. Then I imagined a world that could be real or what I imagined to be real. I was still in no condition to formulate my own judgment. What I said seemed strange to my parents. They probably understood nothing about my world. I didn't understand theirs either. It was a game in which nobody lost, in which you couldn't be alone. There were so many memories and scars.

I tried to imagine what my fellow travelers were thinking about. The man caressing his daughter was thin and tall, with a thick strand of hair falling over a forehead marked by smallpox. It wouldn't have been strange if he was thinking about the bones of his wife and children. Perhaps he had seen them being shot, falling into their graves, and had been unable to do anything—suffering, hoping to survive and one day understand why he'd had to endure so much in the name of his people, and later, in their memory, would start a big business, something that would help them be remembered by future generations. His bony hands played with his daughter's hair. He might also have been plotting to avenge himself on the murderers. When the little girl asked about the rest of the family, the man closed his eyes and bit his lower lip. The little girl kept looking at him and seemed to be thinking: "Come on, Dad, tell me they couldn't have died like the others. Our house will be there like before, all this war is a dream from which we have just begun to wake up."

I looked at her and she looked at me. It was stupid. I was thinking about her, and she was in who knows what part of her inner world. However, there was something in that pair of eyes that stuck like pins into whatever they looked at. The reddish stain covering part of her face gave more intensity to her gaze. It was difficult to guess her thoughts. I looked down and got the impression that she was perplexed by us, perhaps not understanding how, after the war, there were still families that remained intact. Of course she had no way of knowing that I was an only child. Whenever I looked at a man and a woman with a child I thought of the others, of those who had been forced to bend their heads to receive a shot in the back. I couldn't think of a family with an only child, although I was an example.

The rain did not stop. We had to huddle together to get a bit of warmth. We looked like newly born mice.

The country spread out like a wet sheet in front of us. The fields were full of mud, and every once in a while a herd of cows went by mooing, perhaps screaming that they too were affected by the fall and the chilly wind that announced the presence of winter, of another cruel freeze. I stared blindly at the road. Sometimes I sneezed and my mother immediately put her hands on my forehead, looking for the beginning of a fever. How could I explain to her that the ghosts were leaving my world and I was doing all I could to stop them. They, the ghosts, would be witnesses to the fact that I had endured, surviving the savage, genocidal hand of the beasts and their slaves.

❖

I woke up to see a man in a raincoat and a huge hat sitting in front of us. He looked at us as if we carried the plague. His pale face and round nose, red and full of holes, made me remember, I don't know why, the Devil's Whip, that beast who had quenched his blood lust at the Stone Cross in Ladyzhin. There was something familiar. The square shoulders, the too-well-kept hands, the inquisitive eyes, almost glaring at us with hatred. A while later I realized that the others in the truck did not like him either.

The girl with the birthmark shuddered and pointed at him with a trembling hand. The man had no chance to move. The hard hands of the refugees pinned him down. "He's a Nazi trying to hide among us," a woman said. A man moved over and began to stroke his face. "Your face is like a girl's. How about if we slice it into pieces so that we can each have a souvenir?" and he took out a knife. Nobody said a word. We all went blank. We had no proof that he was a Nazi. It was only a suspicion based on the trembling hand of a little girl. Another passenger said firmly: "The best thing is to give him to the Russians, they'll know what to do. We might be making a mistake." We began to stomp on the wooden floor of the truck. It stopped. Two soldiers, with their weapons at the ready, looked up. The man with the knife pointed to the one in the raincoat: "Nazi, he's a Nazi." The two soldiers looked at each other and indicated to those who were holding the man to let him go. They made him get out of the truck. They searched him and found a gun and two bullets plus half a bottle of vodka. They took him over to an officer. Shortly afterwards we heard two shots and the man with the raincoat fell down shirtless on the side of

⚜

the road. The soldiers turned to us: "Nazi," they repeated and climbed back into the truck, which started to move again.

I looked around and once again saw the sullen faces of the passengers. It was hard to tell that anything out of the ordinary had taken place. I shrugged, wondering how in hell that guy had gotten into the truck. Perhaps he had jumped as it passed; it was certainly moving slowly enough. I surely did not remember anything other than seeing him almost on top of us, looking at us. What method did the Russians use to identify Nazis?

Images of Iasi came back to me as if being projected from somewhere else. I saw the sister of the pregnant girl shouting that one should be born cursing. Cut. My blind ghost asking to see what we did not see. Quantities of corpses emitting a foul smell. Coming into Iasi, the vodka, the drunkards. The exit from the basement, the anguish, the return and once again the exodus.

Flashes crossed my mind. They made me shake my head and open my eyes to keep looking at the wet fields and the trees bent forward. The never-ending rain. All the faces dripping water, tears, and blood. Drawn, dry faces, with dull eyes, with the exception of the madman who kept grabbing at the strange imaginary bodies that bothered him so much. The girl with the birthmark slept on her father's shoulder while he kept moving his long, dirty fingers through her mass of hair. His gaze was fixed on the floor and he was biting his lower lip.

My mother threw part of her shawl over my head. I yawned, gratefully. I was tired and hungry, but at least I had a goal. I wanted to dream about Bucharest.

I slept for quite a while, and when I woke up, dawn was visible on the horizon. My hands and the rest of my

⚜

body felt numb with cold. I hardly felt the warmth of my mother's flesh next to mine. With my eyes half-closed, barely aware of the faint light of dawn, I started to rock back and forth, looking for a bit of warmth. I found the cold stare of the girl's father. I did not pay much attention at first. After all, he was free to look where he wished. But his insistent staring made me stop. As he looked at me, I thought, he was surely remembering one of his sons. I reminded him of something he had lost. He looked again and nodded. This intrigued me, since I had not said a word. I kept rocking.

Some dogs were barking near a fence. A group of farmers were singing en route to their work. When they saw the truck, they started to wave at their liberators. The other passengers woke up upon hearing the shouts of happiness. They had been liberated from the German occupation and were now returning to their previous condition. The pain gripped my throat and clutched at my gut. They had a right to cheer the victors, but what about us? How could we cheer anybody? In Czernowitz all we found were stones. My mother's tears had mingled with the foundation of what had been our home. That was our liberation...

We saw the same expression on the face of every Jew we met along the way. They moved slowly, mumbling about the terrible massacre. We kept wandering along the roads, seeing the ruins, feeling the burden of having survived the hell. One more step, we're almost there, nothing. This was the routine of any survivor from the death camps, and many left their captivity to die in the dampness of a liberated camp, only to go crazy and hang themselves by their own belts. They couldn't endure the loneliness, their survival crushed them, and some found

❖

no way out other than suicide. A smaller group tried to avenge their own and ended up being killed at the front. The laughter of the farmers did not enrage us, we simply felt envious. We, too, would have wanted to cheer our liberators.

After a long ride we stopped in order to pick up some meager provisions given to us by the Soviet soldiers. We ate silently, savoring each morsel, sunk into a strange lethargy. Perhaps it was the rain and the gray skies. We kept seeing more trucks full of soldiers and refugees, and finally turned onto the road that would take us to Bucharest, the city where my father expected us to be reborn, to return to our human condition, something that was difficult for me to comprehend. The war had left its miserable mark on me, on everything I did. I had responded according to the circumstances. My credo was to survive no matter what the cost. This was a difficult task, since I had entered in one life and had come out in another. Circumstances had turned me into an accommodating being, someone who acted upon the first stimulus, and now in this truck, wet to the bone, with the rain dripping on my face, I was trying to understand the concept of liberation and rebirth. My survival was centered on the constant memory of the anguished faces of the people who had been forced to bow in front of the graves to receive the shot in the back of the neck. I swallowed hard. The image of the cheering farmers came back. I opened my eyes to be sure of my surroundings. Nothing had changed, trucks en route to Bucharest, where my father had pinned his hope of survival.

I shuddered when I felt the cold wind from the Ukrainian steppes. I licked my parched lips and felt pain. I looked ahead. The trucks kept advancing in the midst

❖

of non-stop noise. The noise, my burning lips, the face of the girl with the birthmark smiling, her father's fingers quietly on her hair. Rebirth was not an easy thing.

My eyelids hurt and felt swollen, like small balloons. Figures seemed to be distorted. I went back to the memories I had preserved from before the war. I shook my head and a few drops of water fell into my mouth. By my side someone was saying that he had relatives in Buenos Aires. He was a young man with three fingers of his right hand missing. He talked about a new life in America, of the possibility of starting anew in a South American country. "Buenos Aires is a mixture of all the cities in the world. There are people from everywhere. They all talk fast and like something called the tango and also roasted meat. My relatives kept asking me to move there before the war and— Well, I hope to be able to get to Buenos Aires." The old lunatic stopped waving his arms, looked at him with envy, and pursed his lips. He didn't again for a long time. The girl with the birthmark kept looking at me. I sometimes smiled at her and she smiled back. I felt my face burning and rolled into myself like a worm. She laughed, and her father began stroking her hair again. It was a stupid situation, but I enjoyed it.

In the middle of this truck a whole world full of new forms was being born. We felt it, but could not do anything about it.

We saw Bucharest in the distance. A big mass that became bigger as we got closer. My father stroked his beard nervously, and my mother turned to dry a tear that danced for a moment on her lower lid. Our goal was near. The trees surrounding the city were in front of us. They were half bare, but different from the other trees we had seen before. They raised their branches to the sky,

❖

proudly challenging the rain. At an angle, was the con-
fluence of the Ilfov and Dîmbovi Rivers. A light shiver ran
through my father's body. He was facing his goal, and
now needed to start the rebirth. My mother and I looked
at him and he answered: "Well, we're here, and we'll see
what happens when we step into those streets." We
shrugged. The traffic increased. Cars and trucks went by
carrying troops, foodstuffs, clothing, and refugees. The
girl fell asleep in her father's arms. I opened my eyes wide
and felt them burn, but didn't close them. I wanted to see
every detail and raise my arms to heaven to indicate to
the fallen that here came one who had endured. I
laughed inside. I was being carried away by my emotions.
I felt like a hero, and here I was no more than one of the
thousands of refugees who arrived in the city every day.
I stuck my hands back into my pockets and stretched my
legs to let the blood circulate. I could see the buildings.

Many of them had been destroyed by bombs. But
there were people living in the half-destroyed houses.
They stuck out their faces like mice and quickly pulled
them back inside. When we drove onto the city streets we
felt a wave of safety. At least our pilgrimage had reached
a zone of rest, a place affording some relief from the lives
we had endured over the past days and years, full of
mud, smelling of explosives and decomposing human
bodies.

It had been a long time since I'd seen so clean a room
as the one we now occupied. In my reverie I had forgotten to say goodbye to the soldiers who had transported
us here. When I raised my hand to wave, the truck had
already turned. I looked at the people who were walking
past. They didn't seem to notice anything out of the ordinary. To them the arrival of refugees had become a daily
routine.

⚜

"This is the goal, Israel," I said to myself. "The people you see in the street have already been reborn, and you'll soon be walking like them, without worrying about what is happening around you." My mother shook me and I saw the plate of soup they were placing in front of me. It was warm and smelled greasy. The occupying troops of the Red Army went by, looking at a girl every once in a while. I ate without paying too much attention. Many of those waiting for their ration were talking about King Michael. I didn't understand their preoccupation with the welfare of the king. They were saying that the Communists were pressing him to allow some freedoms. I did not understand things very well in those days. Every once in a while my head went blank. I was wandering in the delicious vacuum of not being, even though I was. When the little girl with the birthmark said goodbye I did not answer. I felt as if the last of my ghosts was leaving.

We spent the winter in Bucharest, living in a small two-room apartment. It was cold and my hands would get numb. Sometimes I thought my brain would ooze out through my nose. However, I kept enduring, thinking about the space between reality and fantasy.

My father found a job, and my mother found part-time employment. They started earning a living and I found rebirth looking at the snow that fell on the half-destroyed roofs. My mother talked about her cousins in South America. I imagined Buenos Aires. It was the only place I had heard about. But they were talking about Colombia, a country surrounded by two oceans and which gave enough immigration visas so that we could settle there. My mind flew, trying to imagine that place.

There were many people in the building where we lived, some of them quite peculiar. A redheaded woman who readily told everyone why her marriage had ended

❖

went up and down the stairs singing obscene songs. Standing by her door, she would take out a brush and start brushing her hair. It was her daily routine. She worked in a liquor factory, but she herself did not drink. I remember her well because once she took me by the shoulders and, looking into my eyes, told me that all men were bad. I bit my lips without knowing what to answer, and she, satisfied with what she had said, went to look for her brush.

At night my father would tell us his plans. He would save some money and we would move somewhere else. My schooling was included in his plan. After the winter I would start school to become somebody in this life. My mother nodded.

I left one morning on my way to school. I had a pad of paper and a pencil. I didn't look at all like that boy who, only four months before, had been ready to risk his skin for an ear of corn. I thought about Moshe, Isaac, and Mordechai, about all my friends and all the children the beasts had massacred in their lust for blood.

On the way to school that first day, their faces kept looking at me from the stones I kicked and from the walls the workers had already started to repair. Why did they, who were also children, not have an opportunity to be reborn? School was for children, and they could well have been my schoolmates. I sat down on the sidewalk and began to cry. I didn't go to school that first day. It was my time to start to remember them so as not to ever forget them. Happy people passed by, still celebrating the liberation. I smiled. All those people who offered their lives, who were forced to cross to the other side of the Bug, there at the Stone Cross, needed to be liberated too,

⚜

and the only way to do so was not to forget them ever, to make them live in the pages of my story.

Wandering through the streets of Bucharest under reconstruction, I started my rebirth by reactivating my memories, engraving them with fury into my brain. I found another boy who had not gone to school either. "I won't go until my father comes back," he said. "And where is he?" I asked. He stuck his finger in his nose and answered: "I don't know, no one will tell me."

I looked at the spring sky. Birds were coming back to build their nests. I stuck my hands in my pockets. "You have to go on," I said to myself and said goodbye to the waif, who had started to play with some pebbles. I walked for a while and then stopped. I had gone forward, without obstacles, I had gone forward! I breathed deeply, realizing that I was alive, and felt alive.

I no longer had to endure. I was committed to keep living, to filling myself with the vitality I had seen buried in the graves after the shot in the back of the head from the murderous enemy. In a corner, a few feet away from the apartment where we were living, I said: "Well, lady life, I hope you will allow me to accompany you. Do you know about the millions of innocents murdered by the Nazi assassins who are now living in the night star?"

❖

Epilogue

Miami, June 24, 2003

In 1946, in Bucharest, Rumania, Israel Lapciuc started school for the first time in his life. He was then aged 12. He completed all of his elementary school studies in just one year. For this accomplishment he was awarded a special diploma for excellence and achievement. The Joint Distribution Committee helped Israel and his parents, Perla and Samuel Lapciuc to locate relatives living in Colombia who were able to get them visas to immigrate there.

While waiting for their visas, they moved to Belgium where Samuel and Perla worked pressing clothes, and Israel, thanks to the ORT, resumed his studies and found part time work as a mechanic, earning some money for his immediate expenses.

A few months later, the Lapciucs moved on to Marseilles, France, There, they boarded a ship bound for Colombia, South America. They arrived in Medellín in 1948. Samuel, like many Jewish immigrants, started to work as a peddler and Israel went into high school, all the while learning the new language in a new and foreign environment.

In 1952, Samuel and Perla bought a small textile workshop. Shortly after Israel graduated from high school, he won a small lottery. With the proceeds, he was able to go to France to study textiles.

He studied first at the Sorbonne, improving his French; then, he went on to L'Ecole Textile de Lyons. From there he moved on to Germany to further specialize in textile engineering, receiving a scholarship from a fund created by the German government for Holocaust survivors.

After graduating, he returned to Colombia to work with his parents in their small workshop. He brought his knowledge into the business, improving and modernizing the workshop and making it into a modern factory. Today the factory is one of Colombia's finest vertically integrated textile manufacturers, employing over 600 workers.

In 1961 he met Tania Fraiman, born in Peru of Russian Jewish parents, who had emigrated in 1929. They wed shortly thereafter in that same year. They have three sons: Marcos, Isaac and Yair, all born in Colombia. Perla Lapciuc died in Medellín in 1968

In 1972, Israel became President of the small Jewish Community of Medellíin for a period of 4 years. In 1975, Samuel Lapciuc was kidnapped by leftist guerrillas. After his father's release, Israel and his family moved to Miami due to security concerns and also to look for a stronger and safer Jewish community in which to raise and educate their children.

In Miami, he started a new business in wholesale electronics and distribution as well as real estate, keeping his textile factory running in Colombia.

Their three sons are all married and all live currently in Miami Beach.

Marcos is married to Tiffany, Isaac to Sandra and Yair to Bassy. Israel and Tania have 11 grandchildren, so far.

⚜

Index of Names and Places

(Compiled by Markus Thiel)

Aleph group 62
America, American(s) ix, xiii, 355, 393
Antonescu (Marshal) xiv, xv, xvi
Aryanization xii
Auschwitz xi, 308

Babi Yar 315
Balta (Camp) 311
Balti (see Belz)
Belgium 398
Belz, Beltsy xii, 21, 329, 350–353, 355–356, 359
Belzec, Belzek xvi, 308
Berlin 318, 376, 382
Bershad 227–230, 232–235, 237–239, 241–242, 244, 249- 250, 252–253, 257–259, 262, 264–265, 271–272, 274, 278, 281–282, 284, 286–288, 290–291, 294–300, 305–308, 311–312, 315–317, 319, 321, 324, 326–331, 339
Bessarabia xii, xiv, xv, 359
Bialik 345
Black Sea xiv
Bucharest xv, 353, 355–356, 368, 382, 384, 386, 390, 392–393, 395, 397–398

Buenos Aires 393, 395
Bug (River) xv, 46, 145–146, 150–151, 154, 158, 160, 166, 168, 170, 175–176, 181, 194, 221, 229, 238, 242, 255, 263, 267–268, 274, 308, 313, 342, 346, 350, 368, 396
Bukovina xii, xiv, xv, 359
Bulgaria xii
Bialystok 303, 309

Calarasi xiii
Carpathian Mountains xii
Chelmo 170
Czernowitz, Chernovtsy xii, 1, 21, 23, 33, 39, 70, 76, 81, 86, 92, 104, 143, 350, 391
Colombia 395, 398–399
Communists xiv, xvi, 24, 395

Dalnik xiv
Des Pres, Terrence xiv
Dimbovi (River) 394
Dnieper (River) 309
Dniester (River) xii, xv, 350

Eastern Europe xiii
Eastern Galicia 309

Eight O'clock Way   298,
   300–301, 306, 308,
   310–311, 324
Einsatzgruppen   xii, xiv
England   345
Europe   ix, xi, xiii, xv, 147,
   200, 269, 324

Fascism   318
Final Solution   xi, 147, 288,
   325
Floss, Dr.   142
France   xi, 399

Germany, Germans   ix, xii,
   xiii, xv, xvi, 1, 3, 6, 8–9,
   11–12, 17, 20–23, 27,
   31–32, 36, 38, 41, 43,
   48, 50, 54, 58, 64, 67,
   70, 73, 76, 86, 91, 100,
   114, 118, 134, 141, 148,
   150, 159, 166, 169–170,
   191, 196–197, 200, 202,
   205, 208–211, 215, 229,
   238, 247–248, 264, 269,
   282, 288–291, 294–295,
   298, 300–309, 311-313,
   315, 317–318, 320–322,
   324, 326, 333, 336–339,
   343, 346–347, 352–354,
   356, 358–360, 363–366,
   369, 371, 373, 375–376,
   382–384, 391, 399
Gestapo   48, 61, 63, 68, 70,
   170, 297–300, 307
God   viii, 14–16, 20, 24–26,
   45–47, 54, 60, 65, 71,
   84, 90, 99, 108, 141,
   170, 180, 186, 188–189,
   196, 205, 207, 210, 218,
   225, 267, 277, 310, 323,
   334, 366, 377

Gypsies   xii, 176

Haggadah   96
Hasid   84 (see also: Satmar
   Hasidim)
Hatikvah   121
Hebrew   153
Hitler   176
Holocaust   x, xiii, xiv
Holocaust survivor(s)   x, 399
Holy Land   21
Hungary, Hungarians   xi,
   xiii, xvi
Hungarian Jews   xiii, xvi

Iasi, Jassy   xii, 356,
   359–361, 363–365, 367,
   369, 371–372, 375 -376,
   382–385, 390
Ilfov (River)   394
Israel   ix, xvi, 108, 180
Christ, Christians   159, 163,
   203

Jassy   (see Iasi)
Jew(s)   vii, viii, xi, xii, xiii,
   xiv, xv, xvi, 3, 15–16,
   24–26, 28–29, 31–36,
   38–39, 41–43, 45, 47–48,
   51, 54–55, 57, 67, 80,
   82, 86, 110, 129, 132,
   137–142, 147–148, 157,
   159, 166, 170–171, 176,
   183, 191, 197, 201–202,
   204, 209–212, 215, 219,
   227, 229, 235, 238, 251,
   258, 273–274, 293–294,
   298–299, 301, 303,
   308–310, 320, 324–326,
   336, 338, 345, 378, 391,
   398–399
Jewish Council   62, 66, 68,
   70

❖

Jewish National Committee
    308, 321
Jewish Problem   xi, 325
Jewish resistance   286–287,
    289–290, 294–295,
    307–308, 312, 330
Joint Distribution Committee
    398

Katznelson, Yitzhak   x
Kiev   315
Kishinev   xii
Krakow   309

Ladyzhin   177, 193,
    233–235, 242–243, 263,
    267, 274–275, 313,
    318–319, 325, 346, 370,
    389
Litzmannstadt   170, 309
Lodz   (See Litzmannstadt)
Lyons   399

Magen David   (see also: Star
    of David) 224
Maidanek   325
Medellin   399
Miami   vii, 398–399
Michael, King (of Romania)
    395
Mogilev-Podolski   xii
Moldavia   xv
Molotov   248

Nazi, Nazi Germany   xii, xiii,
    xv, 5, 11, 22, 30, 33,
    55–56, 64, 137, 142–143,
    224–225, 257, 302, 304,
    311–313, 318, 363, 366,
    371, 383–384, 389–390,
    397
Nikolayev   313

Oder (River)   309
Odessa   xiv
Office of Displaced Persons
    318, 324
Oswiecim   (see Auschwitz)

Palestine   xvi, 251, 321
Panzer   (Tank)   298
Peoples's Army   167
Peru   399
Podolia   309
Poland   xi, xiii, 64, 308–309,
    384
POW camp   366
Prut (River)   xii

Realpolitik   xv
Red Army   1, 8, 17, 269,
    282, 300, 315, 318,
    322–323, 326, 331, 343,
    345, 361, 366, 375, 382,
    384, 395
Reich, Third   xv, 73,
    138–139, 148, 157, 170,
    176, 245, 273, 275, 278,
    292, 302
Romania, Romanians   ix,
    xi–xvi, 1, 33, 136–138,
    142, 145, 149, 176, 209,
    227–230, 234, 236,
    238–239, 246–247, 264,
    288, 301–302, 304–305,
    308, 315, 353, 386
Romanian Army   xiv,
    304–305
Romanian Jews   xi, xv, xvi
Romanization   xii
Russia, Russians   41,
    163–164, 167, 184, 201,
    203, 213, 252, 264,
    266–267, 269, 272, 274,
    277, 282–289, 294,

❦

298–299, 301, 306–308,
312–313, 315–316,
318–323, 326, 331–332,
335–336, 338–340, 342,
344, 346, 352–353,
355–356, 358, 360, 364,
366–369, 374–375,
382–383, 389–390, 399
Russian Jews   399

Satmar Hasidim   xi
Satu Mare   xi
Sighet   xi
Shoah   x
Siberia   161
Silesia   309
Sobibor   308
Sorbonne   399
Soviet Union   ix, xi, xii
Soviet troops   xiv, 145, 371
Srul, Esther   153
SS   24–25, 28, 30–35,
38–39, 41, 44–45, 55, 66,
80, 86, 88–90, 92–93,
100, 129, 131, 136–143,
147–149, 162, 171, 176,
183–184, 197–198, 217,
228, 245–246, 256, 273,
275–276, 282, 287–289,
298, 300–301, 304–305,
310–311, 320, 326, 327
Stalingrad   xv, 269, 282,
315, 375
Star of David   (see also:
Magen David) 338
Stone Cross   165, 242–243,
255, 313, 316, 319, 389,
396

South America   355, 393,
395, 398

Talmud   19
Torah   47, 92
Transnistria   xv, xvi
Transylvania   xi
Treblinka   308
Tulchin   xii

Ukraine, Ukrainians   ix, xiv,
xv, 91, 147–148, 150,
155–157, 161, 165–166,
168–169, 172, 174–176,
178–179, 196, 210, 228,
269, 288, 301, 305, 308,
313, 315, 327, 346, 350,
384, 392
Ukrainian Jews   xvi
Ukrainian troops   145
Umi   91
Uman   107, 177–178, 182
United States   ix

Vienna   xii
Vilna   309
Vlasov (Marshal)   91, 145,
315, 327
Volhynia   309

Walachia   xv
Warsaw (Ghetto)   41,
302–303, 308
Wehrmacht   xii
Wiesel, Elie   xi
White Russia   309

Yiddish   153, 203, 226

❖